Authoritarian Capitalism

Also of Interest

Brazil in the International System: The Rise of a Middle Power,
edited by Wayne A. Selcher

**Brazil: A Political Analysis*, Peter Flynn

The Future of Brazil, edited by William H. Overholt

International Politics and the Sea: The Case of Brazil, Michael A.
Morris

Brazil: An Industrial Geography, John P. Dickenson

**The Continuing Struggle for Democracy in Latin America*, edited by
Howard J. Wiarda

*Technological Progress in Latin America: The Prospects for Overcoming
Dependency*, edited by James H. Street and Dilmus D. James

**From Dependency to Development: Strategies to Overcome Underdevelop-
ment and Inequality*, edited by Heraldo Muñoz

Latin America, the United States, and the Inter-American System,
edited by John D. Martz and Lars Schoultz

Corporatism and National Development in Latin America, Howard J.
Wiarda

**The Challenge of the New International Economic Order*, edited by
Edwin P. Reubens

**Change in the International System*, edited by Ole R. Holsti, Randolph
M. Siverson, and Alexander George

A Select Bibliography on Economic Development: With Annotations,
John P. Powelson

*Available in hardcover and paperback.

Westview Special Studies on Latin America and the Caribbean

Authoritarian Capitalism: Brazil's Contemporary Economic and Political Development
edited by Thomas C. Bruneau and Philippe Faucher

During the past decade, the potential offered by Brazil's size, resources, and location has begun to be realized. There are, however, a number of international and domestic obstacles to the country's continued development, as indicated by its extreme inflation rate and its foreign indebtedness. There are also serious questions about the social and political results of the Brazilian approach to development: Brazil has become something of a test case for whether the Western, or capitalist, orientation can achieve development in more than strictly economic terms.

Emphasizing key aspects of Brazil's economy, politics, and society, the authors present an overall analysis of the present system and provide a base from which to assess Brazil's future development.

Thomas C. Bruneau is professor of political science and director of the Centre for Developing Area Studies at McGill University. He has published several works on Brazil, including *The Political Transformation of the Brazilian Catholic Church* and *Religiosity and Politicization in Brazil: The Church in an Authoritarian Regime*.

Philippe Faucher is assistant professor of political science at the University of Montreal and directs the university's Groupe de Recherche sur L'Amerique Latine.

Authoritarian Capitalism: Brazil's Contemporary Economic and Political Development

edited by Thomas C. Bruneau
and Philippe Faucher

Westview Press / Boulder, Colorado

Westview Special Studies on Latin America and the Caribbean

Published in 1981 in the United States of America by
    Westview Press, Inc.
    5500 Central Avenue
    Boulder, Colorado 80301
    Frederick A. Praeger, Publisher

Library of Congress Cataloging in Publication Data
Main entry under title:
Authoritarian capitalism.
    (A Westview special study)
    Bibliography: p.
    1. Brazil--Economic conditions--1945-   --Addresses, essays, lectures.
2. Government business enterprises--Brazil--Addresses, essays, lectures.
3. Industry and state--Brazil--Addresses, essays, lectures. I. Bruneau,
Thomas C. II. Faucher, Philippe.
HC187.A798   338.981   81-10411
ISBN 0-86531-220-6   AACR2
ISBN 0-86531-283-4 (pbk.)

Composition for this book was provided by the editors.
Printed and bound in the United States of America.

Contents

vii

viii

Tables and Figures

ix

Figures

Foreword

The chapters in this book arose from a series of seminars held in the Winter and Spring of 1980 at the Centre for Developing Area Studies of McGill University. The seminars were organized and coordinated by the co-editors with the assistance of a group of graduate students specializing in Brazil. It was felt that the current development processes in that country were so important that a series of high-level seminars was justified in order to discuss the details as well as the general "model" of development. The co-editors have researched extensively in Brazil: Bruneau works on the Church, religion, and development, whereas Faucher works on the state and issues of political economy.

The contributors were invited to present papers on particularly important areas of the state, economy, and society. The co-editors and graduate students then made a number of comments and suggestions which the authors might use in their revisions. Through the selection of the specialists and a certain coordination of the suggestions for revision it was hoped that an integrated work would result. We feel that this is indeed the case in this book, and we are confident that the most important issues in the Brazilian development strategy have been dealt with.

The series of seminars was put on with support from the Ministry of Education of Québec in its FCAC programs. The Centre for Developing Area Studies also provided facilities and extensive clerical assistance. The Faculty of Arts and Sciences of the University of Montreal has provided technical assistance in preparing the final manuscript. To these three institutions we extend our thanks.

A collected work of course requires the support of a great number of people. We should like to thank the contributors, who not only presented stimulating papers but also revised them and met deadlines. We owe a debt of gratitude to Betania Pena, who translated Roberto da

Matta's paper from Portuguese, and to Darlene Pearson and Robert Young for their assistance with Faucher's paper. Judith Sabetti has assisted at all stages of this endeavour, and the typing is but the most obvious element of her broader contribution. Johanne Mercille performed remarkably in putting the material on the word processor and coping with all the necessary changes. Finally we would like to thank Joan McGilvray for the excellence with which she carried out the demanding job of copy editing the entire manuscript.

Thomas C. Bruneau
Philippe Faucher

Contributors

Werner Baer is professor of Economics at the University of Illinois, Champaign-Urbana. He specializes in the study of Latin American economic development and has published four books and a score of articles on the Brazilian economy. His most recent book is The Brazilian Economy: Its Growth and Development.

Thomas C. Bruneau is professor of Political Science and Director of the Centre for Developing Area Studies at McGill University. He specializes in the study of Brazilian development with particular emphasis on the role of the Catholic Church. More recently he has also researched and written on politics in Portugal since the April Revolution. He has written two books and a dozen articles on Brazil and Portugal. His most recent book is Religiosity and Politicization in Brazil: The Church in an Authoritarian Regime.

Roberto da Matta is professor of Anthropology at the Museu Nacional in Rio de Janeiro. He has been head of that department as well as a visiting scholar at Cambridge University and a Tinker Visiting Professor at the University of Wisconsin, Madison. He has published four books; the most recent one to appear in Portuguese and English is Carnavais, Malandros, e Herois (Carnivals, Rogues, and Heroes).

Kenneth Paul Erickson is associate professor of Political Science and Director of Inter-American Studies at Hunter College of the City University of New York. His book The Brazilian Corporative State and Working-Class Politics won the 1978 Hubert Herring Memorial Award. He has coordinated the Energy Policy Seminar at Hunter College and is the author of "The Political Economy of Energy Consumption in Industrial Societies," in International Energy Policy as well as "The Energy Profile of Brazil," in National Energy Profiles.

xiv

Peter Evans is associate professor of Sociology and a member of the Center for the Comparative Study of Development at Brown University. He specializes in the study of multinational corporations and development, and his articles have appeared in Economic Development and Cultural Change, International Organization, The Journal of Development Economics, The American Sociological Review, etc. His book is entitled Dependent Development: The Alliance of Multinational, State and Local Capital in Brazil.

Philippe Faucher is assistant professor of Political Science at the Université de Montréal. He specializes in the study of the state and development with particular interest in industrial strategies. His research and writing have focused on the cases of Brazil, Canada, and Peru. His articles include "Croissance et répression, la double logique de l'Etat dépendant: le cas du Brésil" and "Industrial Policy in a Dependent State: The Case of Brazil". His book is entitled Le Brésil des militaires: l'Etat et la structure du pouvoir dans un régime autoritaire.

Adolfo Figueroa is professor of Economics at the Catholic University in Lima, Peru. He has been head of that department as well as visiting professor at the University of Illinois, Champaign-Urbana. He has researched and written extensively on income distribution in Latin America with particular emphasis on Peru and also recently terminated a study on the economics of low-income peasants in Peru. His publications include "Agricultural Price Policy and Rural Incomes in Peru," in M. Urrutia, ed., Agricultural Economic Policies in Latin America.

Ronaldo Munck is Argentinian by birth. After having lectured at universities in England and Ireland, he is presently lecturer in Sociology at Ulster Polytechnic, Northern Ireland. He has specialized in the study of labor and the state in Latin America with particular emphasis on Argentina and Brazil; he has also written on Ireland. His articles on Latin America have been published in Capital and Class Critique, Labour Capital and Society, and Latin American Perspectives. His forthcoming book is entitled Class Politics and the State in Latin America Today.

Riordan Roett is professor of Political Science and Director of the Latin American Studies Program at the School for Advanced International Studies, Johns Hopkins University; he is also Director of the Center of Brazilian Studies. He specializes in the study of political development in Latin America with particular reference to Argentina, Brazil, Paraguay, and Uruguay. He has

served as the President of the Latin American Studies
Association and as consultant or member of such groups
as the Commission on U.S.-Latin American Relations, Council on Foreign Relations, and the National Council on
Foreign Language and International Studies. He has published three books and a dozen articles on Brazil and
Paraguay.

Thomas G. Sanders is senior associate for Latin America of the American Universities Field Staff. He has
studied and written on a variety of topics including politics in Latin America, religion, population planning,
and educational problems. He has written three books
dealing with religion with particular emphasis on Latin
America and Southern Europe. Through the AUFS he has
published scores of articles on Latin America as well as
a number of articles in books and journals.

Francisco Colman Sercovich is Uruguayan by birth and
currently lives in Argentina. He has been a visiting
scholar in England as well as at the Harvard Institute
for International Development. He has been associated
with the Inter-American Development Bank as well as the
International Development Research Centre in Ottawa. His
publications include a number of specialized papers for
the OAS, ECLA, Inter-American Development Bank, and the
Harvard Institute for International Development. His
forthcoming book is entitled State Enterprises, Multinational Enterprises and Technological Change in Latin
America.

Thomas J. Trebat is Senior Latin American Economist
of the Bankers Trust Company in New York. He has spent
a number of years in Brazil as a visiting scholar at various economic research institutes. He specializes in the
study of public enterprises and has co-authored articles
on this topic. His forthcoming book is entitled The
State as Entrepreneur: The Case of Brazil.

1
Introduction

Thomas C. Bruneau
Philippe Faucher

It has frequently been pointed out that Latin America
is paradoxical. Economic growth, massive foreign investment, and grandiose projects in far-flung areas of the
region flourish in the midst of misery, poverty, and
great problems in the distribution of the benefits arising from economic growth. Despite a long tradition of
frequently changing military regimes, some absolutely
infamous, there has been a continuing interest in democratic values and processes.

In order to understand Latin America as the region
enters the decade of the 1980s, it is useful to return
briefly to the era of the 1960s and the first "development decade." During this period, several of the more
important countries in the region, including Brazil,
sought to stimulate economic growth and to establish
democratic regimes. The example of the Cuban revolution
of 1959 was the underlying reason for the support which
the United States provided for these changes; it was
thought that removal of oligarchies, promotion of economic growth, and encouragement of participation by the population would not only lead to development but would
also avoid other Cubas. The development strategies actually implemented varied greatly from one country to
another, but by 1970 it was clear that, while economic
growth was possible, democracy was not. Thus the second
"development decade" was dominated by military dictatorships. The objective of economic growth was retained,
but as democracy was perceived to be unrealiable and inefficient it was replaced by a variety of regimes in
which political participation was strictly limited. In
contrast to earlier periods of "caudillo rule," however,
it was not a single leader who assumed control but rather
the military as an institution with a particular view of
the relation between state and society justified by its
own ideology of national security. Economic growth,
usually to further national security, was encouraged and
toward this aim the state apparatus was perfected and

1

elaborated and its personnel trained to better administer a modern economy. In all instances economic growth was promoted through deepening cooperation with foreign investors and through reliance on foreign loans. During this period political opposition was controlled or even eliminated, the legislature was restricted, and the executive came to rule by decree - although at times its rulings were legitimated by the legislatures. This type of regime appeared first in Brazil in 1964 and later developed in all countries of the Southern Cone, as well as in a few other countries in the region.

The success of these regimes in promoting economic growth and development has been mixed, and in the 1980s we are likely to see significant changes in their approaches or models. The global context is now more constrained and economic growth more difficult. There is no question but that the countries of the region are fully integrated into the world economy and, at their particular stages of development, are very sensitive to negative trends in this economy. The decrease in economic growth raises problems for the legitimacy of these regimes as they have relied more on growth than on the support of the population. Even their justification in terms of the fight against Communism is more difficult now that the political systems have been purged and international alignments have become more complex. What is more, there is not only a substantial backlog of unmet grievances among the working class, but even the middle class, which has supported these regimes, is now smarting from increasing demands which are also unmet. In this context of decreasing legitimacy, the central core of the state has a tendency to fragment, leading to further fragmentation. Now, more than ever, there are many obvious reasons and increasing pressure for the military to return to their barracks.

The processes of industrialization and development under military auspices have substantially transformed the social structures in most of the countries in this region. Industrialization has created an urban working class of significant potential importance in countries such as Brazil. Development has also come to rural areas through the increasing penetration of modern technology, related to international demands, which has transformed rural structures as rural workers move to the cities and create a larger pool of urban workers. Clearly the urban working class must be taken into consideration, but it is precisely this group which these regimes have intentionaly and most completely excluded.

The general points made above have occurred in a number of ways which differ from one country to another. We are presently seeing tremendous changes in Central America, an area which until recently was thought to be all but stagnant. If in 1964 it was Brazil which led the way into authoritarian rule under military auspices, in 1980 it was Peru which moved from this pattern to one a great deal more democratic.

The richness and complexity of the processes of development under authoritarian rule, and the newly perceived limits to this strategy, have stimulated reflection about the theories and concepts to be employed in the analysis of all aspects of state and society. While earlier efforts sought to analyze economics and politics as distinct from one another, today the emphasis is on comprehending them only in relation to each other. The coups which led to authoritarian rule may be seen as responses to political agitation arising from economic crises. The perceived need for economic growth through stabilization has justified the use of repression in the closing of these systems. The main actor in this process, the military as institution, has allowed for a new type of management in these increasingly complex economies. This is a far cry from its traditional role in society. Alfred Stepan's study on Brazil is the first work to analyze how what he termed the "new professionalism" affected the manner in which the military perceived its role in society.(1) The doctrine of national security, with its emphasis on the war against the enemy within which is used as a justification for brutal repression, is probably the defining characteristic of these regimes and justifies their role in all areas of society.

Other analyses have sought to deal with the characteristics of military regimes as they seek institutionalization. Beginning with the writings of Juan J. Linz on authoritarianism, there is now a broad and rich literature on authoritarianism in Latin America. The same may be said for writings on corporatism.(2) Little by little a new approach has been adopted. The writings of Guillermo O'Donnell have helped crystalize an approach which suggests that these "bureaucratic-authoritarian" regimes are not simple military dictatorships. They cannot be considered either accidental or transitory but rather are a stage in the process of Latin American development.(3) These regimes arise out of particular class configurations, and the internal dynamics are linked to the international context. The absence of representation is manifest in these systems and exclusion is severely enforced. The dominant coalition is composed of civil and military technocrats. Industrialization, by means of close collaboration with foreign investment and technology, is the primary goal of these regimes. Order, and the general absence of politics, is considered a necessary condition for investment and thus for development. Despite variations among what might be termed the bureaucratic authoritarian regimes, and the criticisms directed at this concept, this term, and the approach it implies, are the defining themes in the study of Latin America from a political and economic perspective.(4)

Parallel with the study of the political regimes, and more closely related than many would like to admit, has been the analysis of the mechanisms of accumulation in peripheral societies. A great many aspects of these mechanisms have received attention. There has been a great deal of work on inflation and on the efforts of the governments to achieve monetary stability, efforts usually closely related to foreign governments and international institutions.(5) The effects of these measures on the systems of production, capital, and sectoral distribution have also been studied.(6) In all instances foreign investment has increased, with particular emphasis on programs of industrialization. In consequence, there is much discussion about whether these economies have become denationalized. The fight against inflation has, in most cases, led to control of salaries and their maintenance at levels less than inflation. One of the key issues, then, has been to provide evidence on the character of the maldistribution of income as a way to highlight the precise nature of these regimes.(7) Probably the broadest theoretical or conceptual approach which includes most of the above considerations is the dependency school which has received its most convincing formulation in the work of Fernando Henrique Cardoso and Enzo Faletto.(8) This form of analysis is situated within the Marxist approach to the analysis of imperialism and, following studies by the ECLA, has provided the basis for criticism of the theories of development previously prevalent. The concept of dependence, elevated to the status of theory by some, is felt by many to be an improved version of the relationships of domination identified by the Marxists. It rejects, however, the more radical theses of "neocolonialism" and "sub-imperialism."

Arguments over the concept of dependency, as well as confrontation with the complex and dynamic processes in the region, have led to an ongoing elaboration of concepts within this general approach. The mere fact that industrialization and growth does take place has forced a reexamination of Marxist literature on underdevelopment which criticized the earlier liberal literature on development. In 1973 Fernando Henrique Cardoso published his most important article dealing with the concept of associated or dependent development.(9) He was led to develop this concept because the traditional Marxist approaches, as well as those of the dependency school, did not accord well with the actual facts of industrialization and processes of accumulation in the peripheral countries. In his work he has demonstrated how the process of internationalization of the domestic market is linked to an increasing association of the domestic bourgeoisie with international capital, as well as to the increased

importance of the middle class in the state with particular emphasis on the military and technocrats.

Peter Evans has further elaborated this form of analysis for Brazil.(10) He argues that the productive and
financial structure has become substantial enough, and
the state sufficiently developed, that it can now assume
a predominant role in orienting the process of growth and
accumulation. The state, then, possesses the means
whereby it can negotiate with international capital in
order to secure "national interests" as well as meet most
of the demands of the middle classes. Investments must
now be made in such a manner as to respond to local demands. The links of subordination are replaced by links
of association. These take the particular form of an association between foreign capital, the state, and local
capital.

Discussions in Latin America today usually concern
politics, particularly democratization. Until now, however, there has been little theoretical orientation to
this debate for concepts are only now being formulated
and, of course, the outcome of this process is very much
in question. For this last concern, that of democratization, Brazil provides an important case study. We are
not speaking of a model, for the variety of states and
societies in Latin America is such that a model is limited to one country - if that. Still, Brazil, with its
huge size (fifth largest in the world), large but not un-
manageable population (sixth largest in the world), and
its economic strengh (tenth largest in the world), offers
researchers and theoreticians a number of situations and
processes which are of importance for the whole region.
It was in Brazil in 1964 that the new type of bureaucratic authoritarian regime first appeared. The program of stabilization and the fight against inflation
before the economic miracle of the late 1960s was also
thought to be a model. These mechanisms, and their results in terms of the distribution of income, are also of
relevance elsewhere in the region. Brazil's particular
form of state organisation, and its major efforts at promoting development, have made it apparent that growth and
development could be achieved. It was in Brazil that the
tri-pé (a tripod of foreign capital, the state, and local
capital) was recognized as a means to promote such development. It was in Brazil in 1974 that the rhetoric of
the return to democracy began to appear serious. What
is more, in Brazil movements among labor and students,
as well as in the Catholic Church, have been extremely
important in promoting socio-political change.

Much of what is both specific to Brazil and general
for the whole region is included in the chapters that
follow. The theme of this book is the development of
Brazil under a particular form of authoritarian regime.
It examines the most important aspects of the development

process including the state, its reciprocal and changing
relationship with society, and the complex interactions
with several elements of the international or global system. The overall analysis is not static for the concepts
and data indicate that there is indeed a changing situation at all levels. Within these chapters we find that
there is indeed class and technological formation and
even a developing political openness which may be linked
to these larger or more secular processes. However, because of the bureaucratic authoritarian model and the
type of economic system, there is serious doubt whether
the skewed distribution of benefits will in fact allow a
further opening of the system or whether it will be at
most an "elitist" or "supervised" democracy. The character of the cultural system also raises questions as to
the limits of the process.

Philippe Faucher, in his opening chapter, provides
an interpretation of the crisis of the Brazilian regime.
He argues that the process of liberalization is encouraged by the absence of agreement at the political level
regarding the implementation of a stabilization program.
The stalemate of the model of economic growth is manifested by the inability of the regime to realize the objectives stated in the second National Development Plan.
The process of liberalization expresses the demands of
domestic capital for a role in the system, as well as the
pent up claims of workers, intellectuals, and certain
other groups for real democratization.

Public enterprises play a large and important role
in the development strategies of a number of Third World
countries. Their role in Brazil has been the subject of
some debate as to what they indicate about the state, the
processes of development, and their impact on society.
The chapters by Thomas Trebat and Werner Baer and Adolfo
Figueroa are concerned with the behavior of these enterprises. Trebat provides a comparative analysis of the
origins, control, and financial performance of enterprises in Brazil and Mexico. He finds that public enterprises are rather more independent in Brazil than in Mexico. Baer and Figueroa compare the experiences of Brazil
and Peru with regard to the impact of public enterprises
on the distribution of income and find that the impact
has been negative. Here, as in the case examined by Trebat, Brazilian public enterprises appear to be most concerned with furthering their own interests, somewhat concerned with aiding the state, and very little if at all
interested in aiding major sectors of the population.

The Brazilian state has systematically elaborated its
apparatus and its negotiations with foreign capital in
order to maximize the utility of this capital for local
interests. The process of dependent development is characterized in precisely these terms of defining national
interests in order to redefine the terms of dependence.

Peter Evans is concerned with the role of the state in
accumulation and, through his analysis of the petrochemical sector, suggests that efficient production of chemicals is but part of the purpose of the second petrochemical complex in Bahia; of even greater importance is the
integration of a system bringing together foreign capital, the state, and local capital in order to elaborate
institutions for further development. Francisco Sercovich is also concerned with petrochemicals (the third
petrochemical pole in Rio Grande do Sul) in much of his
work, but his chapter in this book focusses on the export
sector in general. He finds that Brazil is reaching a
point in the development of its technology at which it
can compete effectively in the international market.

Whereas Evans and Sercovich are interested in petrochemicals as indicative of processes and structures in
development, Kenneth Erickson is more concerned with the
strategy of the Brazilian state in dealing with the serious situation that 80 percent of its petroleum must be
imported. He provides a comprehensive analysis of this
topic which, as one of the two or three foremost problems
of the country, is of such importance that it alone might
provide the basis for a foreign policy independent of the
United States. Riordan Roett, however, in his chapter
demonstrates that energy is part of an overall strategy
of development and shows how pursuit of this strategy has
led Brazil and the United States to diverge in their foreign policies. The ability, and even need, for Brazil
to diverge says something about the weakness of the United States and even more about the increasing strength of
Brazil.

Since Castello Branco in 1964, presidents have indicated that Brazil would reestablish a democratic political system. Until 1974, however, few took these statements at face value; even after the Geisel government of
1974-1979 there were still doubts that this would occur.
Thomas Sanders demonstrates how the opening, or liberalization, of the system has taken place and describes the
key actors as well as analyzing likely processes in the
near future. A key factor in these is undoubtedly the
labor movement. This has largely come into being under
the process of industrialization during military rule and
has been repressed. How it emerges from this repression
and the terms under which this takes place hold important
implications for the nature of the whole regime. The labor movement is related not only to the state, but to the
whole nature of the strategy of development as analyzed
in the other chapters. Ronaldo Munck provides an analysis of the movement and its changing relationship with
the regime.

The focus of this book is the development of Brazil
under an authoritarian regime. The overwhelming emphasis
comes from the perspectives of politics and economics.

8

All but the most doctrinaire or closed-minded, however,
realize that Brazil is complex and that there are many
levels of meaning as well as perspectives from which to
approach the country. For this reason, we have included
a somewhat different approach in the chapter by Roberto
da Matta who provides an analysis of the Brazilian system
from an anthropological perspective. From a reading of
this chapter one can appreciate, at several levels of
analysis, the nature of the development task as well as
the implications of this form of development for the
society.

It is our hope that these chapters will provide an
overall interpretation of Brazilian state and society as
it undergoes yet another transformation while entering
the decade of the 1980s. These chapters should indicate
the nature of the development process in Brazil as well
as its implications for the society as it is now constructed.

NOTES

1. See Alfred Stepan, The Military in Politics:
Changing Patterns in Brazil (Princeton: Princeton University Press, 1971).

2. See, for example, James Malloy, ed., Authoritarianism and Corporatism in Latin America (Pittsburgh: University of Pittsburgh Press, 1977).

3. For the original statement see Guillermo O'Donnell, Modernization and Bureaucratic-Authoritarianism:
Studies in South American Politics (Berkeley: Institute
of International Studies, 1973).

4. The most complete collection dealing with this
theme is undoubtedly David Collier, ed., The New Authoritarianism in Latin America (Princeton: Princeton University Press, 1979).

5. Mario Henrique Simonsen, Inflação: Gradualismo
x Tratamento de Choque, (Rio de Janeiro: APEC, 1970).
See the articles of Albert Fishlow, "Some Reflections on
Post-1964 Brazilian Economic Policy" and Thomas Skidmore,
"Politics and Economic Policy-Making in Authoritarian
Brazil" in Alfred Stepan, ed., Authoritarian Brazil:
Origins, Policies, and Future (New Haven: Yale Universi-
ty Press, 1973).

6. See the now classical contributions of Francisco
Oliveira, "La economia Brasileña: critica a la razon
dualista," El Trimestre Economico 40 (April-June 1973)
and José Serra and Maria da Conceição Tavares, "Mas alla
del estancamiento: una discusion sobre el estito de de-
sarrollo reciente en Brasil," in José Serra, ed., Desar-
rollo Latino-Americano (Mexico: El Trimestre Economico,
1974), pp. 203-248).

7.   Ricardo Tolipan and Arthur Carlos Tinelli, eds.,
A Controvérsia Sobre Distribuição de Renda e Desenvolvimento (Rio de Janeiro: Zahar Editores, 1975) and Albert
Fishlow, "Brazilian Size Distribution of Income," American Economic Review, May 1962, pp. 391-402.
    8.   Fernando Henrique Cardoso and Enzo Faletto, De-
pendency and Development in Latin America (Berkeley:
University of California Press, 1979).
    9.   See Cardoso's article in Alfred Stepan, ed., Au-
thoritarian Brazil: Origins, Policies, and Future (New
Haven: Yale University Press, 1973).
    10.   Peter Evans, Dependent Development: The Alli-
ance of Multinational, State and Local Capital in Brazil
(Princeton: Princeton University Press, 1979).

2

The Paradise That Never Was:
The Breakdown of the
Brazilian Authoritarian Order

Philippe Faucher

The military regimes of Latin America are frequently classified as totalitarian. On this view, repression is seen as the means to achieve growth. Furthermore, because authority is strongly centralized and all forms of representation are prohibited, it is equally apparent that the international bourgeoisie is the basis of support for these regimes. The state is reduced to the role of mere agent for international capital. Even taking into account the simplification necessary to understand such complex phenomena, this analysis is almost always misleading. The current debate regarding democracy raging among the intelligentsia prompts us to reconsider, by means of political analysis, the military regimes presently in power.

The Brazilian situation is perhaps the most striking example. When the dictatorship first came to power it appeared that it would follow the same course as other military dictatorships. This was supported by the fact that it was the bourgeoisie, the pillars of industry and finance associated with imperialist capital, who profited most directly from the stabilization of the economy, the partial closing of the political system, the elimination of the leaders among the workers and peasants, the purging of all progressive elements, the concentration of revenues, and the opening of domestic markets to foreign capital. Since dictatorship favors the exploitation of work and the realization of profits, it has become, in the words of Florestan Fernandes, the "paradise of the bourgeoisie."(1) This paper examines the support systems that maintain the Brazilian bourgeoisie and its state. It commences with an examination and discussion of the doctrine of the hegemony of the international bourgeoisie in order to underscore the preponderant role of the state. It is important to clarify the precise nature of the association between the state and the bourgeoisie. This association is an example of dependent development.

It is necessarily contradictory and conflicting and cannot be contained within the model of an authoritarian regime. The purpose of this study is to show how the process of political liberalization(2) has been incorporated into the structure of the bourgeoisie-state relationship in the context of the critical growth situation and the present international economic situation.

This paper is divided into three parts. The first demonstrates that since 1964 the Brazilian bourgeoisie has been isolated from the centers of power by the military and the bureaucracy; a dependent society is fundamentally different from the advanced capitalist economies. Thus, contrary to the analyses of monopoly capitalism, it is the state which exercises tutelage over the entire bourgeoisie. The second part discusses the second National Development Plan (1975-1981), which can be considered as an unequivocal expression of the autonomy of the Brazilian state. The discussion centers around the failure of the reformed growth model proposed by the Geisel government and its difficult relations with certain sectors of the business community. At this conjuncture the Brazilian state appears as the principal obstacle to the exercise of power by the dominant class. The government's attempts at conciliation, and the economic crisis now raging, are clear indications that the tutelage of the state has not resolved the central question of the power struggle between the hegemonic and nonhegemonic factions of the bourgeoise. The third part of this paper examines the process of political liberalization. The process of increased political openness within the system will be presented as the necessary result of the government's attempt to achieve a different legitimization within a framework of conciliation between the various elites. Simultaneously there has been an increase in democratic demands by classes and fractions of classes excluded from the regime. The fundamental question of the democratization of Brazilian society occurs precisely at the juncture of these movements.

ECONOMIC POWER VERSUS BUREAUCRATIC CENTRALISM

One cannot understand the political process in Brazil if one assumes that military dictatorship is the ideal form of government for the bourgeoisie. On this assumption the speeches on democracy by representatives of the state would become merely a cynical ploy aimed at appropriating the ideas of the opposition and manipulating the masses. It is therefore necessary, if we wish to analyze the present political liberalization, to show why the static notion of the state as an instrument of high finance or capital is not the most effective model for a society set on the path to associated dependent development.

It is consistent with observations of advanced capitalist societies, where the bourgeoisie is hegemonic, to
postulate the state as an instrument of high finance.
This is not the case in dependent societies because their
bourgeoisie is characteristically nonhegemonic. In fact,
it is interesting to observe that the dominant class in
these societies is generally incapable of imposing its
interests on society as a whole without a totalitarian
exercise of power. In comparison with those in dominant
societies, the dependent bourgeoisie is weak; this condition and its effective control by the state apparatus
render it incapable of assuming the role of the governing
class in realizing a political objective.(3)

In dependent societies, the implantation of modern
industrial capitalism was imposed from the outside and
led to varying degrees of changes in social relations
without modifying the colonial order of commercial relations. The absence of a dynamic internal core, in the
form of a governing class, has prevented the classes from
becoming agents in the creation of a new social order and
the destruction of the former social relations. The specific features of dependent societies develop not from
the class structure, but rather from the make-up of the
social relations upset by the intrusion of industrial
capitalism as the dominant mode of production.

It should be stressed that structural heterogeneity (social and economic) and the frustration
of the hegemonic potential of the new bourgeois
sector are deeply rooted in the foundations of
late peripheral development. The class structure that emerges from the process of capitalist
development in peripheral formations is historically marked by the fragmentation and heterogeneity of the social forces in presence in Brazil.(4)

It is precisely the weakness and the heterogenous nature of the dominant class which explains and justifies
the military coup d'état. The division of the bourgeoi-
sie(5) means that each faction works towards the realization of its own particular interests, which may lead
it into conflict with other sectors. The level of solidarity of the bourgeoisie is particularly low; it does
not assume the role of dominating class unless its long
term interests are directly threatened. Its economic
power does not presuppose its capacity for political organization. The absence of a political objective uniting
the different factions of the bourgeoisie into a governing class may provoke recourse to military intervention.

In a very definite sense, the bourgeois fractions were not able to translate economic dominance into political direction. To contain the
popular forces and restore an increasingly exclusive order, they were forced to renounce the
direct exercise of power. The military became
the sustainers of the development projects of
an elite that lacked internal homogeneity, had
diverging interests, but shared the need for
order and a long-run interest in accelerated
capitalist growth. None of the groups present
in the new pact of domination was able to join
hegemony over the others and hence to legiti-
mately implement its interests as if they were
the interests of the nation.(6)

The mode of accumulation favoured by the military
government is characterized by what Fernando Henrique
Cardoso calls "the internationalization of the internal
market."(7) Production is dominated by foreign capital
which controls the most dynamic sectors of production
that act as the driving force for growth. Only a small
proportion of the population has access to the consumer
market. The export revenues from the traditional sectors
contribute necessary funds for essential imports. The
international financial market furnishes the funds needed
both to redeem the debt and to pursue expansion.

Once the period of stabilization was over, there is
no doubt that the bourgeoisie as a whole greatly benefited from the economic growth of the 1968-1973 period
(the "miracle"). Because the economic policy was aimed
not only at maintaining but also at stimulating the
rhythm of growth, it was clearly directed towards the interests of the bourgeoisie, both national and foreign.

In ensuring the domination of the bourgeoisie, the
state becomes, in its turn, a political agent:

As the political "condensation" of a social relation of domination it /the state/ expresses
the correlation of forces prevailing in society,
the diversity of interests, the stresses and
contradictions embedded in the movement of civil
society. Hence its relative autonomy vis-à-vis
civil society. As a political and bureaucratic
apparatus the state becomes a most strategic
agent in interest intermediation, articulating,
organizing and selecting socially determined
interests.(8)

It is in this way that technobureaucracy greatly centralized its power, even going so far as to exclude the bourgeoisie from the decision-making processes. A serious

displacement has existed since 1964 between economic power and its political expression at the level of the state
organs in charge of the management of the growth model.

The state take-over of the entire economic policy was
evident immediately following the coup d'état. The bourgeoisie was excluded from the elaboration of the economic
stabilization program and its claims (demanding the end
of credit restrictions in order to limit the severity of
the recession), which it had been advocating since 1965
before the Conselho Counsultivo de Planejamento (the Consultative Planning Council, CONSPLAN), were ignored.(9)

Economic growth was not only encouraged by the state
at the regulation level (favorable welcome to foreign capital, monetary and fiscal policy promoting investment
and consumption), but was also stimulated by a strong,
direct participation by the state in financing and production. This intervention (which also characterizes
dependent development) was permitted by the political
weakness of the bourgeoisie, and by the serious division
of the dominant class into factions and groups with divergent interests.

Economic policy generally aspires to ensure the most
propitious conditions for growth. In doing this the
state created the conditions of its own expansion and,
throughout the entire period, the development of the public sector was at least as important as that of the private sector. The technobureaucracy occupied the position
in the economic plan which was left vacant by a bourgeoisie which did not perceive itself as a hegemonic class.
(10) The state, rather than placing itself at the service of this class, which was not aware of its potential,
instead used the leeway which it possessed to increase
its hold on the definition of the development model. It
is even possible to point to certain instances where the
representation of the business community in the economic
decision-making organs was plainly manipulated. In this
respect, the planning process is noteworthy. In fact,
although the business community was strongly represented,
this presence became merely symbolic and without any real
influence in the content of the plan.(11) The state
presented, in the name of the general interest of the capitalist class, a text which bore no real relation to the
decisions of the administrators of the various sectors.
The completely symbolic nature of bourgeois representation in the state administrative machinery obliged entrepreneurs to present their demands individually before the
appropriate administration. The power of intervention
was displaced from the central organs to the sector agencies, whose autonomy was thereby increased. Each agency
had a tendency to develop its particular objectives, and
to assess requests according to the support it would be
able to mobilize for the realization of its own objectives. This influence game was rendered necessary by the

closing of channels of participation. It resulted in the atomization of economic policy and increasing incoherence in state intervention.

To this first fragmentation process was added another, i.e., the autonomy of the state favored the manifestation of divergent interests between the different agencies, particularly between the state enterprises and the sector bureaucracies.(12) The former, adopting the logic of expansion and conforming to the laws of the marketplace, had a tendency to develop their production without conforming to regulations (on rising prices, import limitations, and debt limitations) aimed at harmonizing growth.

These factors clearly show a dichotomy in an economic policy whose decision-making is totally centralized at the executive level (first by Roberto Campos, Minister of Planning during the Castello Branco government, then by Delfim Netto, Finance Minister under Costa e Silva and Medici, by President Geisel himself, and finally again by Delfim Netto under the present Figueiredo government). Implementation was split among the sector bureaucracies and state enterprises. These agencies, as the sole area of penetration by the individual interests of entrepreneurs in the state apparatus, used their influence to increase their power and their margin of maneuverability. (13) This state of confusion flows necessarily from the military decision (supported by the technobureaucracy) to simultaneously close off the political system and the privileged access of the capitalists to the machinery of economic intervention.

This situation had no immediate consequence. Indeed, who worries about representation when the rate of growth exceeds 10 percent and the rate of real profit reaches 25 percent in certain sectors? In such circumstances, the executive had the means to satisfy essential demands and to prevent, at great expense, the formation of bottlenecks. Discrimination in the distribution of aid and in the application of regulations remained very slight.(14) The absence of open conflict may lead one to believe in the existence of a consensus between the different fractions of capital and the state, but the growth during the 1968-1973 period hid the level of initiative by the state and the incoherence of government decisions. This became apparent the moment decline appeared. Thus the closing of the means of access to the economic intervention mechanisms, which led to decision-splitting and multiplication of unrelated programs, becomes a factor which generates inflation:

> Correcting imbalances requires that the real income growth rate of some groups within society decline relative to other groups. However, if

(a) those who benefit from the unequal distribution insist that their incomes accompany the
aggregate growth rate, and (b) those who don't
benefit refuse to accept a decline in their relative income, and (c) all have enough influence
to express their wishes, the natural result is
inflation.(15)

It became essential to rationalize economic policy
and to ensure that the executive assumed more direct control of the bureaucratic machinery. The internal crisis,
caused by the reversal of the expansion trend of the national economy, was aggravated by the need to reconcile
the divergent interests of many groups. The solution to
the crisis which began to be evident in 1973 is fundamentally political.

Let us quickly sum up the problem. The participation
of the state in the growth model is open to two interpretations. First, the economic intervention of the state
may be understood as the expression of the accord of the
public policies with the interests of the dominant class.
Their nonparticipation in the decision-making organs is
then not important given that the policies do aid the
accumulation process. The state does not possess any
autonomy under these conditions other than, at the most,
a certain bureaucratic rigidity. In this case economic
intervention of dependent states is merely the manifestation of general capitalist tendencies.

The other interpretation sees the economic intervention of the state in underdeveloped countries as a basic
expression of the autonomy which flows directly from its
dependent condition. The association with foreign capital is never without a national resistance which the
state, because of the weakness of the local bourgeoisie,
attempts to express. The nonparticipation of the business community and the absence of bourgeois representation, combined with the double process of the centrali-
zation of decisions and the atomization of policies, show
how much autonomy (other than just organizational) is
held by the various bureaucratic machines.

Four arguments have been presented which tend to show
that the dependent state is not to be considered as the
instrument of capital: the fundamental thesis of class
fragmentation in a dependent society, the nonrepresenta-
tion of the bourgeoisie in the organs of decision-making,
the contradiction in the economic policy, and the inter-
bureaucratic rivalry.

In the Brazilian situation, the debate cannot be settled merely by examining the accelerated growth period
(1968-1973) which prevented dissension and imbalances
from becoming apparent. Examination of the decline which
corresponds to General Geisel's government should advance

our argument. In fact, if the state intervention expresses the interests of capital, certain adjustments towards the interests - as far as they can be recognized -
of the hegemonic fraction of the bourgeoisie should limit
the effects of the recession on capital. Where accelerated growth permitted avoiding a policy choice by allowing
the expression of substantial autonomy from the state,
recession would require a definition of economic policy.
In conjunction with the atomization of policies of the
state an effort would be made to create coherence, at the
risk of accentuating the imbalances (inflation, debt).
The bourgeoisie, which until then had profited from
growth without directly assuming its management, is likely to demand real power of management and control over
the mechanism of economic intervention (which risks creating a power struggle). Whereas the system had econo-
mized on debate (a relative economy since it cost dearly
to all the victims of repression and censorship), it became essential to reestablish the channels of communication and political participation in order that the
choices, which must be made, would be the result of, if
not a consensus, at least a compromise by the bourgeoisie.

The three elements just mentioned - the bureaucratic
rationalization, the demand for access to the mechanisms
for economic intervention, and the resumption of the debate on the orientation of the development model - comprise key guide posts that will direct our analysis of
the most recent period.

THE BREAKDOWN OF THE CLASS ALLIANCE

Despite what the Brazilian government has publicly
claimed, it is not the 1973 rise in oil prices which was
responsible for the almost simultaneous decline in the
economy. As early as 1970, the "miracle" was showing
signs of strain.(16) Expansion was carried out only by
means of a heavy indebtedness undertaken to finance large
public projects (Itaipu, Tubarão, Ferrovia do Aço, etc.)
and to pay for private sector imports. The "oil crisis"
nevertheless upset the international capital market. The
dramatic price increase abruptly shifted demand and created, for a limited period of time, a relative shortage,
thereby causing interest rates to soar. With international capital becoming both more expensive and less
available, the Brazilian authorities were obliged to face
a declining rate of growth and to consider new alternatives.

It is in this context that the II Plano Nacional de
Desenvolvimento (the Second National Development Plan,
II PND) was proposed on 10 September 1974. This is an
interesting indicator which expresses all the ambivalence

of the state towards national development and the participation of foreign capital while reaffirming the absolute
priority given to the pursuit of growth. In retrospect,
the movement of both the Brazilian and international economic situations toward a crisis prevented the attainment
of the objectives of the II PND and showed it in its true
light, that is, as a political manifesto emanating from
the Brazilian state.

The II PND expresses the spirit of nationalism and
the desire for autonomy which characterize the techno-
cratic-military coalition controlling the bureaucratic
apparatus. This is an unequivocal demonstration of state
autonomy. On the other hand, the coalition which held
power fully realized that it needed a legitimate basis
in civil society, mainly within the bourgeoisie. The
principal proposal of the II PND aimed at reinforcing
national private entreprise.(17) There are two corol-
laries to this main objective: to define the field of
activities of the public sector and to circumscribe the
activity of foreign capital.(18)

The government proposal clearly expresses the desire
to adapt the tri-pé in order to reinforce its weakest
member - national capital.(19) The priority given to national industry was obviously the result of the alarming
increase in the trade deficit (particularly in the capital goods sector).(20) But one should not overlook the
political aspect of this phenomenon. Although the period
of stabilization (1964 to 1967) caused a marked denation-
alization of the economy, in relative terms due to the
numerous bankruptcies of small and medium-sized national
entreprises and in absolute terms due to the purchase of
these enterprises by multinationals (the creation of new
undertakings with foreign capital began to escalate in
1968), the ensuing growth permitted the strengthening of
a Brazilian national industry, often associated with but
never subordinated to foreign capital. This national
sector needed the protection and assistance of the state
and, of course, demanded participation in decision-making
processes. This emerging faction of the bourgeoisie
wished to assume its role of class leadership on a political level.

The II PND propounds a set of policies designed to
maintain a high rate of increase in the GNP (10 percent).
The viability of the model depended on the balance between the public sector and private initiative, and in
the private sector this viability hinged on the balance
between national and foreign enterprise. This search for
balance implied a limitation of expansion in the public
sector. Private national enterprise was to be strengthened through programs supporting mergers and the formation of holdings. Foreign enterprise was to take account
of national priorities and thus government agencies (Bank

of Brazil, CACEX, CDI, CPI, etc.) were to closely scruti-
nize any requests (repatriation of profits, import authorization, grants, tax credits and exemptions, price
fixing, etc.).

The producers of capital goods were particularly affected by this policy statement. Resolution 9, on 31
March 1977, by the Economic Development Council reaffirmed in a concrete fashion the measures for the support
of capital-goods production. The government thereby undertook to promote participation by the national private
sector in its projects. Under this resolution, the Banco
Nacional de Desenvolvimento Economico (National Bank for
Economic Development, BNDE) must grant priority to the
financing of projects in the national private sector.
The state favors and wishes to perfect the model of tripartite association (public enterprise, national and multinational private enterprise) by imposing conditions and
demanding guarantees. Thus all associations must involve
a substantial investment by the foreign partner in the
form of risk capital and an actual transfer of technology, and the studies and principal engineering works must
be carried out locally by or in collaboration with Brazilians. With regard to its investment authorizations
(the responsibility of the Industrial Development Council, CDI), the administration must ensure that new businesses not compete unnecessarily with already established
producers and, in fact, public enterprises are only permitted to import machinery and equipment if there is no
local producer of these articles.(21)

The II PND proposals assume a collective savings rate
for the whole period (1975-1981) equal to approximately
35 percent of the national product or its equivalent in
foreign debt.(22) From the outset the project was not
feasible. The harmonization of interests which was facilitated by growth became increasingly difficult in a
crisis situation. Experience has shown that national
capital is hit hardest by production slow-downs and requires state protection against competition by multinationals. Public enterprises saw their working margin
reduced by the shortage and high price of credit in international markets. Foreign companies protested the
controls imposed on price fixing, the obligatory investigation for import authorization, the delays imposed for
obtaining funds for the repatriation of profits, etc.
The real and perceived difficulties associated with the
lack of government consultation, added to the total absence of control by the bourgeoisie of the tools of economic intervention - President Geisel had totally centralized the decision-making processes of the Economic
Development Council (CDE) over which he presided - led
the bourgeoisie to publicly oppose not the plan itself,
but rather its lack of implementation and the behavior
of the regime regarding it. Thus between 1974 and 1976

a debate arose in which many denounced what they perceived to be a state stranglehold on the economy.(23)
     This debate is important in understanding the nature
and extent of the changes presently taking place. The
debate on state control was the first public demonstration by the Brazilian business community since 1964. It
shows the alienation of the dominant class in the face of
the inability of the regime to make the necessary adjustments to give a new impetus to the process of industrialization. It also indicates the dilemma in which the
regime found itself and the powerlessness of the bourgeoisie itself to develop (even if to its own advantage)
an alternative. This debate clearly expresses the rupture of the interdependent association between the various factions of the bourgeoisie and the technocratic-
military coalition.(24)
     Until 1976, the local bourgeoisie remained discreet
and only joined in the debate at a relatively late date.
In fact, the very survival of the Brazilian business community depended on the protection and patronage of the
state (this is especially true for the capital goods sector it controls). While the international sector denounced both the controls placed on it and the advantages
enjoyed by public enterprises, the capital goods sector,
in contrast, protested the excessive constraints imposed
on its markets by foreign capital and, paradoxically, the
lack of autonomy of the state enterprises.(25) Yet it
was the capital goods sector which benefited most from
state generosity on the eve of the publication of the II
PND. In this respect the signs are clear and irrefuta-
ble. The assistance given to the basic sectors by the
CDI between 1973 and 1977 increased from 5 percent to 18
percent of the total investments, while the aid given to
the automobile and consumer goods sectors decreased from
5.5 percent to 2.6 percent. The participation of the national industry in supplying equipment approved by the
CDI rose from 35 percent to 68 percent.(26) For its
part, the BNDE created new agencies (Embramec, Fibase,
Ibrasa) with a view to supplying fixed capital to businesses or to financing projects at preferential rates
(for the years 1975 and 1976, FINAME, a subsidiary of
BNDE, set at 20 percent the monetary correction applied
to its loans whereas the current inflation rates for
those years were 29 percent and 46 percent respectively).
(27) Given such conditions, why would the national capital goods industry decide to take part in the debate
against state economic intervention?
     The II PND forecast a fabulous $43 billion investment
for the capital goods sector. This investment effort was
to be based entirely on the state enterprises which were
responsible for the vast equipment programs (electricity,
steel, transportation, communications, petrochemicals,

etc.) and on their ability to seek financing in international markets. This euphoric prospect led many businesses to increase their production capacity in view of the anticipated increase in demand. For example, the capacity for the production of machinery for the years 1975 to 1978 (until September) went from 115 to 131 (1972 = 100). Although the turnover more than doubled between 1972 and 1976 (the value of deliveries went from 100 in 1972 to 215 in 1976, 231 in 1977, and 250 in 1978), this was not enough to maintain this level of activity. Thus, after an initial increase, orders steadily diminished from 1975 on. Taking the year 1972 as a base, the index 100 represents 32.4 weeks of activity. The index for this period rose to 135 in 1975 only to diminish progressively to 127 in 1976, to 112 in 1977, and to dip to 97 in 1978.(28)

The reasons for this decline are twofold. Businessmen, anxious not to allow competitors to monopolize the excess demand, launched ambitious investment programs, thereby profiting from the extremely favorable financing conditions offered to them. They presumed that the public enterprises had the capacity to adapt to the new orientations of industrial policy. However, these did not respond to the expectations of the executive. Once the national bourgeoisie realized that the promises made to it would not be honored, as we will see below, as early as 1976 it allied itself with the criticism of the government's economic policy.

Brazil also found itself confronted with the structural constraints of the international division of labor. Neither the state nor the public enterprises possessed the autonomy which the II PND assumed they had.(29) In fact, the government project consisted of maintaining internal demand and of stimulating private investment by means of large scale projects. However the decline of economic activity, which was felt as early as 1973, reduced the demand for equipment goods (steel) and services (energy, transport) produced by the public enterprises. The unused capacity of industry reduced both the revenues and the self-financing ability of the public sector. This situation upset the "national autonomy" strategy and altered the importance of the national private sector's participation in the realization of the projects.(30) Thus the large public enterprises were obliged to submit to the requirements of the international financing agencies in order to realize their projects. Participation with these agencies usually entails conforming to a whole series of conditions. In particular, the agencies require that contracts of purchase be awarded by an international call for tenders which in effect virtually eliminates local producers. The World Bank laid down this condition for the whole of the steel plan, even though its participation represented only 10 percent of the resources necessary for the project.(31) In this instance, the World Bank also made the following demands on the Brazilian government: (1) that eventual changes of ownership of shares in steel enterprises would not be made without prior consultation with the Bank, (2) that any alteration of the price of steel would be submitted for evaluation, and (3) that a substantial part of the coal necessary for the production of steel would be imported from the United States.(32)

A similar situation occurred in the case of the iron ore project at Tubarão which is a joint venture of the state-run Siderbras company together with the Japanese firm Kawasaki and the Italian firm Finsider. The equipment was to be sold by the foreign partners and this represented their participation in the project. In May 1976, the total estimated investment rose to $1.9 billion. The shareholders' agreement provided that the capital for Tubarao was to be approximately 25 percent of this amount. The participation of each foreign enterprise was fixed at 24.5 percent or 49 percent in all, the equivalent of $236.4 millon. The cost of the equipment reached $1.2 billion of which 30 percent was to be produced locally while the rest, $800 million, was to be imported. If one assumes a profit margin for the sale of equipment of 25 to 30 percent, this means that Kawasaki and Finsider would obtain a profit of between $200 and $250 million. This amount corresponds to the capital investment of the foreign partners.(33) Thus their participation in the capital of the enterprise is made through their supplying the equipment. However, even though they did not actually participate in the financing of the project, Kawasaki and Finsider nevertheless obtained a veto power on the principal questions relating to the life of the enterprise. In fact, article 11 of chapter III of the agreement established that the Board of Directors be composed of five members, three nominated by Siderbras and two by the associated companies. The consent of at least four directors is required for all those questions pertaining to contracts for the purchase of coal and iron ore, changes affecting capital, new investments, etc. On the other hand, if one partner wishes to withdraw, it may do so without penalty. Thus, once the equipement is supplied, the foreign partner may obtain reimbursement for its investment and be freed from its option to purchase a portion of the production.(34)

The Brazilian business community denounced both the meager part they were allowed in the supply of equipment (30 percent) and the controlling power of the foreign partners; moreover, they voiced doubts about the viability of the project (particularly concerning the flow of production onto the international market).(35) Foreign participation is indispensable, not only for the technology it brings, but because it guarantees outlets for production the Brazilian market would not be able to absorb. Under these circumstances, the Brazilian partner is in a difficult bargaining position. Enough pressure was finally brought to bear on the government of Brazil for it to promise to review the Tubarao agreement.(36) However, it is hard to tell whether this decision was due to the denunciations of the local bourgeoisie or whether the project was suspended because of the falling price of steel on the international market. It is noteworthy that the famous nuclear agreement with Germany was similarly denounced for the minimal participation of Brazilian production and for the controlling power reserved for the foreign partner.

To realize major investment projects, most under - developed countries have little choice but to ask for international financing. Under the laws of the world market, public enterprise is faced with the following alternatives: either to continue its activity with the result that the bulk of its equipment must be imported and control will be out of its hands, or to give preference to national producers at the risk of seeing the projects endangered for lack of financing or markets. Given the importance of these projects, and the prominence gained by the public sector, to accord preference to local industry would induce a recession.(37) As long as the regime has no other source of legitimacy, growth remains the primary objective. In such circumstances the union of state enterprises and large-scale national enterprises, so desired by the II PND, could not be realized.

Strikingly symbolic of the government's effort to open new sectors of activity, acquire technology at the lowest possible cost, and obtain access to foreign markets, while leaving local businessmen trailing, is the petrochemical complex of Camaçari in the State of Bahia. The most recent studies clearly show the extent of the costs as weighed against the few advantages which Brazil has to gain from this strategy.(38) The creation of a petrochemical integrated complex in the State of Bahia is a political decision (the opening of a new sector, production autonomy, and a concern for the regional distribution of economic activities were among the criteria which influenced the decision) because the project does not meet the criteria of economic feasibility. Therefore, such a project can only be put into action by the state. The national and foreign private sector will undertake such a venture only if the state gives sufficient guarantees as to the viability of their investment. It is precisely because this is a political decision, and because the state assumes the costs, that the tripartite association is able to be formed.

Study of the methods of management and financing reveals, as in the Tubarao case, that the foreign partners
have preserved a legal right of veto over the decisions
of the Camaçari Board of Directors.(39)   A survey of the
tripartite association experiment in the petrochemical
sector showed that the state assumes the financial risks
almost entirely while the foreign companies retain authority over the future development of the petrochemical
industry, power which in no way corresponds to their financial participation or to the risks they run.   From
this example, Martins concludes that the bureaucracy uses
its association with foreign capital to legitimize its
role as entrepreneur.(40)   These conditions demonstrate
the voluntary and utopian character, considered by some
to be emancipatory,(41) of the PND proposals for an association of the public sector and national capital.

The deep disillusionment which followed the repeated
failure of the public sector to stimulate economic growth
caused repercussions among the bourgeoisie.   Never before
had it been necessary to question the economic model and
the authoritarian nature of the regime.   Once they clearly understood the coalition of interests which excluded
them, the entrepreneurs began to associate themselves
with those who demanded a liberalization of the regime.
Thus in 1976 the local bourgeoisie came to see democracy
as the form of government best able to understand and
defend their interests.   This date also marks the end of
the class alliance tri-pé and ushers onto the political
scene social forces (workers, students, intellectuals)
which had previously been restrained by artificial means.
(42)   The bourgeoisie did not act out of a spirit of
magnanimity, but instead applied a rather cynical cost/
benefit approach to the regime.   It opposed the regime
from the moment that the concrete benefits it received
did not outweigh the costs associated with authoritarianism.

Since 1976, several articles in business journals
have documented the growing dissatisfaction with the government's evident inability to control the economic situation and to implement its development program.   The
year 1977 began with two statements favoring political
liberalization, democratization, and free elections: one
by the Minister of Industry and Commerce, Severo Gomes
(who, soon after this, was forced out of the cabinet),
(43) and the other by a business leader, José Papa Jr.
(president of the Federation and Commercial Centre of the
State of São Paulo).(44)   This public taking of sides led
other sectors of the industrial bourgeoisie to declare
their allegiances.   The principal business associations
pronounced themselves to be in favour of a democracy:
these associations included ANFAVEA, ABDID, ABMAG/SIMESP,
ABINEE, FIESP.(45)   Note that this stance was by no means

unanimous: there was a marked split among the factions
of the bourgeoisie.(46)

A few days later another document signed by eight
influential industrial leaders was published. This became the manifesto of the democratic bourgeoisie.(47)
It stressed the government's commitment to the priority
of the capital goods industry and addressed itself explicitly to the crisis of the tri-pé:

> We realize that the desired equilibrium among
> the three principal protagonists of the process
> of industrialization is far from being attained.
> National private enterprise suffers from a dis-
> quieting fragility, public enterprise has es-
> caped from the control of society and foreign
> enterprise has no clear or adequate norms to
> discipline it.(48)

Analysis of the economic situation reveals three factors: distortion of the financial structure caused by
the systematic recourse to outside financing, absence of
a policy directed at absorbing technology, and lack of
control and definition for the orientation of spending
by the state and public enterprises. The signatories
pointed out that no industrial policy can be realized
without the active participation of entrepreneurs, that
economic development cannot be attained at the cost of
great social inequality, and that the power relationships
between workers and employers must be worked out by direct negotiation. In short, the authors opted for a
democratic regime.

It is this second manifesto which received the greatest support from the business community. Its stance in
favor of democracy united the nationalistic bourgeoisie
and the representatives of foreign capital. Both these
factions opposed the growing role of the technobureaucracy as any increase in its power means a greater arbi-
trariness in state intervention. The nationalistic bourgeoisie hopes to gain access to the machinery of economic
intervention in order to direct economic policy in its
own interests. Foreign capital wishes to reduce controls
which limit the viability of its investments.(49) For
both these factions, the conflict revolves around state
power; this coalition of forces requires the creation of
a political dimension, or liberalization. If one admits
that the growth model must be modified and that the international economic situation no longer allows the pre-
sumption of access to world markets (capital, market outlets), this crisis forces a greater contribution from the
local markets. In a dependent society, mediation between
national and foreign interests is handled by the state.
The regime's crisis has reached such proportions that its

ability to negotiate the conciliation necessary for market division must be legitimized through the opening of political debate.

This chapter has detailed the main factors pertaining to the definition of class alliance relative to the process of dependent development, and has explored the factors responsible for the conflict which provoked the split and initiated the crisis on the political level. We have seen how, in 1976, the public was made aware of the split between the technocracy responsible for the bureaucratic machinery of economic intervention and the state enterprises and the local bourgeoisie, especially the capital goods sector. The crisis of this model or plan divided the bourgeoisie and revealed the incompatibilities among the various factions.

Although the crisis of the Brazilian model is most clearly expressed on the economic level, its solution is actually political. It is in this context that one must understand the announcement by the government of the instigation of reforms leading to liberalization. Political analysis also helps interpret the varying contents of the demands for democracy, which have increased since 1976.

DEMOCRACY BY DECREE?

At the beginning of his mandate in 1974, President Geisel announced his intention to liberalize his regime. However, his rule did not bring about any dramatic changes; in fact, he exercised the discretionary powers available to him under Institutional Act No. 5 (AI No. 5) as often as his predecessors. This waiting period was necessary to allow the concept of democratization to develop so that the goals of the executive could be assimilated by all levels of government (states and municipalities) as well as by the state machinery (bureaucracy, police, etc.) and by the ruling elite. President Geisel abrogated AI No. 5 in June 1978 and transferred power to General Figueiredo in March 1979. General Figueiredo began his term of office with a decree of partial amnesty for political prisoners and exiles. The reform of the political system, initiated several months ago, has resulted in the formation of new political groups with an eye to the approaching deadline for legislative elections in 1982. Political liberalization is clearly a goal of the regime.

Nevertheless, we must question these government proposals in the light of the impasse in the attempt to restructure the growth model. At the outset, two observations must be made. First, if the existing military government is committed to a process of democratic liberalization, then it must have become convinced that the

regime is doomed in its present form. Second, the government will do everything within its power to keep control of, and to manipulate, the process of liberalization. The regime will only allow the minimum amount
of concessions necessary to obtain from civilian society
a social base from which it may secure a majority representation. The recently initiated reforms tend in this
direction. The election process will only be reestablished if the government's political strategists (headed
by General Golbery do Couto e Silva) are convinced that
forces favorable to the regime are assured of a comfortable victory. It would be out of the question for the
military to transfer power to the existing civilian opposition. Since a true democracy requires recognition
of the principle of alternation of government, we can
only refer to recent changes as the beginnings of a process of liberalization. These observations suggest that
the actual redemocratization of political life in Brazil
will come about only through a victory for the opponents
of the military regime, a culmination of their struggle
since 1964.

What are the factors which have led the regime to
search for a new form to exercise power? We have discussed the structural factors which resulted in the
breakdown of the power-sharing pact between the state and
the bourgeoisie, as well as the contradictions within the
bourgeoisie which prevent the clear expression of some
political direction by a hegemonic faction. Certain political indicators illustrate the crisis of the authoritarian regime. First, there was the 1974 electoral victory of the opposition, when it received 60 percent of
the vote despite all the obstacles which it encountered.
This victory forced the government to grossly manipulate
the electoral system (1976 Falcão Law, Pacote de Abril
in 1977) in order to protect its majority in the Congress
and the Federal Senate. It became obvious in 1974 that
most of the opposition was concentrated in the richer
districts of Brazil (São Paulo, Rio de Janeiro, Rio
Grande de Sul), uniting the workers as well as the middle
class (civil servants, teachers and employees) who enjoy
the most direct benefits of the regime.(50)

This last observation brings us to the second reason
for this movement towards a change within the regime:
the wear and tear of power manifests itself by a dangerous erosion of the military institution. After sixteen
years in power, the army finds itself in the same position as a government party increasingly weakened by internal dissension. President Geisel's succession brought
to light several of these conflicts. A growing cleavage
appears to separate a more professional military group,
which wants to preserve the integrity of the institution,
from the politicians who are mainly interested in keeping
themselves in power.(51) The successive dismissals of

Generals Hugo Abreu and Silvio Frota, and the rapproche-
ment of Euler Bentes with the civil opposition, demonstrate the irreconcilable nature of the divisions within
the armed forces. However, the problem goes deeper than
this. Since the military has held a power monopoly for
the past sixteen years, they are blamed for all the ills
of Brazilian society; for problems which the dictatorship
has not solved, or has even worsened. The armed forces
are associated with the pitiful living conditions of the
majority of the population, with torture, and with corruption. This image is not acceptable to many career
officers, the majority of whom do not actively participate in the government and receive only indirect benefits from its favors. Furthermore, the ideological cement of the regime, the doctrine of national security
which justified a merciless war against communism, no
longer rings true since the government established diplomatic relations with the M.P.L.A. in Angola (against the
advice of the Americans), and has made overtures towards
China and Eastern Europe. We may also presume the existence of concerns within the armed forces regarding the
possibility of a swift reversal of the present situation,
in which case the military would be obliged to publicly
justify its flagrant contravention of basic human rights.
How could the government justify its role as the defender
of the nation if the people view it as a dangerous enemy?
These considerations confirm the political crisis of the
regime both at the political level, in the system established by the regime, as well as within the military institution. These factors also corroborate the fact that
the political domination of the army is no longer based
on a hegemonic power bloc.
    The status quo can no longer be maintained in light
of these mounting tensions. But can we truly expect
liberalization, even if it is a stated goal of government? Have the previous crises not been resolved, instead, by a greater use of force, repression, and authoritarianism? We cannot dismiss the possibility of a violent closing of the barely-parted curtain of repression.
This would, however, be an extremely precarious solution.
Such measures would result in a profound divison of Brazilian society. The armed forces would be the first and
most harshly affected institution. A government which
attempted this would find itself on thin ice, and would
likely be sunk by a settling of accounts. The only solution, therefore, is greater liberalization. The following discussion will deal with this liberalization, the
hopes to which it has given rise, and its limits.
    The government's goal in liberalization is to allow
a political system broad enough to give rise to a new
power pact, one which would restrict the influence of
social forces seeking a change in the regime. Any liberalization must provide an honorable exit for the army, as

well as leading to the formation of a responsible civilian government. We must not forget that we are faced here with a very limited plan of democratization. The regime hopes to broaden its social base by cooptation, while forbidding a real debate on a national scale. In my view, this solution would seem difficult to achieve. It demands a minimum of consensus within the government, and presumes that there exists an economic and political plan capable of defusing the crisis and providing a rallying point. Yet, as we have seen, the group in power has only one utopia to propose: the second National Development Plan. The apolitical realism of Mario Henrique Simonsen, Minister of Planning and a passionate advocate of monetarism during the early months of the Figueiredo regime (March-August 1979), did not survive attacks from the combined opposition of the bureaucracy and the business community. Delfim Netto returned to the helm with only pragmatism, optimistic speeches, and authoritarian methods to offer as a solution. The authorities evidently have no alternative proposal. Deprived of any concrete social foundation, they remain in power thanks to the weight of inertia.(52) Although the military regime is not supported actively by any significant class or group within Brazilian society (it can neither invoke a state of emergency nor produce a collective project to legitimize the regime), it manages to stay in power only because the different forces within civilian society have not been able to organize their diverging interests into coherent and articulate political organizations capable of assuming the political and economic leadership of the country.

Since General Figueiredo became president, Brazilian political life has centered entirely on the formation of a political direction. The business community has stopped publicly opposing the government, since the industrialists do not wish to overshadow the organization of political parties. Rather, they prefer to channel their collective demands through the political system while they avoid playing the role of the opposition. However the bourgeoisie appears seriously ambivalent towards the liberalization plans. The Brazilian bourgeoisie is not aware of itself as a class, and is concerned with losing the rather inglorious, but comfortable, protection of the state. Thus the bourgeoisie is demanding guarantees from the state before it participates in the liberalization process. These guarantees are obviously related to free trade unions and opposition parties. While the bourgeoisie accepts the working class as a social actor, with the right to assert its legitimate demands in the workplace, it is reluctant to accept it as a political actor on a national scale.(53) Thus the government strategy in establishing the rules of formation of political parties consists entirely of the development of a right-wing formation, while promoting the break-up of opposition forces.(54)

Since the abolition of the two party system in November 1979, the politicians (old and new) have begun an agitated search for a coalition to accept and represent them. The initial project of the government has been accomplished; the opposition is divided into five factions while the governing party has remained united despite strong internal dissensions. The Democratic Party (PD), led by José Sarney and Jarbas Passarinho, enjoys a comfortable majority in the Congress and the Senate. The most moderate opposition, the liberal right, is found in the Popular Party of Tancredo Neves and Magalhães Pinto. The most prominent opposition party is composed of a group (of "moderates" and "authentics") formed from the former official opposition party, the Brazilian Democratic Movement (MDB). This latter party preferred to remain united, despite their great differences, in order not to divide the opposition and thus, according to them, play the government game. Ulysses Guimarães, Teotônio Vilela, and Miguel Arraes are the most influential personalities of the Brazilian Democratic Movement Party (PMDB). Because they wished neither to recoup the spoils of a dictatorship nor to collaborate with men who form part of that system, the unions (led by the metallurgists of Sao Paulo where the last strike in mid-1980 was brutally suppressed) decided to form the Workers Party (PT) which is directed by Luis Inácio da Silva (Lula). Even before his return from exile, Leonel Brizola's credibility was suspect. Irreparably implicated with president João Goulart, who was overthrown in 1964, he remains, as far as the right is concerned, a dangerous agitator. On the opposition's part, Brizola has compromised himself by association with European social democracy (mainly German). He is today a moderate who, through his various and contradicting stands, has lost his right to lead and revive the Brazilian Labor Party. (The Labor Party formed the workers' base in the last Vargas government and the populist governments which followed it). Even the name of the party was taken away from him by Ivete Vargas (a distant relative of President Vargas) who, together with ex-President Jánio Quadros, has revived the tradition of the Brazilian Labour Party (PTB). Brizola has since formed the Democratic Labor Party (PDT).

Exactly as the military calculated, the proximity of power, and the prospect of being able to assume more direct control following the liberalization of the regime, served as a catalyst for the governing party which remained united. The contradictions within the opposition induced its fragmentation. The groups which were not represented in the old system preferred to create their own organization. The following is a brief examination of the constraints facing the opposition in this new system.(55)

To check the military's strategy requires the opposition movement to seek to reconcile the demands of the workers and the tendency for institutionalization. It would be extremely dangerous in the present situation for it to go beyond the institutional framework proposed by the government. It must be remembered that, at the present, it is the government which has the initiative, which determines the rules, and which decides the timing and the extent of the liberalization process. Any excess will be seized upon by the most authoritarian factions and risks modifying the present relations among the state forces favorable to liberalization. On the other hand, it is desirable that the opposition movement be able to count on a large base of support within organized labor as well as among all other workers.

It follows from these observations that the struggle of the working class is occurring simultaneously on two distinct fronts. The union movement and the workers' political movement are thus separate and distinct. If this distinction is not maintained, it seems clear that one of the conditions necessary for a true redemocratization, opposition representation within the institutional framework, will never arise. The unions must fight for recognition of the democratic principle at the workplace (the right to strike) and demand the formation of mechanisms for negotiating between workers and employers, all of which means putting a definite term to the Ministry of Labor's tutelage. The necessarily precarious balance between union practices and political action, bound up with the constant danger of the collapse of the opposition forces, is at the heart of the debate which has raged for the past several months between the union leaders from the São Paulo industrial belt and the progressive wing of the opposition party (PMDB).

CONCLUSION

The conclusion to be drawn from this study is that, contrary to what is commonly asserted, the military dictatorship received extremely precarious support from the bourgeoisie. In consequence, the legitimacy of the regime, always precarious, was further compromised following the decline of economic growth. In the second part, I demonstrated how the project of a new power pact, symbolized by the proposals contained in the II PND, could not be realized. This failure led the business community to consider that its interests may coincide with a process of political liberalization.

Finally I attempted to explain how the "liberalization" proposed by the government aims at the creation

of a political system which is not necessarily democratic. Democracy can be achieved only by a victory of the
opposition forces. This struggle demands that the movement of those favorable to a full and complete democracy
remains as open as possible to be able to include all opposition forces. It also requires that the leaders of
the movement, resisting populist leanings, take on the
thankless and delicate task of containing their demands
in order to protect the institutional framework and thereby prevent any outbreak of violence.

What are the theoretical implications of my conclusions? The facts detailed above allow us to gauge the
autonomy of the dependent state. The II PND represents
the plan of the technobureaucracy (designated by the term
"state bourgeoisie"). The obvious failure of this undertaking gives us a clear idea of the voluntary nature of
this reformist proposal. The autonomy of the state is
important when it is bound up with the accumulation process. The state possesses a vast potential for negotiation and regulation. This allows it to actively engage
in the definition of a production structure and in the
creation of a market (local and foreign) which will not
be subject to exterior control. However, it is wrong to
believe that the interests of the public sector coincide
with a greater solidarity with the local bourgeoisie.
The state enterprises do not escape the constraints of a
market dominated by imperialist capital. As we have
shown, the public sector contains an emancipatory dimension because it favors and reinforces the creation of a
national economic system. Notwithstanding this, it creates its own contradictions by limiting the expansion of
local production. In this sense one may state that the
development of the public sector in a dependent economy
is legitimized by its association with foreign capital
rather than by its relation with the local bourgeoisie.
(56)

Our study also shows that the process of harmonization of interests among national capital, foreign capital, and the state has been strained to the utmost. The
advantage gained by private national capital from its
privileged access to the state is insufficient to ensure
that its interests are effectively protected. This is
why large sectors of the bourgeoise feel that the political framework is too restricted. By broadening the political system they hope to enlarge their power of negotiation. Our analysis casts doubt on the theory of the tri-
pé and on the true significance of a project such as the
petrochemical complex in Bahia which is supposed to represent the reconciliation of the three sectors.(57) It
is not by the manipulation of the tools of economic intervention that the process of national accumulation will
prevail over the process of accumulation at the world

level. The defence and the development of the local market henceforth must proceed by the democratization (at least partially) of the regime.

In order for production to be shifted to meet the needs of the vast majority of the population, it is imperative that those needs find an expression through the political process. Hence the project to strengthen national accumulation cannot be separated from the debate on democracy.

Does the gravity of the present economic situation endanger this political project? For 1980 the inflation rate should be over 100 percent, while the country needs an input of $20 billion in order to meet its obligations (debt service of $11 billion) and to pay off its oil bill (also almost $11 billion). With credit becoming increasingly expensive (the government is considering appealing to the International Monetary Fund), strong pressure will be brought to bear to ensure that a policy of stabilization will be followed; this necessarily means an even greater decline in economic activity. As a probable scenario, we can easily imagine that tensions will become more accentuated. Workers will resist any deterioration in their buying power and in their working conditions. The economic crisis will affect first and foremost small and medium sized business as well as national enterprises. It is highly probable that it will give rise to a new wave of denationalization of the economy and to added pressures for a reduction of the controls applied by the sector bureaucracies. Under these conditions the liberalization process will result in the weakening of the state and its capacity for intervention, and will not have the effect of democratizing its access in order that its policies can be oriented toward "the national interest." Furthermore, it is conceivable that social and political conflicts will attain such a level that they will induce the formation of a new alliance between the different factions of the bourgeoisie and the state, thereby making possible the maintenance of the military dictatorship.

I wish to thank the CAFIR program at the University of Montreal for helping fund this research.

NOTES

1. Florestan Fernandes, A Revolução Burguesa no Brasil (Rio de Janeiro: Zahar Editores, 1975), p. 359.
2. The term "political liberalization" is used for want of a better expression to designate the process begun in 1974 of opening a political dimension in the system. I am perfectly aware of the ambiguity which can

result from the use of terms found in official documents. This is, therefore, not to be taken as an endorsement of the government's plan nor as a prediction that the outcome of this process will be the democratization of the regime. This paper continues the reflections on the relationship between the political system and economic accumulation in dependent societies. In particular, it is intended as an attempt to define the limits of state autonomy by showing the importance of the conflicts in relations among the local bourgeoisie, the state, and foreign capital. This is based on the fascinating research carried out by Fernando Henrique Cardoso, Guillermo O'Donnell, Philippe Schmitter, Alfred Stepan, etc. and more recently developed by David Collier, ed., The New Authoritarianism in Latin America (Princeton: Princeton University Press, 1979); Peter Evans, Dependent Development: The Alliance of Multinational, State and Local Capital in Brazil (Princeton: Princeton University Press, 1979); E.V.K. Fitzgerald, The State and Economic Development: Peru since 1968 (Cambridge: Cambridge University Press, 1976); Ronaldo Munck, "State Intervention in Brazil: Issues and Debates," Latin American Perspectives 6, no. 4 (Autumn 1979): 16-31; Jonathan Fox, "Has Brazil Moved Toward State Capitalism," Latin American Perspectives 7, no. 1 (Winter 1980): 64-86.

3. Sérgio Henrique Abranches, "The Divided Leviathan; State and Economic Policy Formation in Authoritarian Brazil" (Doctoral thesis, Cornell University, 1978), p. 32.

4. Ibid., pp. 158-159.

5. The bourgeoisie is not only divided according to the sector of productive activity it is engaged in, as in any capitalist society, but also along the lines of its relation with foreign capital. In a dependent country, one must distinguish between a bourgeoisie compradore and a domestic (or local) bourgeoisie. This last concept designates the fraction of the bourgeoisie which, while having its own basis of accumulation, is limited to foreign capital and profits from it (see Nicos Poulantzas, Les classes sociales dans le capitalisme aujourd'hui (Paris: Seuil, 1974), p. 71. In this paper, when the term bourgeoisie is used, I refer to the class as a whole. In the analysis I also refer to specific factions of the bourgeoisie, and each time the sector considered is specified.

6. Abranches, "The Divided Leviathan," pp. 157-158.

7. Fernando Henrique Cardoso, Autoritarismo e Democratização (Rio de Janeiro: Paz e Terra, 1975), p. 73.

8. Abranches, "The Divided Leviathan," p. 435.

9. Cesar Guimarães, dir., Expansão do Estado e Intermediação de Interesses no Brasil (Rio de Janeiro: IUPERJ, 1979), p. 195.

10. Eli Diniz Cerqueira a Renato Paul Boschi, "Elite Industrial e Estado: uma Analise da Ideologia do Empresariado Nacional nos Anos 70," in Carlos Estevam Martins, dir., Estado e Capitalismo no Brasil (Sao Paulo: Hucitec-Cebrap, 1977), p. 177.

11. Guimarães, Expansão do Estado, p. 177.

12. Abranches, "The Divided Leviathan," pp. 164-165.

13. Sergio Henrique Abranches and Sulamis Dain, A Empresa Estatal no Brasil: Padrões Estructurais Estrategias de Ação (Rio de Janeiro: Relatório do Grupo de Estudos Sobre o Setor Público, FINEP, 1978), p. 30.

14. This was clearly apparent in the policy of attribution of grants for investment applied by the Industrial Development Council. Thus in 1977 only 37 of the 2,888 requests for financing presented to the Industrial Development Council were rejected. On this subject see Luciano Martins, A Expansão Recente do Estado no Brasil: Seus Problemas a Seus Atores (Rio de Janeiro: IUPERJ-FINEP report, 1977); Sérgio Henrique Abranches, "The Divided Leviathan"; Philippe Faucher, Le Brésil des militaires, l'État et la structure du pouvoir dans un régime autoritaire (Montréal: Les Presses de l'Université de Montréal, 1981).

15. Pedro S. Malan, "The Brazilian Economy: Its Directions in the 80's" (Washington: Center of Brazilian Studies, School of Advanced International Studies, No 3, Occasional Paper Series, January 1980), p. 10.

16. On the Brazilian economic crisis see: Edmar Bacha, "Issues and Evidence on Recent Brazilian Economic Growth," World Development 5, no. 1/2 (1977); R. Bonelli and P.S. Malan, "Os Limites de Possivel: Notas Sobre o Balanço de Pagamentos e Indústria nos Anos 70," Pesquisa e Planejamento Económico 6, no. 2 (1976); Theotônio dos Santos, "The Crisis of the Brazilian Miracle," Working Paper 20, Brazilian Studies/LARU (April 1977).

17. By the term national private enterprise, I refer especially to the capital goods industries (equipment, machinery) whose production is directly linked to orders from the state.

18. Carlos Lessa, "A Estrategia de Desenvolvimento 1974-1976, Sonho e Fracasso" (Thesis presented for the position of full professor, Federal University of Rio de Janeiro, 1978), pp. 16-17.

19. Folha de São Paulo, 7 January 1979.

The association of national capital, foreign capital, and the public sector forms the tri-pé. Their combined interests determine the model of associated and dependent development and, on the political level, the authoritarian regime. The whole forms what is known as the "Brazilian model" which is characterized by the closing of the political system, the exclusion of the masses and intermediary groups from state functions, the elimination of any opposition, a strong concentration of revenues,

the penetration of foreign capital, and a heavy indebtedness on the international financial markets.

20. In 1973 and 1976, (before and after the rise in
oil prices) the machines and equipment represented the
major import. In 1973 the importation of machines cost
$2,142.5 million, while oil cost $710.8 million. In 1974
the figures are respectively $3,107.7 million and $2,
759.5 million. Opinião, 28 August 1975, p. 11.
21. Folha de São Paulo, March 1979.
22. Lessa, "A Estrategia de Desenvolvimento," p.
163.
23. See the analysis of this debate put forward in
Faucher, Le Brésil des militaires.
24. Luiz Carlos Bresser Pereira, O Colapso de uma
Aliança de Classes (São Paulo: ed. Brasiliense, 1978),
p. 127.
25. Lessa, "A Estrategia de Desenvolvimento," p.
132, p. 149. It is adviseable to point out that this
criticism addresses itself in a lesser fashion towards
Petrobras, which for historical reasons directs a greater
proportion of its orders to local producers.
26. Folha de São Paulo, 7 January 1979.
27. Folha de São Paulo, 28 December 1978.
28. Ibid.
29. Lessa, "A Estrategia de Desenvolvimento," p.
148.
30. Maria da Conceição Tavares, "Ciclo e Crise: O
Movimento Recente de Industrialização Brasileira" (Doctoral thesis, Federal University of Rio de Janeiro, Rio
de Janeiro, 1978), p. 116.
31. Carlos Estevam Martins, Capitalismo de Estado e
Modelo Político no Brasil (Rio de Janeiro: Graal, 1977),
p. 269.
32. Ibid, p. 270.
33. O Estado de São Paulo, 12 August, 1978.
34. O Estado de São Paulo, 29 September 1978.
35. Jornal da Tarde, 30 June 1977. O Estado de São
Paulo, August, September, October 1978.
36. Jornal da Tarde, 11 October 1978.
37. Carlos Lessa, "A Estrategia de Desenvolvimento,"
p. 157-159. The chapter by T. Trebat in this book shows
how important the state sector is in the Brazilian economy. The chapter by Baer and Figueroa stresses the capi-
talistic nature of public firms. Their work confirms the
government's concern to make public enterprises responsible for the core of the investments in the second half
of the 1970s.
38. Luciano Martins, "La joint-venture etats-firme
transnationale-entrepreneurs locaux au Brésil," Sociologie et Sociétés 9, no. 2 (October 1979): p. 178. Francisco Colman Sercovich, in his paper "State-Owned Enterprises and Dynamic Comparative Advantages in the World

Petrochemical Industry," (Harvard Institute for International Development, Development Discussion Paper no 98, May 1980), is more confident than is Martins on the possibilities of the Brazilian project for autonomy in the petrochemical sector. The implicit hypothesis according to which Brazil can penetrate the world market by taking advantage of the game of competition on the international level, is, in the opinion of this author, unrealistic to warrant sharing the optimism of Professor Sercovich for the realization of the third petrochemical complex.

39.   This question of veto is mentioned by Luciano Martins, "La joint-venture etats-firme," p. 182, and by Peter Evans in his chapter in this book. Martins accepts this while Evans rejects it on the grounds that emphasizing domination by international firms in characterizing the process of accumulation represented by Brazil's integrated petrochemical complexes is misleading. I believe that the right of veto by the foreign partners in the joint ventures clearly shows the limits of the negotiating power of the dependent state in these types of associations.

40.   Martins, "La joint-venture etats-firme," p. 186.

41.   Martins, Capitalismo de Estado, p. 255. One finds this optimism in its technocratic version in the article by Sercovich, "State-Owned Enterprises."

42.   Bresser Pereira, O Colapso de uma Aliança, p. 125.

43.   O Estado de São Paulo, 9 February 1977.

44.   Veja (São Paulo), 7 February 1977, p. 72.

45.   Ligia Maria Leite Pereira, "Bourgeoisie industrielle et capital étranger au Brésil: 1956-1977" (Doctoral thesis, Ecole des Hautes Études en Sciences Sociales, Paris, 1978), p. 417.

46.   A group of one hundred businessmen sent a letter to the President of the Republic expressing their disagreement with the role of the state, which they felt to be excessive, and publicly demanding to know whether the current debate on liberalism was not really a return of the communists. (Gazeta Mercantil, 2 June 1978). Certain signatories were members of the movement for the defence of Tradition, Family and Property (T.F.P.). Despite its outmoded tone, this document cannot be ignored. It evokes the alarmist speeches of the period from 1962 to 1970, but is now directed, not against the worker or student movements, but rather against the nationalist faction of the bourgeoisie. Among the many signatories of this letter (many of whom have not been revealed publically) are those in the civil construction business sector. This group is the most neo-liberal in the economic sphere (although it hopes the government will multiply projects, it opposes their regulation in any form), the most reactionary on the political and social levels, and the most directly dependent on international

finance capital (necessary for the realization of the large infrastructure projects).

47. The eight signatories are: Cláudio Bardella; Severo Fagundes Gomes; José E. Mindlin; Antônio Ermírio de Morães; Paulo D. Villares; Paulo Vellinho Laerte Setubal Filho; Jorge Gerdau Johannpeter; O Estado de São Paulo, 27 June 1978.

48. Ibid.

49. Peter Evans, Dependent Development, p. 270.

50. Bolivar Lamounier and F.H. Cardoso, Os Partidos e as Eleições no Brasil (Rio de Janeiro: Paz e Terra, 1975).

51. Movimento, weeks of 4 and 11 June 1979.

52. Francisco Weffort, et al., "Debate: A Crise Politica e Institucional," Revista de Cultura Contemporânea 1, no 2, (January 1979): p. 56.

53. This reluctance has expressed itself in the growing fear manifested by the government and the business community in the face of the project of union leader Luis Inácio de Silva (Lula) to launch union activity onto the political scene by the creation of a Workers Party (P.T.).

54. See Thomas Sanders chapter in this book for a comprehensive study of the ongoing process of political reform.

55. Some elements of this discussion can also be found in Ronaldo Munck's chapter in this book.

56. The author borrows in part the formulation of Luciano Martins, "La joint-venture etats-firme," p. 186. This conclusion is also found in the article by Ronaldo Munck, "State Intervention in Brazil: Issues and Debates," Latin American Perspectives 6 (Winter 1979): p. 29.

57. This criticism is aimed primarily at the work by Peter Evans, Dependent Development. The present author's reservations are based on three points: (1) Evans minimizes the divergences of interests and the contradictions among local capital, the state, and foreign capital, (2) he assumes too great an intervention ability on the part of the state, and (3) he does not sufficiently emphasize the weakness of national capital and attaches too much importance to the political negotiating power of this faction of the bourgeoisie without giving sufficient importance to the closed nature of the political system and the authoritarian nature of the regime.

3
Public Enterprises in Brazil and Mexico: A Comparison of Origins and Performance

Thomas J. Trebat

Governments throughout Latin America have found public enterprises to be useful and flexible tools of development policy. The reasons for the creation of public enterprises often vary from country to country within the region and so, too, does the financial performance of public firms. The object of this chapter is to trace the links between the origins of public enterprises, including the motivations of policymakers in setting up such firms, and their financial performance. A comparative approach is used to examine large public enterprises in Brazil and Mexico, countries which have experimented widely with the direct participation of the state in the economy. Two questions are asked: (1) what were the motivations of policymakers leading to the creation of public enterprises in each country and (2) in the light of these motivations, what has been the financial (i.e., profits, savings, investment) performance of public firms in Brazil and Mexico.

ORIGINS AND STRUCTURE OF PUBLIC ENTERPRISES IN BRAZIL AND MEXICO

A first point of comparison is that neither Brazil nor Mexico has an accurate count of the number of its public enterprises. While some of the confusion results from a juridicial difficulty in defining what counts as a public enterprise, it also reflects a legacy of weak central control over public enterprises in both countries. Recent estimates put the number of public enterprises at about 600 in Brazil and about 845 in Mexico.(1) The economic activities of public enterprises in both countries include steel mills, railways, oil refineries, hydroelectric projects, and development banks. But public firms are also found in less traditional activities such as data processing, airplanes, insurance, and meat packing in Brazil, and autos, hotels, and shops in Mexico.

As a means of dealing with the complexity of the respective public enterprise sectors, this chapter will focus on a core group of very large public enterprises - no more than fifty in each country. For the most part these firms are capital-intensive operations in the utilities or in the mainstream of industry in each country.

Origins and Structure in Brazil

In both Brazil and Mexico, the origins of the contemporary public enterprise sector are traced to the 1930s and the rise of strong national leaders (Vargas in Brazil, Cárdenas in Mexico) intent on spurring industrialization in their relatively backward countries. The main events in the creation of modern Brazilian public enterprises, more fully recounted elsewhere,(2) include:

1. The formation of the Companhia Siderúrgica Nacional by Vargas in the early 1940s when efforts to attract direct investment by the U.S. Steel Co. in an integrated steelworks in Brazil proved fruitless.
2. The nationalization of the rich Itabira iron ore deposits and the formation of the Companhia Vale do Rio Doce (CVRD) in the 1940s.
3. The founding of the Banco Nacional de Desenvolvimento Econômico (BNDE) in the 1950s to promote long-term investment by both the public and private sectors in basic industries and the utilities.
4. In response to nationalist furor, the creation of the national petroleum monopoly under the aegis of PETROBRAS in the early 1950s.
5. The organization and expansion of nationwide electricity and telecommunications networks in the 1950s and 1960s to replace utilities once owned by foreigners and driven to the brink of bankruptcy by politically inspired rate controls.
6. The creation of many state enterprises in petrochemicals and atomic power in the 1970s for various reasons including the goal of accelerating technology transfers without relinquishing national control of sensitive industries.(3)

By the late 1970s, some 600 Brazilian public enterprises existed in a wide variety of economic sectors. Table 3.1 is a simple listing of some of the more important of the "core" group of the fifty or so largest enterprises.

Table 3.1
Representative Brazilian Public Enterprises

Firm	Type of Economic Activity
Cia. Vale do Rio Doce	mining
Cia. Siderúrgica Nacional	steel
USIMINAS	steel
PETROBRAS	petroleum
PETROQUISA	petrochemicals
Rede Ferroviária Federal	railways
Lloyd Brasileiro	shipping
Cia. Docas da Guanabara	ports
TELESP	urban telephones
EMBRATEL	intercity tele-communications
CIESF	electricity
EMBRAER	airplanes
ELETROBRAS	electricity
Banco do Brasil	commercial banking
INTERBRAS	international trading

Aside from financial sectors, in which entities such as BNDE and Banco do Brasil dominate, Brazilian public enterprises are concentrated in sectors such as transport, utilities, and basic manufacturing which involve large initial investments and long periods before a rate of return on investment can be achieved. This concentration can be appreciated in Table 3.2, a breakdown according to economic activity of employees and net assets of the 224 largest Brazilian public enterprises in 1974. More than 80 percent of the state's equity has been allocated to the traditional sectors, with 13 percent to PETROBRAS alone.

The public enterprise sector in Brazil is much more diverse in its origins and activities than this brief review would suggest. But the main point is that, if we equate size of firm with its importance in the national economy, attention can be focused on relatively few firms operating in relatively few sectors of the economy.

Origins and Structure in Mexico

The key events in the creation of the core group of large Mexican public enterprises include the following:

Table 3.2:
Sectoral Distribution of Selected Characteristics of Public Enterprises, 1974

Sector	Number of Public Firms	Employees	Net Assets (in millions of cruzeiros)	Net Assets as % of Survey Total
Mining	9	15,866	5,892.1	62
Manufacturing	32	102,545	32,496.4	20
Agriculture	3	3,143	64	1
Construction	5	5,317	2,732	15
Public Utilities and Transportation	155	444,274	86,050	88
Commerce	3	2,894	211	1
Services	17	19,311	22,842	27
Totals	224	593,350	150,378	37

Source: Visão, "Quem é Quem na Economia Brasileira" 1975

1. The decision, made during the Cárdenas years of the 1930s, that foreign-controlled "basic services and strategic sectors" should be nationalized; the origins of PEMEX and the national railways can be traced to this era.
2. The formation, also under Cárdenas, of Nacional Financiera to provide long-term investment finance.
3. The creation of a national steel industry symbolized first by Altos Hornos and later by Las Truchas.
4. The nationalization of electricity services and the formation of the Comision Federal de Electricidad (CFE) in the early 1960s.
5. The formation of CONASUPO, a diversified marketing firm with the twin objectives of supporting agricultural producer prices while keeping retail prices low.
6. The bankruptcy of many private firms (e.g., in sugar and miscellaneous manufacturing operations) which were unable to survive in an environment of tight government price controls and were eventually taken over by the state.

While most of the large Mexican public enterprises are rooted in earlier eras, more than 500 were created during the Echeverria "sexenio" from 1970-1976. Little in the way of organized data is available concerning these newly created or nationalized firms, but they tend to be small and to owe their creation to two factors: (1) the contrast between Echeverria's interventionist style and the fiscal conservatism of his predecessors, and (2) the very low level of private sector investment during the period.(4)

As in Brazil, the bulk of the Mexican public sector's equity is concentrated in a few firms. For example, as of 1976 just fifteen public firms accounted for 90 percent of the combined equity of all public firms.(5) Again, a World Bank survey of thirty-four Mexican public enterprises in the manufacturing sector revealed that five firms accounted for 88 percent of the combined value of plants and equipment.(6) Some of the more important Mexican firms are listed below in Table 3.3.

Even within the restricted group of large Mexican public enterprises, certain highly capital-intensive firms dominate. Thus two-thirds of total spending by productive firms subject to budgetary control is carried out by PEMEX and CFE.(7)

Table 3.3
Representative Mexican Public Enterprises

Firm	Type of Economic Activity
PEMEX	petroleum
CFE	electricity
Aeromexico	airlines
Ferrocarriles Nacionales	railways
Complejo Sahagun	diesel engines, trucks, rolling stock
SICARTSA	steel
Altos Hornos	steel
Guanomex	fertilizers
CONASUPO	marketing of food products
NAFINSA	investment banking
Teléfonos de Mexico	telecommunications

Comparisons of Origin and Structure

1. A very basic point is that the public enterprise sectors in both Brazil and Mexico are highly heterogenous. Government-owned firms range from small and innovative manufacturers to large, traditional public utilities. However, in both countries we can identify a core group of thirty to fifty enterprises which, because of their size or influence on resource allocation, are the backbone of the respective public enterprise sectors. With some exceptions, e.g., CONASUPO in Mexico, these tend to be public enterprise monopolies or oligopolies in the utilities, the mainstream of industry, and the financial sectors.

2. The sectoral allocation of public investment is very similar in the two countries. This observation calls attention to common factors influencing policy decisions in both countries. Two of these factors can be highlighted, although others are also present: (1) the scale, risk and financial requirements inherent in those sectors which the state entered clearly exceeded the resources available in the private sector, and (2) foreign private investment was often available as an alternative to public enterprise, but was rejected for political reasons. In considering the role of these two factors, it is helpful to recall the origins of a number of public enterprise counterparts in Brazil and Mexico: PEMEX and PETROBRAS, ELECTROBRAS and CFE, CSN and Altos Hornos, BNDE and NAFINSA, and others.

3. Both Brazil and Mexico use their public enterprises in what the Brazilians call the "empty spaces" of the productive structure, where their main task is to support extensive networks of supplier or customer private firms. Again, except for CONASUPO, neither country has used public enterprise in order to "set the pace" for private enterprise by engaging in direct competition with these firms.

4. Most core public enterprises in both countries are engaged in economic activities (steel, telephones, oil, others) which offer the potential for these firms to earn revenues sufficient to cover current costs (whether or not this is the case in practice).

Important differences in the origins and structure of public enterprises in Brazil and Mexico are also apparent.

1. Social objectives, as opposed to more narrowly commercial ones, have been more important in the creation of Mexican public enterprises than has been the case in Brazil. For example, it is significant that Brazil has no close equivalent to CONASUPO. The point is more general; the Brazilians have rarely founded public enterprises with the primary intention of keeping prices low for consumers. On the contrary, given its history of generally higher inflation and thinner capital markets, Brazil has often founded public firms with the express intention of raising prices to ensure adequate rates of return. The Mexicans have frequently founded public enterprises as a means to reduce "excess profits" and to keep prices low as a subsidy to consumers.

2. A related point is that Brazil has been more concerned that public enterprises grow to meet the demand for their output without acting as adjuncts of public finance. Thus, while no mandate has been issued to maximize profits, a concern for efficiency and profitability has been important in the origins of many Brazilian public forms.

3. Brazilian public enterprises are probably more important than their Mexican counterparts in terms of decision-making and overall resource allocation. First, the Brazilian private sector is, apparently, weaker and smaller relative to state enterprises (and relative to foreign multinationals as well) than is the case in Mexico. Newfarmer and Mueller examined the ownership structure of the fifty largest firms in Mexico and Brazil in 1972.(8) They reported that the domestic private sector owned 38 percent of the assets of the fifty largest enterprises in Mexico, versus 16 percent for the private sector in Brazil. The corresponding ownership shares of the state sector were 42 percent in Mexico and 56 percent in Brazil. (The remaining assets were attributed to foreign multinationals.) The most recent survey of firms in Brazil indicates that the ten largest enterprises in

Brazil in 1978 belonged to the state; similarly, seventeen of the twenty-five largest firms in the same year
were state-owned.(9) Second, public enterprises dominate
commercial banking in Brazil to a much greater extent
than in Mexico. The Banco do Brasil, for example, holds
50 percent of all deposits in the commercial banking system; the government's share is augmented by the market
shares of commercial banks, such as BANESPA and BANERJ,
which are owned by state governments in Brazil.

Third, the tradition of direct state intervention in
the economy is more deeply rooted in Brazil than in
Mexico. Brazil's statist-oriented economic policies,
even under conservative military regimes, contrast with
Mexico's traditions of fiscal conservatism, now once
again embraced by Lopez Portillo after Echeverria's departure from the tradition.(10)

4. A final point of comparison in regard to origins
is that the Brazilian case seems to better illustrate the
argument that successful public enterprise management
will demonstrate a tendency to expand and diversify
beyond the strict confines of the firm's original charter. The growth of subsidiaries of PETROBRAS and CVRD
during the 1970s are, perhaps, the best examples of this
means of public enterprise creation.

COMPARATIVE FINANCIAL PERFORMANCE

For this comparison, three questions are asked about
the financial performance of public firms in Brazil and
Mexico. First, have these firms been profitable in the
sense of generating a surplus over and above current
operating expenses? Second, has the surplus been sufficient to cover a significant portion of the investment
finance requirements of these firms? Third, what were
some of the macroeconomic implications of overall financial performance?

A Current Surplus

A study of Brazilian public enterprises in six major
industries during 1966-1975 revealed that, for the most
part, the firms studied yielded a consistent current
surplus. The railroads are the only major exception to
this general pattern of profitability. Rates of return
on stockholder equity in each of the industries may be
found in Table 3.4.

Profitability varies significantly across sectors in
Brazil. The rate of return has been generally high in
mining (basically, CVRD), petrochemicals, and intercity
telecommunications (EMBRATEL). Profits have been relatively low, but positive, in electricity and telephones.

Table 3.4.
Current Surplus as Percent of Net Worth in Brazilian Public Enterprises, 1966-1975

	1966-1969	1970-1975	1966-1975
Mining	20.6	20.2	20.4
Petrochemicals	22.7	14.7	18.7
Electricity	6.5	8.3	7.4
Steel	- 6.6	4.3	- 2.05
Urban Telephones	7.5	3.3	5.4
EMBRATEL	....	19.7	9.7
Railroads	n.a.	-26.3	-26.3

Source: Thomas J. Trebat, "An Evaluation of the Economic
Performance of Public Enterprise in Brazil" (Doctoral
dissertation, Vanderbilt University, 1978), p. 211.
(This source is hereafter referred to as "An Evaluation.")

The public steel firms lost money in 1966-1969, a
period of price controls and depressed demand for steel,
but were profitable in the 1970-1975 period. As is the
case in many countries, the railroads recorded large
losses in each of the years for which data were available.

In order to gain perspective on the profit performance of public enterprises, we can consider the results
of another study of profitability in 731 large Brazilian
firms in 1974. (11) In this study, Suzigan calculated
an aggregate profit rate of 11.4 percent for public enterprises, as compared to 21 percent for multinational
firms, and 23 percent for private domestic firms.(12)
While the results indicate lower profitability in the
public enterprises, it must be noted that public enterprises, by comparison to private firms, are involved in
much more capital-intensive activities with longer matu-
ration periods. Viewed in this light, the profitability
differentials between public and private firms are probably not unduly large.

Summing up, Brazilian public enterprises have been
generally profitable and, in some cases, highly profitable. This finding is consistent with earlier observations that these firms have not been saddled with many
social as opposed to economic objectives, and that they
have experienced a fairly liberal pricing environment.

By contrast to the Brazilian experience, Mexican
public enterprises have had great difficulty in generating sales revenues sufficient to cover current operating

expenses. With important exceptions, Mexican public enterprises have been forced to rely more heavily than their Brazilian counterparts on government subsidies to avert bankruptcy. Table 3.5 compares current surpluses (i.e., sales minus operating expenses) in percent of total sales on a sector-by-sector basis for selected large Mexican public enterprises during 1972-1978. (Data on shareholders' equity were not available so that profit rates could not be calculated.) The figures in Table 3.5 should be interpreted as the firm's margin on unit sales; in particular, a negative figure indicates the degree to which sales revenues fell short of covering expenses.

The profitable Mexican public enterprise sectors are PEMEX and "other transport," i.e., non-rail transport. PEMEX has undoubtedly benefitted from a favorable oil pricing environment, especially after 1975. The firms included in the "other transport" sector (such as Aeronaves) have also been able to charge prices sufficient to generate revenues in excess of costs.

Obviously, these two sectors constitute exceptions to a general rule in Mexico. By and large, firms do not generate surpluses in their current operations. CONASUPO is an extreme case because it pursues social rather than narrowly economic objectives. Typically, CONASUPO incurs losses equal to 35 percent of its sales revenues, but in 1974-1975, losses which had to be covered by government subsidies amounted to 60 to 80 percent of ordinary sales income.

Table 3.5
Current Surplus as a Ratio of Total Sales in Mexican Public Enterprises, 1972-1978

	1972	1973	1974	1975	1976	1977	1978
PEMEX	.09	.15	.21	.14	.30	.24	.32
Electricity	.06	0	-.08	-.23	-.11	-.29	-.33
Railroads	-.25	-.31	-.41	-.25	-.44	-.38	-.29
Other Transport	.24	.25	.13	.26	.09	.26	.20
CONASUPO	-.18	-.35	-.60	-.82	-.23	-.36	-.30
Steel	...	0	.32	.36	0	-.38	-.61
Misc. Manf.	...	-.09	-.25	0	-.18	-.09	-.08

Source: Secretaria de Programacion y Presupusto, Boletin Mensual de Informacion Economica III, No. 4 (April 1979).

As was true in the case of Brazil, the railroads lose large amounts in Mexico. Between 1972-1978, railroad losses ranged from 25 to 40 percent of sales.

While the verification of losses in CONASUPO and the railroads is certainly not surprising, the pattern of losses in the presumably "healthy" productive sectors of electricity, steel, and manufacturing goes against expectations. While the steel firms do not lose money in every year examined in Table 3.5, profitability declined sharply after 1975. By 1978, the last year considered, current losses amounted to 61 percent of sales. The obviously unprofitable experience of the electricity firms contrasts sharply with Brazil in which the large utilities have been profitable. To judge from the results in Table 3.5, the miscellaneous public manufacturing enterprises have also had difficulty in adjusting prices. They are seen to be money-losing operations in virtually every year considered.

The findings on sectoral financial performance generally support the belief that Brazilian public enterprises, at least during the period under consideration, have been much more concerned with accumulating a surplus which can be used to finance investment spending. One concern in Brazil with regard to the largest public enterprises has been to reduce the strain on the National Treasury. In Mexico, with some exceptions, public enterprises have generally acted to subsidize the private sector by running losses on current operations. Thus it would appear that Mexican firms have been much more dependent on government subsidy than has been the case in Brazil.

Investment Finance

Public enterprises account for large shares of total gross fixed capital formation in both Brazil and Mexico. Data on total investment spending by the public enterprises in each country are not available, but focusing on just the "core group" of large public enterprises in each country illustrates the point. The large Mexican public enterprises considered here comprised 23.5 percent of total investment in Mexico in 1978. The "core" Brazilian firms examined here were responsible for 20.2 percent of all investment in Brazil in 1975. In view of the magnitude of these figures, the ability of public enterprises in each country to finance investment out of their own resources has important implications for the government budget and, thus, for the rate of monetary expansion in the respective economies. As an indicator of financial performance, the self-financing capability of these firms is now considered.

The extent of self-finance in Brazil

Table 3.6 details the self-financing experience of large Brazilian public firms in the mainstream of industry and the utilities. In this table, the concept of a surplus has been expanded to include not only profits but also depreciation allowances. Defined in this way, the current surplus of these firms expanded from 1.2 percent of GDP (Gross Domestic Product) in 1966 to 2.1 percent of GDP in 1975. On the other hand, the investment spending of these firms expanded from 1.9 percent of GDP in 1966 to 5.2 percent of GDP in 1975. Thus the overall deficit of the large public enterprises considered in the study rose from .07 percent of GDP in 1966 to more than 3 percent of GDP in 1975, the last year, unfortunately, for which data are available.

Let us examine this self-finance capacity in more detail. From 1966-1975, the subset of large public enterprises was able to finance from 40 percent to 60 percent of gross investment outlays, using retained earnings and depreciation funds. If the railroads are excluded, the self-financing ratio ranges from 46 percent to 80 percent. Considerable cyclical variation in the ratio is apparent. The decline in the overall self-finance ratio after 1970 coincides with the launching of major investment programs in several sectors. After allowing for such variation, it is possible to conclude that public enterprises annually finance roughly 50 percent of investment outlays. This degree of self-finance compares with a figure of approximately 50 to 60 percent for Brazilian private firms in recent years.

As expected, there is significant variation among public enterprise sectors in regard to degree of self-financing. (See Table 3.7.) The petrochemical firms (principally, PETROBRAS) and the Companhia Vale do Rio Doce have been able to finance up to 100 percent of investment needs out of internal cash flow, although both have also needed significant external funding on occasion. At the other extreme, the railroads depend entirely on outside sources for financing. Firms in the other utility sectors were partially dependent on external finance.

Despite a generally favorable self-financing performance, the public enterprises required large and increasing amounts of external resources to finance their investments. In real terms, the residual demand for finance has increased six times since 1969, although it is highly concentrated in a few sectors. The power firms and railroads absorbed 77 percent of all outside financing in 1970 and 55 percent in 1974. In general, the steel and telecommunications firms require much less external financing, although reliance by steel firms on external financing has increased significantly in the 1970s.

Table 3.6
Overall Deficit of Productive Public Enterprises: Brazil (Percent of GDP)

Brazil	Current Surplus/ GDP	Investment/ GDP	Deficit/ GDP	Self-Finance Ratio
1966	1.2	1.9	-0.7	.60
1967	1.3	2.9	-1.6	.47
1968	1.4	3.1	-1.7	.45
1969	1.5	2.7	-1.2	.54
1970	1.7	3.1	-1.4	.55
1971	1.9	3.7	-1.8	.52
1972	1.8	4.0	-2.2	.45
1973	2.0	4.4	-2.4	.44
1974	2.0	4.4	-2.4	.46
1975	2.1	5.2	-3.1	.39

Source: Trebat, "An Evaluation," p. 322

Table 3.7
Brazilian Public Enterprises: Internal Financing as a Percent of Gross Investment

	1967-1969	1970-1971	1972-1973	1974-1975
Steel	72	100	49	24
Petro-chemicals	69	86	92	88
Mining	100	73	63	95
Electricity	49	37	28	29
Telecommuni-cations	36	47	63	44
Railroads	0	0	0	0

Source: Trebat, "An Evaluation," p. 262.

With the exception of the railroads, Brazilian public enterprises were able to make substantial contributions toward the financing of new investment. The results are, of course, not surprising in view of trends in pricing policies in the public enterprises, particularly the adoption of "realistic" prices in a number of sectors.

The extent of self-finance in Mexico

Results of the investment finance performance of Mexican public enterprises are presented in Tables 3.8 and 3.9. Table 3.8 provides an overview of the performance of nineteen productive public enterprises during 1972-1978. (CONASUPO has been excluded because its pattern of very large current deficits and small investment spending would distort the picture). The overall financial performance of firms studied is characterized by a current surplus which is relatively small in the light of investment finance requirements. The current surplus (sales minus operating expense) in percent of GDP ranges from 0.2 percent to 0.9 percent during 1972-1978; public enterprise investment in percent of GDP ranges from 2.3 percent to 6 percent. In consequence, the overall deficit of the core Mexican public enterprises tends to be much larger than that of the large Brazilian public firms i.e., about 4 to 6 percent of GDP versus 2 to 3 percent in the case of Brazil. Expressed in another way, this means that ability of Mexican public enterprises to finance investment out of internally generated resources was much less than that of their Brazilian counterparts. In the period considered here, Mexican public enterprises typically financed only about 10 percent of investment requirements with internal resources, versus 40 to 50 percent in Brazil.

Table 3.9 provides a sector-by-sector view of the finance performance of Mexican public enterprises in 1972-1978. PEMEX and the non-rail transport sector are seen to be the only public enterprise sectors able to generate any portion of investment finance internally. PEMEX, by far the most important sector in the entire group, generated approximately 40 to 50 percent of investment requirements internally during 1972-1978. The nonrail transport firms actually showed a surplus after investment in a number of years.

The remaining four sectors - rails, electricity, steel, and manufacturing - were unable to contribute toward the financing of investment requirements.

SUMMARY AND CONCLUSIONS

In this chapter we have considered the reasons for, and the structure of, public enterprise in Brazil and

Table 3.8
Overall Deficit of Productive Public Enterprises: Mexico
(Excluding CONASUPO)

	(1) Current Surplus/GDP	(2) Investment/ GDP	(3) Deficit/ GDP	(4) Self- Finance Ratio[1]
1972	.2	2.3	-2.1	.09
1973	.2	2.7	-2.5	.07
1974	.2	3.2	-3.0	.06
1975	.2	6.0	-5.8	.03
1976	.5	4.9	-4.4	.10
1977	.4	4.6	-4.4	.09
1978	.9	5.3	-4.3	.17

1. Equals Column (1)/Column (2)

Source: Secretaria de Programacion y Presupusto, Boletin Mensual de Informacion Economica III, No. 4 (April 1979).

Table 3.9
Mexican Public Enterprise: Internal Financing as a Percent of Gross Investment

	1972	1973	1974	1975	1976	1977	1978
PEMEX	.31	.38	.70	.23	.53	.35	.47
Electricity	.06	0	0	0	0	0	0
Railroads	0	0	0	0	0	0	0
Other transport	.91	.73	.36	1.4	.55	2.14	1.3
Steel	-	-	-	-	1.07	0	0
Misc. Manf.	0	0	0	0	0	0	0

Source: Secretaria de Programacion y Presupusto, Boletin Mensual de Informacion Economica III, No. 4 (April 1979).

Mexico, as well as some important aspects of the financial performance of these public firms. Close similarities were noted with regard to the motivations of policymakers in setting up public enterprises. In both countries, the risk, scale, and financing requirements of key industrial projects simply exceeded the capacity of the respective private sectors, and the state stepped into the vacuum through the creation of public enterprises. Furthermore, in the creation of state firms in both Brazil and Mexico, policymakers were often motivated by a desire to limit the role of foreign enterprises in what were regarded as strategic economic sectors.

While there are close similarities with regard to motivations in the creation of public firms, there are important differences in the attitudes of policymakers regarding the management of public enterprises. Mexican policymakers gave higher priority to social, as opposed to more narrowly economic, uses of public firms, especially in stressing such policies as keeping prices low to redistribute incomes and to stimulate the private sector. Brazilian policymakers seem to have emphasized the capital accumulation and investment uses of public enterprises, preferring to view public firms as close substitutes for private monopolies or oligopolies.

These differences in attitudes regarding the use of public enterprise are reflected in the comparative financial performance of public firms in the two countries, although important similarities in financial performance are also to be noted. Two similarities are clear. (1) Public enterprises in natural resource sectors (iron ore and petroleums in Brazil; petroleum in Mexico) tend to do well. PEMEX, PETROBRAS, CVRD, and other firms able to capture economic rents are profitable and are able to finance internally a large share of investment finance requirements. (2) At the other end of the performance spectrum, railroads fare poorly in both Brazil and Mexico, as is the case in many countries.

The principal difference in performance occurs with regard to the remaining public enterprise sectors considered, e.g., electricity, steel, telecommunications, and others. Almost without exception, Brazilian public enterprises tend to do much better from a financial viewpoint than the large Mexican firms. Although the amount of surplus varies significantly across economic sectors within Brazil, Brazilian public enterprises tend to be profitable and do not depend entirely on the government budget or other external sources for investment funds. The opposite is true in Mexico, even when CONASUPO, admittedly a special case, is excluded from the comparison. Many public enterprises in Mexico appear to be run as adjuncts of public finance.

FUTURE LINES OF RESEARCH

In the absence of additional evidence, we must speculate about the reasons for relatively poorer performance in Mexico. Subject to empirical verification, it would seem likely that, by comparison to their Brazilian counterparts, Mexican public enterprises have to deal with greater restraints on price-setting, more powerful labor unions, a better organized private sector determined to benefit from public enterprise operations, and more political influences in enterprise decision-making. Public enterprise in Brazil may also be attracting better managers. In general, the "control environment" in which public enterprises operate must be quite different in the two countries. Work is needed to determine the impact of the control environment on public enterprise performance. An interesting approach to this issue might be to select certain "twin" public enterprises for detailed case study treatment. CFE and ELECTROBRAS would be good candidates for such treatment as would PEMEX and PETRO-BRAS.

This chapter did not consider the macroeconomic context within which public enterprises operate in Brazil and Mexico. But, clearly, the operations of large public enterprises have important implications for the government budget, the rate of monetary growth, the balance of payments, the amount of external debt, and so on. The reader will recall, for example, that despite the somewhat better performance of Brazilian public enterprise, the overall deficit of the core group of public enterprises in both countries was large.

It is not a coincidence that in recent years policymakers at the macroplanning levels in the two countries have moved to place the spending and borrowing operations of public firms under much tighter controls.(13) Thus the Secretaria de Programacion y Presupusto and the Ministerio de Hacienda y Credito Publico have assumed increased supervisory responsibilities in Mexico, while the newly created Secretaria Especial para o Controle das Empresas Estatais has analogous functions in Brazil. Investigation of the evolution of these agencies would be welcome.

NOTES

1.   The Brazilian estimate comes from Visão, "Quem é Quem na Economia Brasileira," 1976; the Mexican estimate is reported in Rene Villarreal and Rocio R. de Villarreal, "Las empresas publicas como instrumento de politica economica en Mexico," Trimestre Economico XLV, no. 2 (1978): 217.

58

2.   For a succinct review, see: Werner Baer, Isaac
Kerstenetzsky, and Anibal Villela, "The Changing Role of
the State in the Brazilian Economy," World Development 1
(November 1973):   23-24.
3.   The extensive use of joint ventures as a means
to extend state ownership in the petrochemical industry
is recounted in Peters Evans, Dependent Development: The
Alliance of Multinational, State and Local Capital in
Brazil (Princeton: Princeton University Press, 1979).
4.   cf. Carlos Tello, La politica economica en Mexico, 1970-76 (Mexico, D.F.: Siglo Veintiuno Editores,
1979).
5.   Villarreal and Villarreal, "Las empresas publicas como instrumento," pp. 221-222.
6.   International Bank for Reconstruction and Development, Mexico's Manufacturing Sector: Situation, Prospects, and Policies (Washington: IBRD: 1979), p. 29.
7.   E.V.K. Fitzgerald, "Patterns of Public Sector
Income and Expenditure in Mexico," Institute of Latin
American Studies, Technical Paper Series, No. 17 (Austin,
Texas: Office for Public Sector Studies, 1978), p. 11.
8.   Richard S. Newfarmer and Willard F. Mueller,
Multinational Corporations in Brazil and Mexico: Structural Sources of Economic and Non-Economic Power (Washington, D.C.: GPO, 1975), pp. 53 and 106.
9.   Conjuntura Económica 33, No. 9 (September 1979):
Special Supplement.
10.   For an elaboration on this and other related
points, see Thomas J. Trebat "Mexican and Brazilian Economic Development: A Comparative Perspective of Lega-
cies, Patterns, and Performance," (xerox), May 1979, esp.
pp. 28 to 37.
11.   Wilson Suzigan, "As Empresas do Governo e o Papel do Estado na Sociedade," in Fernando Rezende, ed.,
Aspectos da Participação do Governo na Economia (Rio de
Janeiro: IPEA/INDES, 1976), pp. 77-134.
12.   Ibid., p. 102.
13.   The author develops this point in detail in
Thomas J. Trebat, The State as Entrepreneur: The Case
of Brazil.   (Cambridge: Cambridge University Press,
forthcoming).

4
State Enterprise and the Distribution of Income: Brazil and Peru

Werner Baer
Adolfo Figueroa

Does increased state participation in the economy have positive, negative, or neutral impact on socio-economic equity? This is an important question for those Latin American countries which in recent decades have experienced a steady growth in both the traditional role of government in the economy, as well as in the number and size of state enterprises and financial entities. During the same period most of these countries experienced substantial increases in the concentration of income.

These trends are paradoxical. One might have assumed that inequalities would appear more frequently in private market-oriented economies, whereas the participation of state entities in productive enterprises, banking institutions, and public utilities would lessen them.(1) Our purpose in this chapter is to search for ways in which state enterprises and financial entities might have contributed to increased inequalities by analyzing the cases of Brazil and Peru. Does it make any significant difference in equity whether enterprises are in state or private hands? Both countries experienced drastic changes in the orientation of their regimes in 1964 and 1968, respectively; the participation of the state in the economy of each accelerated, yet the inequalities persisted or even worsened.

THE STATE IN THE BRAZILIAN ECONOMY

A close observer of the post-1964 Brazilian economic scene stated that one of the cornerstones of the regime's policies was a "...liberal market-oriented economic philosophy..." and that it "...tended to reverse the trends of the previous Brazilian government: from state planning to market orientation, from protectionism to export promotion, from nationalism to internationalism, and from structuralism to monetarism...."(2) It is thus ironic that the presence of the state in the economy, which was

already considerable by 1964,(3) should have grown at an
accelerated pace under supposedly market-oriented administrations. The increased role of the state in the economy is related to Brazil's efforts to speed up economic
growth through rapid industrialization. On the eve of
industrialization the economy was primarily oriented to
the exportation of primary products, and the private sector lacked the financial, technological, and organizational capacity to handle the task of industrialization
by itself. The alternative was to rely on the foreign
and state sectors. The state established firms in activities (such as steel) where multinationals had no interest, but which were considered essential for a successful
industrialization program. It also created enterprises
in sectors where it did not want foreign dominance, for
example in petroleum and mining activities.

The Brazilian state's involvement in infrastructure
enterprises began before the industrialization spurt.
Although railroads had been built by foreign firms in the
nineteenth century, the rate-of-return guarantee which
the government had to give to attract them became so
onerous that most of the railroads were gradually bought
out by the state in the first decades of the twentieth
century. Similarly, the original provision of power and
telecommunications was in the hands of foreign firms until the post-World War II period. As controlled tariffs
made investment for private foreign firms unattractive,
the state - through newly-founded enterprises - gradually
dominated most of these sectors.

State involvement in the financial area goes back to
the nineteenth century, when neither domestic nor foreign
financial institutions were available to provide sufficient commercial credits for the expanding agricultural
sector. This accounts for the growth of the Banco do
Brasil, owned by the government, and in the twentieth
century for the appearance of many commercial banks owned
by individual state governments. After World War II, as
the industrialization process was intensified, the lack
of an adequate capital market led to the creation of the
National Bank for Economic Development (BNDE), which
first concentrated on financing state enterprises, later
shifting to financing investment projects in the domestic
private sector.(4) Government-owned development banks
were also created at the regional and individual state
level.

The number of state enterprises has grown considerably since the early post-World War II period. The federal government owned about thirty firms in 1949 (twelve
in the power generation field, five in the financial sector, six in transportation, two in industry, and one in
mining); state and local governments owned thirty-four
firms. By 1978 there were 584 state enterprises (of

which 186 belonged to the federal government); 488 government firms were nonfinancial and the rest consisted
of banks and other types of financial organizations.

Much of the increase in the number of government
firms occurred after 1967, when Brazil's administrative
reform law was instituted. It encouraged the decentralization of public administration through the creation of
state enterprises in order to increase the efficiency of
the public sector. Many of these new government firms
acquired a dynamism of their own, leading to a substantial growth in their activities.(5)

Table 4.1 provides a general picture of Brazil's
urban economy according to the main ownership sector.
It will be noted that state enterprises had important
shares of assets and/or sales in mining, metal products
(they were dominant in steel), chemicals and petrochemicals, electric power generation, transportation, and
telecommunication.

In the second half of the 1970s state-owned banks accounted for over 55 percent of deposits. State banks
were also responsible for 65 percent of the combined
loans of the 50 largest banks. The federal and state
governments together constitute the most powerful investment banker in the economy, accounting for about 70 percent of all investment loans.

Since the second half of the 1960s, much of the in-
crement in the national savings rate has been through the
forced savings programs, whose funds have been deposited
with government banks (such as the BNDE, the Housing Bank
(BNH), and the federal savings banks - the Caixas Econo-
micas). This accounts for the large role of the state as
a long-term lender.(6)

The substantial increase of the state presence in the
Brazilian economy after 1964 was related to the policy
makers' goal of again achieving a high rate of growth.
They were therefore obliged to take steps which substantially strengthened state enterprises, financial institutions, and regulations. Thus the development plans of
the late 1960s and 1970s called for massive investments
in sectors which were already dominated by state firms:
steel, public utilities, mining, and petrochemicals.
These investments were considered important complements
to other policy actions taken to stimulate growth in
areas dominated by either the domestic private or the
multinational sector.

To increase the efficiency of state enterprises, much
greater independence was granted them than in the past
in the areas of pricing, employment, investment decisions, etc. This led to a substantial dynamism in a number of state firms, both in their original activities and
in new sectors, as they expanded through the creation of
subsidiaries.

Table 4.1
Brazil: Shares of Domestic, Government, and Multinational Enterprises in Net Assets, Employment, and Sales
(Percentages) 1977

	Net Assets				Employment				Sales			
	DE	GE	MULT	TOT	DE	GE	MULT	TOT	DE	GE	MULT	TOT
1. Mining	.7	75.2	24.1	100.0	.3	65.5	34.2	100.0	.1	67.3	32.6	100.0
2. Manufacturing	26.1	37.5	36.4	100.0	36.9	11.5	51.6	100.0	24.1	25.2	50.7	100.0
2.1 Non-Met. Minerals	50.6	–	49.4	100.0	53.3	–	46.7	100.0	47.2	–	52.8	100.0
2.2 Metal Products	27.5	51.5	21.0	100.0	39.3	37.6	23.1	100.0	30.9	45.8	23.3	100.0
2.2.1 Steel	13.6	72.9	13.5	100.0	18.6	61.3	20.1	100.0	14.1	70.6	15.3	100.0
2.3 Machinery	36.7	2.3	61.0	100.0	24.0	3.9	72.1	100.0	14.6	3.7	81.7	100.0
2.4 Electrical Machinery & Communication	5.9	–	94.1	100.0	12.7	–	86.7	100.0	8.7	–	91.3	100.0
2.5 Transport Materials	30.6	7.0	62.4	100.0	22.3	3.2	74.5	100.0	15.4	2.9	81.7	100.0
2.6 Wood Products	84.2	–	15.8	100.0	77.8	–	22.2	100.0	82.1	–	17.9	100.0
2.7 Furniture	85.2	–	14.8	100.0	84.1	–	15.9	100.0	85.0	–	15.0	100.0
2.8 Paper and Paper Products	46.8	12.3	40.9	100.0	69.0	4.1	26.9	100.0	78.0	1.0	21.0	100.0
2.9 Rubber	23.1	12.5	64.4	100.0	24.0	4.2	71.8	100.0	15.5	9.5	75.0	100.0
2.10 Leather and Hides	67.2	–	32.8	100.0	55.5	–	44.5	100.0	47.8	–	52.2	100.0
2.11 Chemicals	3.7	84.3	12.0	100.0	9.9	53.9	36.2	100.0	6.5	73.3	20.2	100.0
2.11.1 Chemicals & Petrochemicals	1.8	28.9	59.3	100.0	3.7	10.0	86.3	100.0	4.6	18.5	76.9	100.0
2.12.2 Fertilizers	38.0	56.9	5.1	100.0	64.8	27.4	7.8	100.0	60.2	39.6	0.2	100.0
2.13.3 Petroleum	1.3	97.7	1.0	100.0	2.5	96.7	0.8	100.0	2.4	95.7	1.9	100.0
2.12 Pharmaceuticals	11.5	–	88.5	100.0	4.3	–	95.7	100.0	5.0	–	95.0	100.0
2.13 Perfumes, Soap, Candles	82.3	–	17.7	100.0	85.6	–	14.4	100.0	91.3	–	8.7	100.0
2.14 Plastic Products	49.6	–	50.4	100.0	31.6	–	68.4	100.0	21.5	–	74.9	100.0
2.15 Textiles	56.2	–	43.8	100.0	59.9	–	40.1	100.0	44.0	–	56.0	100.0
2.16 Clothing, Shoes, Textile Products	40.7	–	59.3	100.0	51.8	–	48.2	100.0	46.2	–	53.8	100.0
2.17 Food Products	37.9	–	62.1	100.0	37.6	–	62.4	100.0	34.4	–	65.6	100.0
2.18 Beverages	85.1	–	14.9	100.0	85.5	–	14.5	100.0	79.3	–	16.7	100.0

Sector	DE	GE	MULT	Total	DE	GE	MULT	Total	DE	GE	MULT	Total
2.19 Tobacco	100.0	–	–	100.0	100.0	–	–	100.0	100.0	–	–	100.0
2.20 Printing & Publishing	40.8	–	59.2	100.0	45.3	–	54.7	100.0	26.8	–	73.2	100.0
2.21 Miscellaneous	92.2	5.1	2.7	100.0	85.2	6.3	8.4	100.0	94.2	3.3	2.5	100.0
3. Construction & Engineering	84.9	–	15.1	100.0	–	79.5	20.5	100.0	–	69.8	30.2	100.0
4. Public Utilities	16.7	76.3	7.0	100.0	40.5	52.4	7.1	100.0	37.5	33.4	29.1	100.0
5. Services	51.2	15.1	33.7	100.0	82.3	2.2	15.5	100.0	38.0	16.8	45.2	100.0
5.1 Commerce	84.2	7.8	8.0	100.0	92.5	6.8	0.7	100.0	100.0	–	–	100.0
5.2 Storage	90.9	8.9	0.2	100.0	100.0	–	–	100.0	51.7	46.8	1.5	100.0
5.3 Transportation	–	100.0	–	100.0	25.6	73.4	1.0	100.0	9.3	88.7	2.0	100.0
5.4 Communications	–	100.0	–	100.0	–	100.0	–	100.0	–	100.0	–	100.0
5.5 Other Services	83.5	–	16.5	100.0	82.4	–	17.6	100.0	90.7	–	9.3	100.0

DE – Domestic Enterpise; GE – Government Enterprise; MULT – Multinational Enterprise

Source: IPEA and Visão, August 1978.

64

THE STATE IN THE PERUVIAN ECONOMY

The Revolutionary Military Government that took over Peru in 1968 had a program of social reform. One component of these reforms was the change of the liberal economic system towards one with state intervention. In the post-World War II period Peru had been considered one of the economies where liberalism was running strong.(7) Moreover, Peru was taken as an example of successful liberalism, with rapid export-led growth. It was only in the 1960s that industrialization policies were emphasized. These patterns of growth, however, contributed to furthering unequal income distribution and to external dependence. The military's reforms aimed at reversing both these trends; the increase of the role of the state was to be an important instrument in achieving these goals.

The logic of the policies was based on the premise that income distribution depends upon the distribution of property among individuals. Thus, as there was a high concentration of the means of production, a basic change in the distribution of income would come from a change in the property structure. In addition, the military government considered that capitalism in Peru had failed to bring social progress and the economic system should therefore be changed to a more pluralistic economy with other forms of ownership besides private property. The importance of capitalism was expected to decrease through the creation of labor-managed firms (through land reform, for instance) and state firms. This change in the property structure would lead, the military government assumed, to a more equal income distribution.(8)

The most notable change in Peru since 1968 has been the increased presence of the state in the economic process. Very few state firms existed up to that time: a steel firm (founded in 1964), a fertilizer corporation, and a couple of hydroelectric plants were among the most important as well as the development banks for agriculture, industry, and mining. At present, however, there are nearly fifty state enterprises in operation, covering most productive sectors.(9)

The origins of these enterprises are diverse. One group emerged from the nationalization of foreign companies, as was the case in petroleum and mining (PETROPERU, CENTROMIN). Another group grew out of the take-over of domestic firms which was intended to eliminate part of the domestic oligarchy from the social scene. The best example was the take-over of fishing firms (PESCA-PERU) and of firms belonging to the Prado family. The third group consisted of newly-created state enterprises which were established as part of the above mentioned scheme to achieve a pluralistic economic system. The state

reserved for itself the production of some strategic
products, such as steel, chemicals, fertilizers, and
cement.

The outcome of the reforms has been a substantial increase in state participation in the economy. As Table
4.2 shows, 16 percent of GNP was produced by state enterprises after the reforms as compared to 1 percent before
1968. The labor force share of the GNP also increased,
from a negligible amount to 6 percent. The increase of
the state's share in the financial sector was even more
pronounced. In 1974, 63 percent of total bank credit was
supplied by state-owned banks, whereas before 1968 the
proportion was only 36 percent (see Table 4.3). Thus,
at the macro level the increase of state participation
has been substantial. In sum, in both countries state
enterprises have significantly increased their share in
the economy. Brazil, however, has had a longer tradition
of managing state firms than Peru.

Table 4.2
Peru: Pattern of Enterprise Ownership (in percentages)

Sector	Pre-Reform		Post-Reform	
	GNP	Labor Force	GNP	Labor Force
1. State	11	7	26	13
(Government)	(9.7)	(7.3)	(9.7)	(7.3)
(Enterprises)	(1.2)	(0.2)	(16.3)	(6.2)
2. Domestic Capital	30	19	21	11
3. Foreign Capital	20	10	8	3
4. Coopera- tives	–	–	6	9
5. Modern Sector (1-4)	61	36	61	36
6. Traditional Sector	39	64	39	64
Total	100	100	100	100

Source: E.V.K. Fitzgerald, The State and Economic Development: Peru since 1968. (Cambridge: Cambridge
University Press, 1976).

66

Table 4.3
Peru: Credits of Development and Commercial Banks, 1966-
1974 (in billions of soles)

	1966	1970	1974
Development Banks	8.7	15.5	37.5
Associated Banks*	-	7.3	15.1
Total State Banks	8.7	22.8	52.6
Private Banks	15.7	15.9	30.8
Total Bank Credit	24.4	38.7	83.4
State Share (%)	36%	59%	63%

*Government-owned commercial banks.

Source: Fitzgerald, The State, Table 31.

STATE ENTERPRISES AND THE DISTRIBUTION OF INCOME

State firms have had an impact on the distribution
of income and/or equity through their actions on different fronts: pricing policies, choice of technology, employment and wage practices, location of economic activities, purchasing practices, and state-owned banks through
their lending policies. A characteristic of state firms
in post-1964 Brazil and post-1968 Peru has been their
dominance by technocrats (Brazil) and military officers
(Peru) bent on maximizing the economic power, growth,
and/or efficiency of their operations. It is therefore
in order to consider how the above mentioned policy measures of state firms affected the distribution of income
in each country.

Brazilian state enterprises can be found in sectors
whose technology is capital intensive - steel, petrochemicals, public utilities. It should be noted that although state firms account for 37.5 percent of net manufacturing assets, they employ only 11.5 percent of the
labor force (Table 4.1). Trebat found that since the
mid-1960s there has been a substantial increase in the
capital/labor ratio of state enterprises. In 1975 the
average state firm employee was endowed with 3.5 times
the capital of 1966 (Table 4.4). There are a number of

reasons for these trends: the incorporation of the latest technology in new investments, the lumpiness of investments in a number of state sectors, such as petrochemicals and hydroelectric projects, and the decline in
employment in railroads from about 160,000 in 1966 to
133,000 in 1975.

Table 4.4
Brazil: Capital/Labor Ratios in Selected Public Enterprises, 1966-1975 (in thousands of constant 1970 cruzeiros per man-year)

	1966-68	1970	1975
Mining	64	123	283
Steel	122	100	227
Petrochemicals	42	118	374
Communications	58	60	169
Electricity	366	368	734
Railroads	...	8	67
Average for Public Enterprise (excluding Railroads)	104	163	384

Source: Thomas J. Trebat, "An Evaluation of the Economic
Performance of Public Enterprises in Brazil," (Doctoral
dissertation, Vanderbilt University, 1978), Table 21.
(This source is here after referred to as "An Evaluation.")

To the extent that technology influences the distribution of income, i.e., high capital/output ratios resulting in a high proportion of value added going to capital, ceteris paribus, it would seem that state firms
have contributed to an increase in the concentration of
income.

Since 1966, emphasis in Brazilian public firms has
been on efficiency and it would seem that this has been
interpreted by state firm managements as a signal to
adopt capital-intensive technology and savings on employment. The average capital/output ratio increased from
about 2.3 in the mid-1960s to roughly 5.0 in the mid-
1970s. Along with these trends, a notable increase of
labor productivity is evident in Brazilian government
firms. Trebat's estimates show that while labor productivity increased by 44 percent in the manufacturing sector between 1966 and 1975, it rose by 137 percent in
state enterprises in the same period.(10)

In their anxiety to minimize investment costs and maximize efficiency, state enterprises often favor foreign suppliers of capital goods over domestic ones. This is especially the case in Brazil, which has a fairly substantial capital goods sector. The reasons given for this preference are the higher quality, shorter delivery time, and better servicing and pricing of foreign suppliers. Although these factors have been a matter of dispute (in 1978 and 1979 there was considerable public controversy in Brazil over the small share of domestic capital goods firms in the building of a new steel mill - a joint venture of a state firm with a number of multinationals - and over the share of local firms in Brazil's nuclear program), a decision in favor of efficiency, which usually involves ordering foreign equipment, has often prevailed. The impact of such actions on the distribution of income is through the adoption of more capital-intensive techniques (with imported technology). Also, the importation of equipment decreases the opportunity for creating jobs in high technology sectors, and the increase of foreign indebtedness of state firms could have a regressive impact on equity later on, a point which will be discussed further below.

Wages paid by public enterprises in Brazil range from the average wage in manufacturing (in the power generating and railroad sectors) to levels substantially above this average in state steel, mining, and petrochemical firms.(11) In the period 1970-1975, while productivity of state firms increased by 74 percent, employment increased by 19 percent and wages rose by 56 percent. Remuneration of management in Brazilian state firms was competitive with the private (domestic and multinational) sectors.(12) Thus, although wages in state firms are high, their growth lagged behind productivity increases and hence contributed to the income concentration trends within these firms. The remuneration hierarchy prevalent in private firms in Brazil was also notable in state enterprises and was another factor contributing to income concentration.

As in Brazil, state firms in Peru operate in the "modern sector." They are large and capital-intensive when compared to the average firm in the country. It may be that state firms are less capital-intensive than private firms in similar fields, but these are marginal considerations if one takes into account the more substantive difference between "modern" and "traditional" firms. In this respect a greater state participation has not helped to reduce technological duality in Peru. Table 4.2 shows, in fact, that a very small proportion of the labor force is employed by state firms.

The growth pattern of state firms also indicates a much more rapid investment in the more capital-intensive

industries of Peru. Table 4.5 reflects the tremendous
weight of petroleum in total investment; this is the most
capital intensive industry in Peru and elsewhere.

Table 4.5
Peru: Gross Fixed Investment by State Enterprises (in
millions of soles)

Sectors	1970	1975	1976	1977
Petroleum	698	19,049	24,950	20,193
Mining	1	5,224	4,071	3,274
Electricity	1,640	1,892	4,038	3,532
Industry	428	1,486	3,243	5,050
Total*	3,852	32,194	40,074	36,300

* Total is sum of four above sectors, plus other smaller
state enterprises.

Source: Banco Central del Peru, Memoria 1977, Table 14.

Aggregate demand for labor seems to be independent
of state or private firms, at least for unskilled labor.
The increased bureaucracy in state enterprises has generally meant more employment for those in the middle classes.

STATE ENTERPRISES AND EQUITY

How different is the economic behavior of a state
firm and a private firm? When both have monopoly positions in their market, the economic analyst becomes concerned about the equity and efficiency results of their
operations.

Pricing Policies

Whenever executives of public enterprises are given
independence from outside interference, they prefer
pricing policies which allow their organizations not only
to cover current costs, but also to maximize the internal
generation of funds for expansion, i.e., to maximize
profits. The general policymaker, who is primarily concerned with controlling budget deficits to combat inflation, would probably support such policies since they
eliminate the necessity for inflationary subsidies for
deficit-ridden public firms. Other general policy makers, however, might prefer external controls over pricing
by public firms; some would want to use such control as

an instrument to combat general inflationary pressures, while others might want to achieve some equity objectives.

Since the mid-1960s, most Brazilian public enterprises were allowed to follow the first objectives mentioned above. Their prices kept pace with and at times surpassed general price increases in the economy (see Table 4.6). Part b of Table 4.6, which contains indexes comparing prices of public enterprises with prices of industrial products, reveals that since 1964 three periods can be observed. From 1964 to 1966 a period of "corrective inflation" prevailed when the relative prices of many public enterprise goods and services increased substantially. In the years 1967 to 1969 prices of these goods and services rose at more or less similar rates to those in other sectors of the economy. In the 1970s one again observes a rise in the relative price of public enterprise goods and services.(13) One product which was not allowed to accompany the general price increases for a long period of time was steel. Steel firms were used, in fact, as instruments for combatting inflation in the late 1960s.

We may conclude in the Brazilian case that pricing by public firms tended to favor the position of state firms in their attempts to stay ahead of inflation and to generate more internal funds. This had a regressive impact (mainly in the urban sector) since prices and tariffs of many public firms (especially those in such public utilities as electricity, and urban and suburban transportation) fall proportinately more heavily on the population in the lower income urban groups. One should also remember that all this occurred at a time when wage increases fell behind the rise in the general price level.

For the other main products supplied by state enterprises, the price increase shows mild or ambiguous incidence on equity (petrochemicals) or on export products (iron ore). The decline in the relative price of steel, on the other hand, benefited mainly the rich. Finally, rural real incomes are not affected significantly by these prices.

The pricing of Peruvian state enterprises was closely linked to the country's general economic performance. In the 1968-1974 period Peru experienced rapid economic growth and price stability. Most of the social reforms were carried out during this period - reforms in land tenure, industry, mining, fishing, and education. Social property (labor managed) firms were created and most of the state enterprises originated in this period. The years 1975-1980 are characterized by substantial difficulties, including growing inflation, a stagnating economy, and a considerable economic recession in the last

Table 4.6 (a)
Brazil: Price Indexes and Annual Rates of Change of Prices for Public Enterprise Output,
1960-1976 (1965-1967 = 100)

Year	Steel	Rate of Change	Petroleum	Rate of Change	Iron Ore	Rate of Change	Electrical Energy	Rate of Change
1960	7		6		12		4	
1961	9	29%	10	87%	15	25%	6	50%
1962	18	100	13	30	20	33	8	33
1963	31	72	24	77	28	40	15	100
1964	54	74	45	100	63	125	30	100
1965	84	55	80	78	91	44	68	126
1966	99	18	99	24	99	9	98	44
1967	117	18	120	21	111	12	134	37
1968	152	30	155	29	138	24	156	16
1969	196	29	195	26	165	20	202	29
1970	253	29	225	15	199	21	257	27
1971	319	26	276	23	235	18	305	19
1972	360	13	350	27	266	13	366	20
1973	432	20	401	15	293	10	405	11
1974	653	51	641	60	391	33	512	26
1975	960	47	881	31	621	59	744	45
1976	1,197	25	1,398	59	978	57	894	20

Source: Trebat, "An Evaluation," Table 31.

Table 4.6 (b)
Brazil: Comparisons Between Implicit Price Indexes for Public Enterprise + Products and Industrial Products Price Index, 1965-1976 (1966 = 100)

Year	(1) Implicit Price Index for Public Enterprises	(2) Implicit Price Index for Public Enterprise excl. Petrochemicals	(3) Price Index for Industrial Products	(4) Ratio of (1)/(3)	(5) Ratio of (2)/(3)
1965	79	79	75	1.05	1.05
1966	100	100	100	1.0	1.0
1967	122	132	125	.98	1.06
1968	152	149	163	.93	.91
1969	193	191	196	.98	.97
1970	236	245	229	1.03	1.07
1971	288	299	269	1.07	1.11
1972	349	348	312	1.12	1.11
1973	395	390	358	1.10	1.09
1974	473	513	463	1.02	1.11
1975	812	751	599	1.36	1.25
1976a	1,153	961	818	1.41	1.17

Source: Trebat, "An Evaluation," Table 32.

few years. These problems were accompanied by severe balance of payments deficits.(14)

As part of a policy to control inflation, selective price controls were applied beginning in 1973-1974. The government even subsidized some "basic commodities" of the consumption basket in order to implement price controls. Several of the "basic commodities" were either produced (petroleum and derivates) or traded (imported food) by state enterprises, so that in many cases state enterprises were subject to price controls and received transfer funds from the government as compensation. This has been the case for almost all state firms producing for the domestic market.

The policy of price controls and subsidies contributed to a difficult economic and financial situation for state firms. Government subsidies also went to private firms, but these did not seem to have the same difficulties. Of course, many factors in addition to considerations of relative efficiency may explain this difference. The major beneficiaries of pricing and subsidies were the urban groups, whose consumption basket was the primary political concern (see Table 4.7); on the other hand, subsidies applied to imported food clearly worked against rural incomes.(15) Thus pricing policies increased overall inequality in the distribution of income in the period 1973-1977.

It was unfortunate that state enterprises were obliged to face price and foreign exchange controls, inflation, and contraction of domestic demand shortly after beginning their operations. The economic environment was not a very auspicious one for the "growing years" period of state enterprises in Peru. In evaluating the performance of state firms, this fact must be taken into account.

Existing evidence has led to the hypothesis that pricing policies of state firms in both countries contributed to an increase in inequality. The reasons for this are quite different. In Brazil, while state firms were allowed to use their pricing power, their policy followed the market rules for monopoly-type enterprises with their negative effects on equity. In Peru, however, price policies were not allowed to be independent of general government policies. Ironically, their subsidized prices were more beneficial to the higher income groups in urban centers than the poorer rural population. If our argument that both higher pricing, in one case, and subsidization, in the other, have led to increases in inequality seems paradoxical, it must be remembered that commodities involved and income pyramid composition differ in both countries.

Table 4.7
Peru: Incidence of Subsidies by Regions, 1975

Real Residence	Subsidies by Families 1975 (in soles)	Income by Family 1972 (in soles)	Total Subsidy (%)	Population Distribution (%)
Metropolitan Lima	6.500	118.000	56.3	20.0
High Strata	14.400	219.500	20.8	3.0
Medium Strata	6.900	111.900	19.8	7.0
Low Strata	3.700	56.400	15.7	10.0
Other Cities	2.400	60.000	25.9	25.5
Rural area	900	22.000	17.8	54.5
Total Peru	2.600	51.000	100.0	100.0

Source: Ministerio de Economia, Convenio ENCA. Inciden-
cia de los Subsidios en los Ingresos de las Familias en
el Peru (Lima, 1976), p. 4.

Location

The regional distribution of state enterprise activities has reinforced regional inequities in the distribution of income. In Brazil, over 30 percent of the population in the early 1970s lived in the poverty stricken
Northeast, while 42.7 percent lived in the more prosper-
ous Southeast and 17.7 percent in the South. Most government steel firms were located in the Southeast. With
the exception of its capital-intensive petrochemical
operation in Bahia and some oil wells in the Northeast,
most of Petrobras' operations were located in the Southeast; in the mid-1970s about 80 percent of petroleum
refining took place in that region. Similarly, investments in state power-generating projects resulted in the
fact that roughly 65 percent of installed power capacity
was in the Southeast and only 12 percent in the Northeast. Thus, in the matter of location, the bias of state
firms has been to favor efficiency over regional equity.
In Peru, the pattern of investment of state firms is
also not favorable to a more regionally balanced growth
as the activities taken over by the state are mainly nat-
ural-resource oriented. The result of this type of development is already known - regional imbalances occur.
The impact of mine exploitation on regional development,

for instance, will always be very small, regardless of whether the firm is state or privately owned. The Southern Sierra region, which is the most depressed area in Peru, has not benefited from the presence of state firms. In effect, it would seem that state enterprises have the same criteria in allocating resources on a regional basis as do private firms.

Financing

The method of financing the expansion of state enterprises has clearly distributive implications. In order to maximize their economic and political independence, these firms prefer to maximize the capacity for self-financing. To the extent that this is achieved by pricing policies, the impact on the distribution of income would be negative. Government subsidies to state enterprises, however, can also be regressive if these are allocated to firms providing key inputs to the private sector and if the subsidies are financed by a regressive tax system. Finally, foreign borrowing may have a regressive impact if the future burden of these loans on the balance of payments leads to devaluation of the currency, a condition which will be more keenly felt by the lower income groups, and if future repayments come from tariff increases which also fall more heavily on these groups.

In the second half of the 1960s and in the 1970s, Brazil's public enterprises financed a large proportion of their gross investments from retained earnings and depreciation (varying from 40 to 60 percent in the 1966-1975 period; see Table 4.8). In some sectors, the proportion of internal financing declines substantially during major expansion programs, such as power generation; the decline in steel is due to a combination of expansion and controlled prices. Railroads, however, have always relied almost entirely on outside financing. In the mid-1970s about 12 percent of financing came from specific taxes (a regressive source) and 17 percent from foreign loans.

In contrast to Brazil, state enterprises in Peru depend very much on external funds (government and private) to finance their capital formation as their savings have become negative. If transfers (subsidies) from the government are taken into account, the internal creation of savings would be even more negative, as Table 4.9 shows. This table also reflects the sources for financing capital formation, and it is clear that government funding has been very important.

Several reasons can be given for this situation. The official explanation is that "...it is attributable, on

Table 4.8 (a)
Brazil: Investment and Surplus (Profits and Depreciation Allowances) for Public Enterprises, 1966-1975 (values in thousands of current cruzeiros)

	Total Investment	Surplus	Residual	Self-Finance Ratio	Self-Finance Ratio Excluding Railroads
	(I)	(S)	(I-S)	(S/I)	
1966	1,026,395	616,083	410,312	60%	81%
1967	2,040,069	954,412	1,087,657	47	56
1968	3,044,573	1,382,662	1,661,911	45	51
1969	3,566,512	1,923,310	1,643,202	54	63
1970	6,317,567	3,489,137	2,828,430	55	63
1971	10,134,055	5,219,835	4,914,220	52	59
1972	14,065,013	6,395,576	7,666,437	45	53
1973	20,833,411	9,230,277	11,603,134	44	50
1974	31,953,318	14,712,189	17,241,129	46	54
1975	52,674,045	20,697,205	31,976,840	39	46

Source: Trebat,"An Evaluation," Table 35.

Table 4.8 (b)
Brazil: Internal Financing as a Percent of Gross Investment (average yearly figures)

	1967-1969	1970-1971	1972-1973	1974-1975
Steel	72%	100%	49%	24%
Petrochemicals	69	86	92	88
Mining	100	73	63	95
Electricity	49	37	28	29
Telecommunications	36	47	63	44

Source: Trebat, "An Evaluation," Table 36.

the one hand, to investment programs with no proper financing and, on the other hand, to the price and subsidies policy adopted by the government in order to control inflation...."(16) Another reason has to do with the inefficiency of Peruvian state firms. Although studies are not available to show the magnitude of the inefficiency involved, it is a common assumption that state firms are poorly run bureaucratic extensions of the government, and lack a committed, qualified cadre of technocrats.

Table 4.9
Peru: State Enterprise Financing (millions of soles)

Origins of Funds	1970	1975	1976	1977	1978	1979
Internal (Current Government Transfers)	2,086	-3,645	-2,510	143	30,613	74,719
	(-)	(4,735)	(4,801)	(2,248)	(4,982)	(779)
Government Domestic Borrowing	1,504	7,385	10,932	9,796	10,656	17,107
External Borrowing	-413	18,317	20,998	13,339	-12,460	-5,694
	1,660	10,649	10,906	15,199	17,783	-26,117
Total Fixed Investment	4,837	32,706	40,326	38,477	46,592	60,015

Source: Banco Central del Peru, Memoria 1979, Table 13.

Therefore, part of the government transfers to state firms is needed to cover such inefficiencies while the other part is used to offset the effects of price control on their revenue. In any case, government funds have alternative uses and, instead of paying for the inefficiency of state firms, the state could have used its resources to finance many redistributive programs. Due to the shortage of funds, several projects in rural areas, for example, were stopped. In a country such as Peru, where income redistribution policies are badly needed and where government spending is one of the basic instruments to achieve this, it seems unfortunate that so many government funds were used to finance state enterprises.

State Banks

In both countries state banks are a dominant force
in commercial and investment lending. The evidence to
date suggests that they have contributed towards the concentration of economic opportunities, and hence towards
the preservation of the concentration of wealth and its
effects.

In Brazil most of the agricultural credit originates
with the Banco do Brasil, the state-owned bank which is
also the country's largest commercial bank. It has been
estimated that in 1976, of the approximately five million
rural establishments, only 20 percent received credit for
current operations, only 10 percent for investments, and
only 6 percent for marketing. These loans went to the
largest agricultural establishments. It has been shown
that establishments of fifty or fewer hectares received
no credits, although in the 1970 census over 80 percent
of all establishments were of fifty hectares or less.(17)
Since rural credit is heavily subsidized, i.e., the interest rate charged has always been substantially below
the rate of inflation (although Brazil has an extensive
indexing system, this was never applied to rural credit),
it would seem that the state, through its dominance in
agricultural credit, has been an instrument of redistribution in favor of large property owners.

The operations of Brazil's development bank (BNDE)
have also contributed towards increasing the concentration of income. Since the mid-1960s an increasing proportion of its loans have gone to the domestic private
sector and by the second half of the 1970s over 80 percent of its loans were directed to the promotion of that
sector. By that time over half of its resources came
from workers' forced savings, i.e., social security funds
collected from both workers and employers. The purchasing power of these funds was guaranteed by indexing. In
the second half of the 1970s, however, special programs
were devised by the BNDE to bolster the domestic private
sector with loans whose monetary correction (indexing)
would not be above 20 percent. With an inflation rate
substantially above that level, this amounted to a subsidy. Payment for this subsidy could be financed in a
number of ways: reducing the indexing of workers' funds,
which amounts to property redistribution from workers to
capital, reducing the official index used for monetary
correction - which amounts to the same thing, or financing the subsidized part of the loans by general tax
funds which, considering the regressive structure of Brazil's tax system, amounts to a similar redistribution of
income.(18)

It would seem that the pronounced increase of the
share of the state in total Peruvian bank credit would
have had an important effect on income distribution; one

might have expected that cheap credit would go to the
lower income groups. This has not been the case, however. Table 4.3 shows that almost 40 percent of state
credit is supplied by "associated banks" which follow the
practices of private banks. For the development banks,
the practice is not entirely "commercial," that is aimed
at profit maximization, but still the funds go largely
to the more creditworthy clients. For instance, the
agricultural development bank still lends two-thirds of
its total credit to large farms which specialize in export crops (cotton, sugar, rice). While the present beneficiaries are the workers who received the land from the
agrarian reform program, they are one of the smallest
(albeit the richest) groups in the rural sector. Small-
scale farmers of the Sierra region are still out of the
credit system and, in fact, did not get any land from the
agrarian reform.

In sum, the subsidized credit of development banks
reaches neither small-scale enterprises nor the poor
peasants. Poverty in Peru is concentrated in these types
of units of production.

The "Capitalist" Behavior of State Enterprises

As our survey has indicated, there is considerable
evidence that the behavior of state enterprises has not
resulted in greater equality in the distribution of income in either Brazil or Peru and might even, as some of
our evidence suggests, have contributed to an increase
in the concentration of income.

In the case of Brazil, this is due primarily to the
administrative hierarchies of state enterprises (including banks) which are principally concerned with the efficient functioning and rapid growth of their entities.
This emphasis usually works counter to any egalitarian
distributive goals which the central government may have.
One student of Brazil's state enterprise system, Luciano
Martins, has characterized the behavior of state firms
succinctly:

As these entities ....come to count on stable
revenues, administering and reproducing them in
a quasi-entrepreneurial fashion, establishing
their own salary structure, maintaining their
own personnel recruitment procedures and social
insurance system... /there inevitably arises/
an 'esprit de corps' which creates a unique
/institutional/ personality. It is thus not
surprising that these entities behave according
to their own 'logic.' /Their/ staff will identify with the enterprise's problems and goals
rather than with those of the state. It is in

this sense that /one can refer to/ ...the 'au-
tonomization' of firms - the existence of a cen-
trifugal trend within the state apparatus.(19)

In the case of Peru, state firms do not have the same
autonomy as in Brazil. There are several reasons for
this. First, those who administer the firms (both military officers and technical associates) were part of the
larger military establishment running the country. Second, unlike Brazil, Peru lacks both a historical tradition of state firms and a cadre of technicians to run
them. The resulting inefficiency of Peruvian state enterprises has contributed to large deficits in their operations. As these deficits are generally made up out of
state funds, the financial transfers to state enterprises
which this involved had a regressive impact on the distribution of income; the funds, which amounted to 13 percent of the total government budget in 1975-1976, benefited a relatively small part of the population and could
have been used for projects with much greater social
impact.

In short, we are not suggesting that the behavior of
private firms could have been better from an equity point
of view. Rather, it is a question of comparing monopoly
firms - state or private - under a market system. Our
survey shows that state firms did not act to lessen income inequalities. (However, it is worth pointing out
that many of the firms in the private sector are multinationals: thus their resources are not only inequitably
distributed, but part of them may also be transferred
abroad.)

Little is known about decision-making within state
firms and banks, or about the relationship between state
enterprises and the ministries to which they are supposedly subordinate. This is a complex topic which calls
for further case studies. For example, it is likely that
decisions do not simply filter down from the top policymakers to individual state firms, where they are promptly
executed. Indeed, many of Brazil's and Peru's state enterprises are not only economically but also politically
powerful, and often get their own way in opposition to
the wishes of the top economic planners. For example,
it was common in recent years for state firms in Brazil
to import equipment in complete disregard of general
directives from authorities to contain imports. This
type of situation was confirmed by a former president of
a powerful Brazilian state enterprise, who termed such a
situation a "reversão de mando" ("inversion of command
flows.")(20)

One can infer from the case of Brazil that the independent behavior pattern of state entities, which act to
maximize their own efficiency and power, could be considered inevitable. It is easier to establish performance

criteria for state entities which stress efficiency rather than equity, e.g., the profit rate of a firm, the repayment record of loans granted by a loan officer of a state bank, etc. And, once a state entity functions well according to some criteria for efficiency, it acquires political power which places it in a position to disregard - or to influence - central policy decisions affecting its operations. The possibility that this pattern will also occur in Peruvian firms, once they will have improved their operational efficiency, cannot be ruled out.

It remains to be seen whether the trends discussed in this chapter will be reversed following the increases in political freedom which are possible in both countries in the near future. It should be noted, however, that the enormous economic power accumulated by state enterprises could have substantial political influence even in a more open political system.

A FINAL IRONY

If further research sustains our contention that the growing direct involvement of state enterprises in the economy works against the goals of equity, some may claim that more equitable social goals could be more easily achieved in a system in which the role of the state is limited. Rapid growth in an economy dominated by state enterprises results in powerful claims by such entities on the economic surplus for further investments in activities leading to still greater increases in the concentration of economic power. On the other hand, a system in which the nonstate sector is more prevalent could make it politically easier for the government to tax the surplus in order to apply resources in sectors having greater "social equity" impacts. The heroic assumption, though, would be for the state apparatus to overcome political pressure by the domestic private sector and by multinationals to minimize such taxation and to apply state resources in infrastructure investments complementary to their activities.

We wish to thank Paul Becherman for many helpful suggestions.

NOTES

1. Of course, some free market-oriented economists would argue the opposite - that state intervention creates monopolies, which leads to more inequality in the distribution of income.

2.   Donald E. Syvrud, Foundations of Brazilian Economic Growth (Stanford: Hoover Institution Press, 1974).

3.   Werner Baer, Isaac Kerstenetzky and Annibal V. Villela, "The Changing Role of the State in the Brazilian Economy," World Development, November 1973.

4.   Werner Baer and Annibal V. Villela, "The Changing Nature of Development Banking in Brazil," Journal of Interamerican Studies and World Affairs 22, no. 4 (November 1980).

5.   Fernando Rezende, "A Produção Pública na Economia Brasileira," Dados 18 (1978).

6.   Werner Baer, The Brazilian Economy: Its Growth and Development (Columbus: Grid Publishing Inc., 1979), pp. 153-154.

7.   Michael Roemer, Fishing for Growth: Export-Led Development in Peru, 1950-1967 (Cambridge: Harvard University Press, 1970) and Shane Hunt, "Distribution, Growth and Government Economic Behavior in Peru," in Gustav Ranis, ed., Government and Economic Development (New Haven: Yale University Press, 1971), pp. 375-416.

8.   See the articles by Lowenthal and Webb in Abraham F. Lowenthal, ed., The Peruvian Experiment: Continuity and Change under Military Rule (Princeton: Princeton University Press, 1975).

9.   E.V.K. Fitzgerald, The State and Economic Development: Peru since 1968 (Cambridge: Cambridge University Press, 1976).

10.   Thomas J. Trebat, "An Evaluation of the Economic Performance of Public Enterprises in Brazil," (Doctoral dissertation, Vanderbilt University, 1978), p. 187.

11.   Ibid., p. 246.

12.   Edmar Lisboa Bacha, "Hierarquia e Remuneração Gerencial," in Ricardo Tolipan and Arthur Carlos Tinelli eds., A Controvérsia Sobre Distribuição de Renda e Desenvolvimento (Rio de Janeiro: Zahar Editores, 1975), pp. 124-55.

13.   Trebat, "An Evaluation," pp. 220-226.

14.   For a discussion of policies in these years, see Daniel M. Schydlowsky and Juan J. Wicht, Anatomia de un fracaso economico: Peru 1968-1978 (Lima: Universidad del Pacifico, Centro de Investigacion, 1979).

15.   Adolfo Figueroa, "Agricultural Price Policy and Rural Incomes in Peru," Quarterly Review of Economics and Business, Fall 1981.

16.   Banco Central de Reserva del Peru, Memoria 1976.

17.   Paulo Rabello de Castro, "O Impasse da Politica Agricola," in Rumos do Desenvolvimento, Setembro/Octubro 1978.

18.   Werner Baer and Paul Beckerman, "The Trouble with Index-Linking: Reflections on the Recent Brazilian Experience," World Development, September 1980.

19. Luciano Martins, "'Estatização' da Economia 'Privatização' do Estado?" <u>Ensaios de Opinião</u> 2, no. 7 (1978).

20. Fernando Roquette Reis, "Relações entre Empresa Pública e Administração Central: Analise e Recomendações," (mimeographed, 1979).

5
Collectivized Capitalism: Integrated Petrochemical Complexes and Capital Accumulation in Brazil

Peter Evans

The Complexo Petroquímico de Camaçari is reputed to be the largest one-time investment in a fully integrated petrochemical complex ever made anywhere in the world.(2) Its more than twenty plants run continuously, turning out millions of dollars worth of petrochemical raw materials, plastics, chemicals, and synthetic fibers each day. Such a complex, on a site not only in Brazil but in Bahia, 30 kilometers outside of Salvador, must be considered an anomaly. Salvador is known for the quality of its carnival, not for the quality of its industrial infrastructure. The Northeast region in which it is located has neither the tradition of industrial entrepreneurship, nor the market for intermediate chemical products, nor the skilled labor force normally considered necessary for the development of technologically advanced process industries. But Camaçari is more than an anomaly; it is a key element in Brazil's recent industrialization. Analysing Camaçari provides important insights into the social bases of that industrialization.

The "Petrochemical Pole," as Camaçari is called, is a worldscale facility which rivals those of Western Europe, Japan, and the United States. The naphtha cracker, designed by and constructed under the supervision of the Lummus company, has a rated capacity of 384,000 tons of ethylene a year. The second generation plants that surround it, turning its ethylene into polyethylene, ethylene oxide, ethylene glycol, styrene, and polyvinyl chloride, its propylene into polypropylene, and its aromatics into DMT, TDI, and other intermediates, are also of worldscale. Together with the third generation plants which make synthetic fibers, plastifyers, surfactants, and a range of other chemical products, they comprise an intricate interlinked industrial city. For some plants, the number of their technological equals in other countries can be counted on the fingers of one hand, and almost all of them are as technologically advanced as recently constructed plants producing the same products in

86

Figure 5.1
The Camaçari Petrochemical Complex (A Partial View)

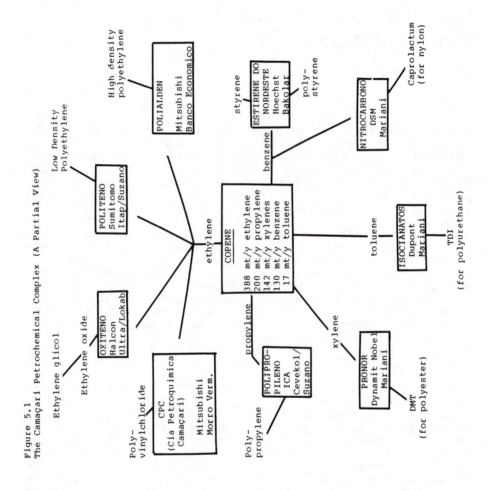

Key to Figure 5.1:

Company names: Are simplified in all-capitals in each circle

Stockholders: Are below company names, with multinational stockholders
                on first line, local private stockholders on second
                line.

                Petroquisa is a stockholder in all companies listed

                In cases of multiple stockholders, only two have been
                listed on each line.

                Bakolar, Cevekol, and Lokab are all Rosenberg holding
                companies.

                Hoechst's ownership is through purchase of Foster Grant,
                Dynamit Nobel has withdrawn.

Products: Only principle products have been listed.

Inputs: Only principle inputs have been listed. For example,
                ethylene is also an input for styrene. Inputs coming
                from sources other than COPENE have not been listed.
                For example, CPC receives ethylene dichloride from Sal-
                gema; Nitrocarbono receives ammonia from Nitrofertil
                (which is also in the pole).

                COPENE's rated capacities are listed in thousands of
                metric tons per year.

the developed countries. Figure 5.1, which provides a
partial view of the complex showing only about one-third
of the plants involved, offers some indication of the
range of firms and products involved.

As of June 1979, the basic complex had twenty separate companies in operation,(3) with another five in the
process of installation and seven more approved for construction. The total cost of the complex, including investment in infrastructure, was estimated at $2.4 bil-
lion. COPENE, which produces the basic feedstocks and
also supplies the second generation companies with steam
and electricity, represents the largest single investment; something on the order of $0.5 billion. The larger
downstream plants represent investments between $100 and
$150 million.(4) Some indication of the scale of the
projects can be gained by comparing Camaçari's capacities
in major thermoplastic resins with existing capacities
elsewhere in the developing world at the time the project
was undertaken.

As Table 5.1 indicates, the Camaçari complex put Brazil in the forefront of the developing world as far as
petrochemical production was concerned. The strength of
Brazil's initiative in petrochemicals is further illustrated by a look at trends in ethylene capacity(5) as
shown in Table 5.2. In 1978, when Camaçari came on
stream, Brazil's productive capacity in ethylene was almost equal to that of all the other Latin American countries combined (the four countries on the table accounted
for virtually total production capacity.) Even oil rich
Mexico was slated to pass Brazil only in 1982. Argentina, which had embarked on its first petrochemical complex
in Bahia Blanca almost twenty years before the inauguration of Camaçari,(6) had fallen by the wayside. Even
after an ethylene facility was finally completed at Bahia
Blanca in 1976, it was unable to start production because
the complementary plant necessary to separate ethane from
the available natural gas feedstock had never been built.
(7) Venezuela's failure in petrochemicals has been even
more ignominious, especially given the longstanding central role of petroleum in its economy. As the Economist
put it, "The Bahia Blanca bloomer is completely out-
classed by Venezuela's failure to complete an ethylene
cracker that was started 25 years ago."(8)

Brazil's success in petrochemicals is not only impressive from an international perspective, it has also
been extremely important in terms of the internal dynamics of capital accumulation. From the middle to late
1970s, the role of leading industrial sector, which
clearly belonged to the automobile industry in the middle
and late 1960s, could be claimed by the petrochemical
industry. The availability of local supplies of basic
and intermediate petrochemicals helped stimulate the
growth of downstream chemical ventures. In addition, the

Table 5.1:
Estimated LDC Capacities in Thermoplastic Resins (1975-1978)

	Low Density Polyethylene	High Density Polyethylene	Polypropylene	Polystyrene	Polyvinyl-chloride
Total LDC Capacity	1334	187	342	693	1991
Latin America	778	110	100	430	664
Argentina	75	---	---	66	---
Mexico	218	---	---	97	232
Venezuela	110	---	---	---	---
Brazil	288	110	100	190	307

Sources: ABIQUIM, 1978; USITIC, 1977.

N.B. USITIC estimates are taken from Chemical Economics Handbook, Stanford Institute, and are for 1975-76. Estimates for Brazil in this source were incorrect, and were replaced by ABIQUIM estimates. ABIQUIM estimates for 1978 were used except for PVC for which Camaçari capacity was included even though CPC was not on stream. USITIC estimates for Brazil were substantially above actual 1978 capacities even though they purported to be for an earlier date. Estimates for other LDCs may therefore also be overstated.

Table 5.2
Ethylene Capacity

	1972 projection of 1980 capacity (UNIDO) (1)	actual capacity 1978 (2)	listed projects for new capacity 1979 (3)	Approx. capacity 1982 (4)
Brazil	485	718	624	1,350
Mexico	210	445	1,000	1,500
Argentina	319	150	170	320
Venezuela	150	200	0	200
U.S.A.		15,000	4,200	19,500
Japan		5,500	800	5,800
Total World		43.000		55,900

Sources:

1. UNIDO, 1972, p. 52, table 56
2. 1978 LA capacity - Oil&Gas Journal, September 1978.
3. projects - Hydrocarbon Processing, February 1979; June 1979.
4. DC capacity - industry sources; LA capacity - based on columns 2 and 3

construction of the Camaçari project and other petrochemical ventures was a boon to the local capital goods industry, not only in providing orders, but also in forcing the acquisition of new kinds of technological competence that might be applied in other process industries.

Both the centrality of the petrochemical industry to the general process of accumulation and the firmness of Brazil's commitment to maintaining its relative international position in the industry were reconfirmed in 1975 when President Geisel announced that another petrochemical pole, with an olefin capacity greater than Camaçari's, would be created at the other end of the country in Rio Grande do Sul. Thus Brazil, a country that has to import 80 percent or more of the petroleum it consumes, continues to keep pace with Mexico in the development of the petrochemical industry, leaving not only other Latin American countries but most of the developing world far behind.

The Brazilian petrochemical industry did not, of course, begin with Camaçari. São Paulo, Brazil's industrial heartland, provided the necessary conditions for the germination of the petrochemical industry in the late 1960s when a local entrepreneurial group managed to put together what is now called the first petrochemical pole, around a naphtha cracker almost as large as the one at Camaçari.(9) Without the engineers, managers, and skilled workers generated by the complex of petrochemical plants in São Paulo, Camaçari would not have been possible.

Including the new complex in Rio Grande do Sul, the so-called "Polosul" which is still in the early phases of construction, Brazil now has three petrochemical "poles," but only two are integrated complexes. The term "complex" is applied on a post-hoc basis to Sao Paulo, but the growth of the industry there was much less coordinated. Some plants are more or less integrated around São Paulo's naphtha cracker (Petroquimica Uniao); others are quite separate. Each of the three poles has something to say about the nature of capital accumulation in Brazil's petrochemical industry, but it is Camaçari which epitomizes the integrated complex and shows most dramatically both the technical and economic obstacles that had to be overcome and the social and organizational strategies that were used to overcome them.

The obstacles to construction of any petrochemical industry in Brazil are obvious but worth reiterating. Adequate local petroleum supplies are missing. The required technology is not the property of Brazilians but of foreign firms. An immense amount of capital had to be raised, a substantial portion of it in foreign currencies, and thus both multinational corporations and international banks had to be convinced that a functioning and eventually profitable petrochemical complex could be constructed in Bahia.

Camaçari as a site had the marginal advantage of being close to one of the few oil fields in Brazil, but the disadvantages were multiple. Despite ten years of effort to draw industry to Bahia through fiscal incentives, the level of industrialization in the state was minimal. The supporting network of specialized industrial suppliers and service firms that cuts external costs for petrochemical plants in Houston or Baton Rouge did not exist. A skilled labor force with experience in process technology plants was also lacking. Complementary downstream manufacturing plants that could take the chemicals produced and turn them into auto parts, polyester clothing, dyes, or paints were nonexistent. Skilled labor, suppliers, service industries, and markets were all in Sao Paulo, insofar as they were available in Brazil at all.

The disadvantages of Bahia were, of course, not due to chance or poor planning. They were deliberate. Brazil was attempting not just to build a petrochemical complex, but to plant a dynamic industrial pole in an area where less extreme attempts to create industrialization did not seem to have worked. The Camaçari pole was an ambitious attempt at the kind of linkage-generating strategy of "unbalanced growth" that Albert Hirschman might have suggested.(10) Its success also implied taking advantage of the potential positive effects of what Hirschman later called "disciplines."(11) The industries being created required precision construction and operation to avoid the possibility that they might quite literally blow up. Thus their successful implantation would ineluctably entail the creation of skilled labor and management at the local level. In the longer run, locally available supplies should call forth the manufacturing firms to provide the pole with a local market and to diversify Bahia's industrial structure.

The theory was attractive, but using the pole as a means of generating external effects on the surrounding environment also meant, by definition, choosing a more difficult environment. By combining the aim of developing a petrochemical industry with the aim of developing the region, Brazil was increasing the risk that the petrochemical complex would fail.

Nationalist strictures as well as regional development aims made the implantation of the pole more difficult. International firms were to be allowed no more than a minority position in any of the firms operating in the pole. Simple state/multinational corporation partnerships of the kind that were forming the basis of the development of petrochemicals in Eastern Europe were also not to be allowed. Local private capital had to be given a role in each of the second generation firms. The firms were to be tri-pés, literally tripods, with their ownership split one-third local private, one-third state, and one-third foreign private.

If the plans for the pole flew in the face of conventional economic and technological logic in the late 1960s and early 1970s when the planning was being done, their implementation flew in the face of international economic trends after 1973 when equipment manufacturers and engineering firms in the developed countries protected their real incomes by increasing their prices along with the price of oil. Reliable estimates of the increases in the costs of building petrochemical plants between 1973 and 1978, when Camaçari came on stream, are not readily available, but informal guesses run between a tripling and quintupling of prices. At the same time the shock to the developed economies cut into the demand for petrochemical products, lowering international prices and cutting into the multinational corporations' enthusiasm for the construction of new capacity.

The explanation for Camaçari and for the Brazilian petrochemical industry in general is essentially a story of institutional and organizational innovation. Without social and organizational innovation, technological and economic logic would have reigned and Camaçari never have existed. Camaçari, in turn, was a key step in the creation of a set of corporate capitalist institutions whose effects will extend well beyond Bahia, and perhaps well beyond the petrochemical industry.

CAPITALIST ACCUMULATION AS COLLABORATION

For those who saw the Brazilian "miracle" in the early seventies as a triumph of free market capitalism, (12) Camaçari is an excellent lesson. It was a key element in Brazil's industrial take-off and bears as much resemblance to ideal typical, laissez-faire, competitive capitalism as a ballet to a boxing match. This does not imply, however, that many of the social characteristics supposed to underlie a Rostowian "take-off" are lacking in Camaçari. New elites, freed from traditional encumbrances and able to gain control over an important part of the society's surplus and direct it toward new productive activities, are part of the story. What is missing is the mythical Anglo-Saxon atomistic individualism that is usually read into the story of capitalist accumulation. Articulation of diverse elite interests and the construction of solidary, cooperative relationships among different elite groups were the keys to the success of Camaçari.

Competition in the sense of each party trying to maximize his own gain at the expense of those from whom he buys or to whom he sells clashes with the nature of an integrated complex. As Otto Perroni, considered by

94

some to be the father of Camaçari, expressed it, "Some petrochemical complexes are the property of a single company, some of various companies, all of them, however, have one feature in common, that is, the cooperative character of the industrial units that comprise them." (13)

"Integration" is not just an abstract concept for the companies that comprise the pole. It is as concrete as the maze of ducts and pipes that connect them. This is especially true in the case of olefins which must be cryogenically stored and are extremely difficult to transport outside of ducts. If COPENE shuts down for more than a few days, then Politeno, Polialden, and Oxiteno will run out of ethylene and have to shut down as well (see figure 5.1). By the same token, if Politeno and Poliaden were to close for more than a few days, COPENE would have no place to store its ethylene and would have to stop production as well. The interdependence of at least some of the plants at Camaçari is as tight as the links that connect different sections of a single factory in other industries.

The technological requisites of petrochemicals, especially olefin production, lead to the development of petrochemical capacity in complexes. Naphtha crackers must be surrounded by a host of second and third generation plants. Given the interdependent nature of these complexes, it is not surprising that major chemical companies like to dominate the complexes of which they are a part by controlling the raw materials center and at least a portion of the downstream plants. In view of the magnitude of the investment and the variety of technologies involved, it is not surprising that even major companies find themselves participating in complexes dominated by others.

The originators of Camaçari had numerous complexes constructed by international capital available as models. The rapid development of the Japanese petrochemical industry after World War II was based on seventeen petrochemical complexes, each of them organized by one or the other of Japan's major chemical firms. At Kashima, for example, Mitsubishi formed a partnership with Kyodo oil to build a refinery, built the central cracking unit itself, and then formed associations with other companies to create the second and third generation users.(14) At Guanyanilla, on the south shore of Puerto Rico, PPG joined with CORCO (Commonwealth Oil Refining Company) to build a naphtha cracker with a rated capacity of a billion pounds of ethylene a year, to be supplied with naphtha by CORCO's refinery. Union Carbide, Grace, and PPG itself put up second generation plants and were joined by Japanese and Taiwanese capital. In Wilton, England, ICI put together its own complex over a period of almost twenty years, gradually adding new plants and new capacity until the complex reached a scale and complexity even larger than that of Camaçari.

All of these ventures share the "health of one is the health of all" character inherent in an integrated petrochemical complex, but none faced as difficult an external environment as did Camaçari. Nor did any of them come close to the organizational complexity of Camaçari. Other complexes may involve five or six major stockholders in the first and second generation plants, but the major stockholders in the first and second generation at Camaçari numbered closer to twenty-four. In addition, foreign ownership came from five different developed countries and the local private owners were an equally diverse group in terms of the range of economic origins they represented.

The variegated combination of owners involved made Camaçari a riskier venture than most. The fate of PPG's Puerto Rican complex provides an indication of the risk involved. The complex came on stream in 1971, but the cracker never exceeded 55 percent of its rated capacity. Eventually CORCO went bankrupt and the central cracker was mothballed, leaving the participants in the complex with several hundred million dollars of theoretically valuable but practically inoperable equipment.

Looking at other complexes provides only a background for understanding Camaçari, not an explanation of how it came to be or how it avoided the fate of the Puerto Rican complex. The inherently collective nature of integrated petrochemical complexes is only one of the keystones of the social organization that underlies Camaçari. Technological integration in itself insures only that failure will be integrated; organizationally Camaçari went several steps beyond existing models.

STATE ENTREPRENEURSHIP

To say that the state played the central entrepreneurial role in the implantation of Camaçari would be correct, but misleading. The entrepreneurial initiatives that led to Camaçari did not emerge from policy decisions made by the state apparatus as a whole, or even primarily from the efforts of individual Presidents and ministers. The entrepreneurial thrust came from a confluence of less powerful influences.

Various political figures and technocrats whose primary interest was in fostering industrial development in Bahia, such as Rômulo Almeida and Governor Luis Viana Filho, played an important role in early initiatives. It was the study by the Bahia-based consulting group, CLAN,

in 1969 which provided the first sketches of what the
pole would be like. The CLAN study, which was directed
by Almeida, was contracted by the state government headed
by Viana. José Mascarenhas, who worked on the CLAN
study, was later made Secretary of Mines and Energy for
the State of Bahia and given responsibility for coor-
dinating support for the pole at the state level.

Political entrepreuneurship at the state level was
essential to the final shape of the pole.(15) There were
good technical economic arguments, as well as powerful
political forces, in favor of simply expanding the petrochemical industry in Sao Paulo rather than attempting a
brand new pole in an unfavorable site. Had these forces
and arguments triumphed, the evolution of the petrochemical industry would have taken on a quite different character. The pressure for a collectively organized plan
of accumulation would have been less, the manueverability
of both international capital and established local capital would have been greater, and institutional consequences would have diminished.

The fact that the first official statement from the
federal government that there would be a pole in Bahia
was made by President Médici while on a visit to the
state in 1970(16) is some indication of the importance
of local political pressure in the origins of the pole.
But initiatives at the national level, from within the
Ministry of Industry and Commerce (MIC), the National
Bank for Economic Development (BNDE), and, most important, from within Petrobras, were at least as critical
in giving Camaçari its eventual institutional shape. The
shaping was done less by overall policy decision than by
informal, personal contacts among the individuals involved. Most of these were more technocratic than entrepreneurial in terms of their roles and training, but the
end result of their activities was entrepreneurial on a
grand scale.

It was through the interaction of mid-career technocrats, like Arthur Candal of MIC, Otto Perroni of Petrobras, and Paulo Belotti of the BNDE, working in informal
groups like the Resolution 2/70 Group,(17) that the plans
for the pole were made concrete. Candal, then assessor
to the Minister of Industry and Commerce, later became a
director of COPENE and still later a director of one of
the local capital groups involved in the pole. Perroni,
who had worked on the original CLAN study, later became
president of COPENE and then executive vice-president of
petroquisa. Belotti, a chemical engineer who had also
worked on the CLAN study, eventually became president of
Petroquisa.(18) Men like these, whose careers took them
through various positions in the state apparatus and occasionally into the local private sector, shared a faith
in the possibility of state entrepreneurship that was not
always felt by others with similiar positions. Support

for the pole, even within Petrobras, was probably not monolithic. There were apparently those within the company who felt that the formation of Petroquisa, and the move toward involvement in industrial activities, was a diversion from the state oil monopoly's legally defined task. Without the support of General Geisel during his term as president of Petrobras, it would have been difficult for those who supported the pole, like Perroni and Belotti, to promote the idea. But, at the same time, without the entrepreneurial initiatives from those lower down it is unlikely that those at the top would have acted.

The initial entrepreneurship was both political and organizational. Someone had to devise the idea of the tri-pé and round up both foreign technologists and local capitalists willing to enter into such ventures. Feasibility studies had to be carried out in order to convince the international banking community to provide some of what eventually became $1.2 billion in foreign currency. Albert Hahn, of the research bureau of the French Institute of Petroleum, was brought in to help with the feasibility studies, and the Japanese Consulting Institute produced the report which determined the exact location of the pole. Gradually the pole changed from imaginative intentions to concrete, detailed plans.

What was involved was neither risking capital to attempt to turn a technological innovation into a productive asset, nor risking the introduction of a new product in an uncertain market. The technology, while up to date, was not the innovative aspect of the endeavor. The market was evident from the existing levels of Brazil's imports, from the high rate of growth in Brazil's consumption of final products, and most of all from the avowed government policy of a "reserved market." The pole could count on government protection of its market from foreign producers through substantial tariffs. Local competition was controlled by the fact that Petrobras controlled the raw materials: through the original law establishing Petrobras' monopoly, no one else could supply naphtha to its steam cracker.

Both the risk and the innovation lay on the organizational side. Could the pole's advocates bring the diverse groups involved together to form a functioning collectivity? Could the downstream firms be convinced that COPENE would actually have the necessary basic inputs on stream when they needed them and that it was therefore not too risky to start committing funds? Would a Brazilian construction company, a Japanese chemical group, and Petroquisa be able to agree on how to produce and sell polyvinyl chloride? Integration is not usually seen as the central task of the classic entrepreneur, but in this case the entrepreneurial role was essentially integrative.

Once the plans had been finalized, the constituent companies approved by the CDI, and the initial financing secured, the required entrepreneurship shifted to a more traditional kind. A technologically difficult construction job had to be undertaken in a difficult environment. If it was not completed successfully the profits of the various companies involved would suffer but, more important, the entire coalition that had been formed in support of the pole would be threatened. Because of the central role of COPENE in the complex, state managers played crucial roles in this stage just as they had in the earlier organizational phase.

COPENE's role in the complex is doubly critical because it is responsible for producing both raw materials and utilities. By taking responsibility for producing the steam and electrical power for the complex, COPENE had shifted the burden of initial investment from the users to itself and had also created a significant saving in operational costs.(19) By the same token, however, failure or serious delay on COPENE's part would result in even those downstream plants which were able to stockpile or truck in their raw materials being unable to operate because they were without power.

Decisiveness and the willingness to risk losing money were essential to pushing through the construction. There was little room for timidity or bureaucratic caution. Fortunately for the complex, the Petroquisa engineers on the site were willing to be entrepreneurs rather than bureaucrats. Perhaps because they knew that they had the personal confidence of those back at the headquarters in Rio, they were willing to take responsibility for the hundreds of modifications necessary to take the project from paper to an erected plant. As one of them put it, "It was not so much being able to make the very best possible decision that was important, it was being able to make a decision at the time it was required so that work could proceed." They were also willing to take responsibility for losses. "If you had to scrap a piece of equipment worth $1 million because using it would have been uneconomical," said one of the engineers in charge of the central cracker, "you just did it."

COPENE's management also took the initiative as far as the central utilities plant was concerned, constructing it before it was necessary as a material gesture to build the confidence of the downstream plants. In some cases, COPENE had to become involved in infrastructure projects that were not officially its responsibility at all. Construction of roads, provision of the water supplies, construction of a port, and other infrastructure investments were primarily the responsibility of the state of Bahia, but COPENE's attitude toward necessary infrastructure was: if it wasn't going to be in place

in time, they would do it themselves. Again, entrepreneurial rather than bureaucratic rules applied.

BOUNDING THE STATE'S ROLE

Given the predominance of state executives and state-
owned firms in the entrepreneurial process that led to
Camaçari, it is tempting to term it "state capitalism."
If state capitalism is used as a label for any process
of capital accumulation in which organizations attached
to the state apparatus play important roles, then the
label fits. But such a broad definition makes most capitalist development into state capitalism and is not
therefore very useful. State capitalism would seem more
usefully restricted to cases of capitalist accumulation
which are centrally planned and directed, in which the
acknowledged prerogatives of the central state apparatus
extend to operational control of industrial organizations. By this latter definition, Camaçari is not
really an example of state capitalism.

To begin with, the ideology of even the state managers involved in the petrochemical industry is in adamant
opposition to state capitalism narrowly defined. The
management of COPENE, for example, is careful to point
out that COPENE is not a state-owned company. Legally
they are correct. Unlike Petrobras and Petroquisa, which
were created by statute, COPENE is legally a corporation
like any other. Furthermore, as of 1979 Petroquisa no
longer held the majority of COPENE's shares. Downstream
companies hold shares in COPENE roughly in proportion to
the size of their own assets. Their combined shares make
up about 46 percent of COPENE's voting stock. After the
start of the complex, a small percentage of COPENE shares
were sold to the public (including the management of
COPENE itself), so that the majority of the stock is now
in private hands.

The image of COPENE as a "private" company should not
be pushed too far. Petroquisa still owns the largest
single block of its shares and is also a major share-
holder in the downstream companies that own most of the
rest of the stock. The possibility of Petroquisa ever
being outvoted on the board of COPENE exists primarily
in theory. In addition, Petroquisa and Petrobras are
COPENE's principal creditors and Petrobras is its only
source of raw materials. Those who claim COPENE is not
a state-owned company do not mean to imply that it has
escaped from the control of its major stockholders. They
are only asserting that COPENE's management does, and
should, have the same operational flexibility that the
management of a large scale capitalist corporation normally has vis-à-vis large stockholders.

A state capitalism (in the sense of accumulation directed by a centralized bureaucracy) interpretation is

inadequate as a means of understanding COPENE. It is even less appropriate for the rest of the pole. Early analyses of the structure of the pole indicated that the major beneficiaries of equity distribution were local private groups. Araujo and Dick claim that local capital was able to translate a contribution of only about 5 percent of total capital and almost none of the technology into control over 30 percent of the equity.(20) The initial structuring of the pole was designed to maximize private capitalism within the limits created by the available resources of local capital groups.

Commitment to local private capital has continued; Isocianatos do Brasil provides a good illustration of this. Initially a tri-pé bringing together Petroquimica da Bahia (the Mariani group), Dupont, and Petroquisa, Isocianatos was one of the most technologically challenging plants in the complex and cost substantially more to build than initially estimated. Surprisingly, Dupont did not feel able to put up the additional investment necessary and instead let its share of the equity sink. Petroquisa was faced with a dilemma: someone had to take up the slack created by Dupont's diminished commitment. If Petroquisa did so unilaterally, it would end up with a controlling interest in the company. The Mariani group had already made a large investment, relative to its resources, not only in Isocianatos but in two other companies in the pole as well. It was not in a position to take over Dupont's share. Nor was it likely that some new investor would be interested in the project as construction was above budget, behind schedule, and still faced difficult technological hurdles before completion.

Statization, in the form of majority control by Petroquisa, would have seemed not only justified as a means of rescuing the project, but almost inevitable. Nonetheless, a different solution was chosen. FIBASE, a subsidiary of the BNDE (National Economic Development Bank), purchased a substantial amount of preferential, nonvoting shares in Petroquimica de Bahia, creating an influx of capital without diluting the Mariani's control of the company. Petroquimica de Bahia then used the cash injected by FIBASE to purchase equity in Isocianatos. Isocianatos remained a "private" company in the sense of having a majority of the equity in private hands. Petroquimica da Bahia's share of the company's eventual cashflow was increased and statism was avoided. An analogous strategy, one designed to preserve local private equity participation, was used when Camargo Corea decided to withdraw from the pole.

Overall, there have been surprisingly few significant shifts in the ownership of the pole's companies since the creation of the original companies and none of these have meant diminished equity participation by private local capital. Examination of the board of directors of COPENE shows that local private capitalists predominate among the representatives of the downstream firms. In addition, it is often the representative of the local capital group who is chosen to preside over the boards of the downstream firms.

It can, of course, be argued that equity control and positions on boards of directors are essentially formalistic indicators - that what really counts is operational control over the companies involved, and that operational control lies increasingly with personnel from Petroquisa. This may be true. Insofar as there has been a shift in operational control over the life of the downstream plants, it has probably been from the multinationals, who tended to have effective operational control during the period of construction, to managers who have come out of the Petroquisa organization. Even if this is the case, however, it is by no means obvious that having executive power exercised by a "Petroquisa man" indicates "state control." Such executives are at least as likely as the managers of COPENE to see their companies as "private."

Perhaps the most clearcut indication of a rejection of a state capitalism model is the new set of rules used in putting together the third pole in Rio Grande do Sul (Polosul). In the Camaçari pole, the initiating role in forming the downstream tri-pé firms was generally played by Petroquisa. Once a foreign partner willing to provide a good technological package on reasonable terms was discovered, a local partner could be added to fill out the tri-pé. In the Polosul, the initiating role was supposed to be played by local capital. Furthermore, there was no requirement that Petroquisa participate in the downstream ventures. In Camaçari there were three conditions for the division of equity: (1) the majority of the equity had to be in Brazilian hands, (2) the majority of the equity had to be in private hands, and (3) Petroquisa's share had to be as large as the share of any other stockholder. In the Polosul, the third condition was dropped. As a result, Petroquisa ended up with the smallest equity share of the three groups in two of the eight Polosul downstream firms and none of the equity in a third.(21) In only one of the newly constituted downstream firms (22) did Petroquisa end up with as large a share of the equity as the largest owner in the venture.

The new rules could hardly have been expected to create local firms capable of standing on their own overnight. In all but the smallest ventures, local capital invited Petroquisa to participate. Nonetheless, the changed requirements indicate a commitment toward the creation of private capitalist organizations that is completely inconsistent with the construction of a bureaucratically centralized state capitalism model. Coupled with the tendency toward relative independence, even on the part of corporations like COPENE which an outsider

would consider state-owned, the persistent efforts to
nurture private capital indicate a model distinctly different from state capitalism.

THE PLACE OF INTERNATIONAL CAPITAL

Scarcely a month after the offical inauguration of
the Camaçari pole, its organizers were shaken by an unexpected accusation. João Cunha, an opposition deputy
from São Paulo, rose in the House of Representatives to
denounce the petrochemical pole, saying, "The Camaçari
(Bahia) Pole is in the service of foreign interests...."
(23) He went on to say that because the stockholders'
agreements in the tri-pé companies required that certain
important decisions be unanimous, the multinational corporations maintained an effective veto over the operations of the companies involved. Consequently, in Cunha's view the financial incentives provided by FINOR
(Sudene) and others to tri-pé firms were illegitimate,
if not illegal, since such incentives were reserved for
locally controlled firms.

Cunha's attack was anomalous in that he had chosen
an ownership structure which was viewed in most quarters
as a nationalist victory and had attacked it as capitu-
lation to international capital. The fact that the
speech was widely disseminated in the press with head-
lines like "Stockholders' agreements give veto power to
multinationals," indicated that Cunha's view was not
merely idiosyncratic but reflected the inherent political
vulnerability of a venture which required cooperation
with international capital. Furthermore, even if Cunha's
arguments were not particularly convincing in themselves,
the underlying thesis they raised seemed plausible. Was
it not likely that whatever the nature of the stockholders' agreements and whatever the division of equity, international capital would somehow come to exercise effective control in petrochemicals? Was it not likely that
the kind of capital accumulation underway in Camaçari was
simply another variation on the general form of accumulation occurring in all capitalist nations, i.e., accumulation under the aegis of multinational firms?

The position that, in a world capitalist system, international capital must be dominant may be defensible as
a general theoretical proposition. Indeed, a careful
examination of the Brazilian petrochemical/chemical industry as a whole might well lead to the conclusion of
dominance by multinationals. But, if one is interested
in characterizing the process of accumulation that is
represented specifically by Brazil's integrated petrochemical complexes, an emphasis on domination by international firms is even more misleading than the state
capitalism label.

When the pole was originally set up, the prediction
that multinational partners would be able to use their
technological superiority and financial resources to
maneuver themselves into positions of de facto control
would have seemed quite plausible. The subsequent evolution of events makes this thesis increasingly less defensible. To begin with, there is the question of changes
in ownership: the only significant ownership changes in
tri-pé firms have not strengthened the role of the multinational corporations, but rather the reverse. The
diminished presence of Dupont in Isocianatos has already
been noted. In another multinational corporation with-
drawal, Dynamit Nobel A.G., which provided the technology
for the production of DMT to Pronor, relinquished its
equity position.

Like changes in equity position, changes in stockholders' agreements have evolved in the direction of increasing local prerogatives. If, for example, one compares Polibrasil, the first polypropylene tri-pé, with
Polipropileno S.A., the second tri-pé,(24) at least one
substantial difference is apparent. In the case of Polibrasil, the marketing function remained in the hands of
the multinational corporation partner. When the agreement for Polipropileno was worked out, this was no longer
considered acceptable. It was felt that a company without marketing expertise was an incomplete company, so the
tri-pé itself, rather than the multinational corporation
partner, was given responsibility for marketing.

Comparison of stockholders' agreements for the third
pole (Polosul) with those for Camaçari also indicates a
substantial change. The unanimity clauses which bothered
Joao Cunha have been eliminated. Their absence has particularly important implications for the use of technology. The tri-pé firms in the Camaçari pole could not,
without the consent of the multinational corporation
partner, expand beyond the initially agreed upon plant
capacity. The technology agreements in the third pole,
especially the one negotiated with respect to the central
cracker,(25) are much more open ended. Expansion of capacity, construction of additional plants, or even the
introduction of new products can all be approved on a
majority basis, which is to say by the Brazilian owners
on their own.

Given that the third pole combines open-ended agreements regarding the use of technology with minority
equity position, it is impressive that there was a sufficient range of multinational bidders to construct a pole
at all. Yet Brazil was able to impose these conditions
and still end up with three to five multinational competitors under consideration for each of the second generation plants. In the case of the polypropylene plant, for
example, there was a choice between Shell, as represented
by Polibrasil, (the São Paulo polypropylene tri-pé), the

Belgian giant Solvay, also heavily involved in the São Paulo complex, Montedison of Italy, and Hercules. A partnership involving Hercules, which does not have any other large scale involvment in Brazilian petrochemicals, was finally selected.(26)

Brazil was not only able to find multinational corporations to join the third pole under conditions more stringent than those imposed on second pole entries, but was able to find a sufficient number of them to prevent any given multinational corporation from enjoying a dominant position in a given product, even as a minority tripé partner. Brazil's success in this regard can be seen in Figure 5.2 which shows the multinational partners involved in the production of major thermoplastic resins in Sao Paulo, Camaçari, and Triunfo (Polosul). From a quick glance at the figure, it is clear that the construction of the Camaçari pole introduced a completely different group of multinational corporations to the production of major thermoplastic resins than the group involved in São Paulo. Similarly, the group of third pole producers is almost completely distinct from the multinationals involved in the second pole. The only representative from the São Paulo complex also represented in the third pole is National Distillers, which was involved in one of the first tri-pés in São Paulo and participates in the third pole through what is essentially a subsidiary of the first tri-pé.(27)

The major chemical multinationals have been obliged to accept an escalating series of nationalist policy decisions as a condition of participating in Brazil's integrated petrochemical complexes. Beginning with the later additions to the São Paulo complex, they were forced to accept the principle of minority participation. Next they were forced to accept the principle of geographic decentralization and the fact that further expansion in certain basic products would have to be done at locations other than São Paulo and chosen by the government. With the third pole they were confronted with agreements which minimized their future control over the use of their own technology. Finally, they have been unable to prevent the development of a structure of production in which there are at least three international firms involved, in partnership with Petroquisa, in the production of each major thermoplastic.

Reviewing the character of the complexes, and especially the evolution between the second pole and the third, it would require rather complicated logic to argue that international capital has had the upper hand in shaping the process of capital accumulation in basic petrochemicals and major thermoplastics. This is not to say that they have suffered. The nominal rates of return for those multinationals involved in joint ventures in Sao Paulo are extremely comfortable. Given the fact that

Table 5.3
Ownership Structure in Brazil's Petrochemical Complexes

Olefins and Major Plastics:

	State*	Tri-pé	State/local	Local/MNC	Local	State/MNC	MNC
Sao Paulo	0	3	1	3	0	1	2
Camaçari	1	5	0	0	0	0	0
Triunfo	1	6	0	0	1	0	0

Camaçari: Basic Complex - Olefins and Aromatics

	State*	Tri-pé	State/local	Local/MNC	Local	State/MNC	MNC
1974 Plan	2	10	2	1	1	2	0
1979 Actual	2	9	1	0	2	1	0
Under Const.	1	2	2	0	0	1	1
Projected	0	0	0	0	4	0	3

*State owned company is largest stockholder and other holdings are dispersed.

CIP (Comissão Interministerial de Preços) sets prices which guarantee 12 to 16 percent returns on total investment, the multinational participants in Camaçari have good reason to expect more than adequate future returns as well. Furthermore, their total risk had been diminished by capital from various government agencies, as well as by fiscal benefits such as a ten year income tax moratorium for firms involved in Camaçari. The rules may not have been entirely to the multinational corporations liking, but neither did they threaten their profits.

Multinational corporations may also have acquiesced to the relatively nationalistic rules laid down in basic and intermediate petrochemicals because they felt that these products were unlikely to be a priority area for them in Brazil, except insofar as they wanted to ensure the availability of inputs for downstream projects. Basic petrochemicals and most intermediates are commodities hard to monopolize without controlling the source of the raw materials. Union Carbide's recent decisions to sell their European petrochemical operations to British Petroleum and license their new low density polyethylene process to Exxon are good examples of the tendency of chemical firms to put diminished emphasis on commodity petrochemicals internationally. In Brazil, heading downstream has the additional advantage of increasing their freedom to operate independently.

The increased freedom available to multinational corporations in downstream firms is apparent from recent developments at Camaçari, as indicated in Table 5.3. The tri-pé has been consistently maintained as the model pattern for the initial structuring of firms in the second and, to some extent, the third generation in all three complexes. This policy scarcely varied at Camaçari between the initial constitution of firms in 1974 and implementation in 1979. But, as the pole has expanded downstream to include new firms that were not part of the original plan, discipline has been relaxed. BASF has a major plant under construction that is essentially wholly-owned. Rhone-Poulenc and Atlantic Richfield both have had wholly-owned plants approved for future construction.

To shape the process of accumulation in downstream proprietary chemicals would be extremely difficult for Brazil without adopting a socialist or centrally-administered state capitalism strategy. Technology in these chemicals is more likely to be exclusive, leverage based on control over inputs is lacking, and the diversity of products and technologies needed works in favor of the multinational corporations. Thus, it is not surprising that the annual reports of multinational corporation subsidiaries in Brazil emphasize future growth in areas like agricultural chemicals.

Figure 5.2
Multinational Corporational Involvement in Major Thermoplastic Resins

Product	Location		
	São Paulo	Camaçari Complex	R.G. do Sul Complex
Low Density Polyethylene	Union Carbide National Distillers	Sumitomo	National Distillers ATO Chemie
High Density Polyethylene	Solvay	Mitsubishi	Hoechst
Polypropylene	Shell	ICI	Hercules
Polyvinyl-chloride	Solvay Huls	Mitsubishi	Rhone Poulenc
Polystyrene	Dow Monsanto	Hoechst	none

Just as it would be difficult for Petroquisa to organize accumulation downstream, it would have made little sense for the multinational corporations to seriously contest the strategy of accumulation that was imposed in the poles. Profitable participation in basic and intermediate petrochemicals was still open to them, even if not on their own terms. The poles opened up opportunities for them downstream that were both profitable and relatively free from limitations on their autonomy.

CONSTRUCTING NEW CORPORATE FORMS

Conventional models of capitalist accumulation do not provide a satisfying account of the social organizational basis for the development of Brazil's integrated petrochemical complexes. The poles are not plausibly accounted for by a private entrepreneurial thrust by a classic capitalist bourgeoisie, nor are they reasonably described as state capitalist accumulation in the sense of a process in which the primary social force is a bureaucratic chain of command leading back to the central government, nor as simply another facet of accumulation under the aegis of multinational corporations. They represent a hybrid form of capitalist accumulation.

Some of the hybrid's features have already been described. Its primary entrepreneurial initiative came from men situated in organizations attached to the state. However, in creating corporate organizations to develop the poles, they insulated these organizations from control by the central state apparatus, both by designing them in such a way that they appeared formally as private firms and by devising ways to include local private capital in their ownership. This combination of connection with the state apparatus and insulation from it proved felicitous in the case of COPENE, allowing the confidence and operational independence necessary to carry out the required entrepreneurial tasks.

Like COPENE, the downstream tri-pé firms are both products of the hybrid and cornerstones of its success. When first created, most of them were artificial organizations, simply an expression of the intention of their major shareholders to work together on a particular undertaking. The real organizations were the companies that held the shares in the tri-pés. The people managing the construction of the downstream plants might nominally be employees of Isocianatos or Politeno, but their past careers, and most probably their futures, lay with Dupont, Mitsubishi, or Petroquisa. None of the tri-pé firms could count on executives who saw their careers and long-term interests as residing in the future of the firm itself. For Camaçari to achieve its goals of producing both petrochemicals and indigenous producers of petrochemicals, this had to change. The evidence is just beginning to come in, but it appears that out of the experience of constructing and operating plants, new corporate entities are being forged.

The best example of a tri-pé taking on a life of its own is Oxiteno, one of the first tri-pé organizations created in the São Paulo pole. It provides a fine illustration of the structural conditions necessary for tri-pés to become real corporations in the modern "managerial capitalist" sense. On the local side, its owners include two of the most powerful indigenous petrochemical groups, the Grupo Ultra and the group headed by Ralph Rosenberg, as well as the Monteiro Aranha group which is also sophisticated and powerful though not heavily involved in petrochemicals. Thus Oxiteno has strong owners who are balanced so that none of them can expect its management to represent their particular interests. On the multinational side, Oxiteno's major owner is unusual: Halcon/Scientific Design received 10 percent of the equity in return for the technology used in Oxiteno's first plant. Since it was a relatively small firm, not a Dow or a Dupont, and since it had practically no operational experience at the time, Halcon had neither the capacity nor the desire to claim an important executive role. Consequently the space normally occupied by multinational personnel was left open to be filled by a relatively autonomous local technical/industrial management whose primary loyalty was to Oxiteno as an organization. The final partner is, of course, Petroquisa. The nature of Oxiteno's relations with its other stockholders also affects Petroquisa's role in the company. Since there is no danger of technical/industrial roles being monopolized by foreigners, Petroquisa has much less reason to want to take an active operational role in company management. Were the firm to perform poorly, Petroquisa, like any major stockholder, might be tempted to step in, but so far its performance has been exemplary.

In São Paulo, where it produces ethylene oxides and its derivatives, Oxiteno is making a return on the order of 20 percent of fixed assets. In Camaçari, an ethylene oxide plant three times the size of the one in São Paulo was constructed on schedule and within budget and was producing final outputs up to specifications within a few days after its start. In the Polosul, Oxiteno will produce styrene, propylene oxide, and propylene glicol, having outbid a set of multinational competitors which reportedly included both Dow and Monsanto, primarily on the basis of being able to offer a technologically innovative new process. With its victory in the third pole, Oxiteno became both the only tri-pé with plants in all three poles and the only truly multiproduct tri-pé.

Those associated with Oxiteno are insistent that its success derives from the superiority of its managerial

system. They see the company as having an internal culture, an esprit de corps, which enables it to attract new
managers, even at lower salaries than they were making
elsewhere. They also see the management as "professional," that is to say as primarily concerned with the future of Oxiteno rather than with catering to the desires
of the major stockholders. This is not to say that the
major stockholders have no say in overall strategy. The
chief operating officer of the company, Paulo Cunha, is
after all the executive vice president of the Grupo Ultra. What Oxiteno's management mean when they talk about
"professionalism" is very similiar to what COPENE's management means when it talks about not being a "state-
owned" firm. In both cases what is being touted is the
relative operational autonomy that is taken as the norm
in the managerial capitalist model as it has emerged in
advanced capitalist countries.

Oxiteno is an extreme case, but similiar trends can
be observed, at least in embryonic form, in other tri-pé
firms. These internal changes are further reinforced by
complementary changes in the competitive position and
internal structures of the local petrochemical groups
which are stockholders in the tri-pés.

CONSEQUENCES FOR LOCAL CAPITAL

The selection of pole participants has had some effect on the relative position of different chemical multinationals within Brazil. Those more willing to collaborate, like the Japanese firms in Camaçari and the French
in the Polosul, have strengthened their position in Brazil in general and in basic petrochemicals in particular.
Those less willing to collaborate, like the German and
American industry leaders, have had to work around the
poles rather than through them. Consequences for multinationals, however, have been much less significant than
consequences for local capital groups.

For local groups, the effects of inclusion or exclusion from the poles is much more critical, both in terms
of consequences for their competitive position in the industry and the effects on their own structures. This is
perhaps most easily seen by comparing the evolution of
the UNIPAR group, which was responsible for the initial
entrepreneurial thrust in basic and intermediate petrochemicals in Brazil(28) and the Ultra Group, considered
by some to be the most important local capital group in
petrochemicals today.(29) The UNIPAR group, having gone
through some difficult times in the early 1970s, is now
again in an enviable position. Its second generation
joint ventures in the São Paulo complex have achieved
"milk cow" status. Constructed before the oil crisis
when capital costs were lower, and having overcome their
initially burdensome financial obligations, these firms

are producing healthy profits and providing UNIPAR with ample resources for expansion and diversification of its investments. More to the point of the present argument, however, is the counterfactual scenario of the UNIPAR group.

Had the UNIPAR group been able to maintain its majority holding in Petroquimica Uniao and its full ownership of the Capuava refinery, it would have been in a position of undisputed leadership within the São Paulo complex. If it had managed to secure a position in one of the more important second generation tri-pés in the Camaçari project as well, it would in all likelihood be the most powerful petrochemical group in Brazil as a whole. Why UNIPAR lost its position in the refinery and in the Sao Paulo cracker is subject to various interpretations, but one thing does seem to be clear. When the group was having trouble maintaining its investments in the cracker in 1974, no attempt was made to infuse funds via purchase of nonvoting shares by official institutions or through some other strategy similar to that used to maintain the equity positions of local capital in the Camaçari pole.

The reasons for UNIPAR's lack of participation in the Camaçari pole are also subject to interpretation. It is clear, however, that UNIPAR was once involved in the plans for the first polypropylene tri-pé(30) which was eventually set up in São Paulo without them. It was also involved in some of the early negotiations over the TDI plant, but again was not included in the final partnership. Looking at the character of UNIPAR's leadership during the early 1970s, it appears likely that the group's orientation was incompatible with the attempt to construct a more collectivized pattern of accumulation. UNIPAR, originally the Capuava or União group, is not only an association built on a family fortune, but is also a group whose early involvement in the industry was based on securing the right to operate a private refinery alongside the Petrobras monopoly. It was, in short, built more in the context of antagonistic relations with state enterprise than cooperative ones. Paulo Geyer, the entrepreneurial figure who shaped UNIPAR's entry into the petrochemical industry and remains its most important owner, does not have either technocratic or bureaucratic predilections. He would be a likely model if one were trying to resurrect a bourgeoisie in the classic individualist mold, but would be rather inconvenient as the most powerful actor in an industry which was trying to develop a more collectivized, technocratic pattern of accumulation.

The contrast between Geyer's career and that of the two leading figures in the Ultra group could not be more clearcut. Hélio Beltrão, President of the group, is a staunch defender of local private enterprise(31) but made his career first of all within the public services(32) and continues to play an active role in this area. The group's rising executive vice-president, Paulo Cunha, has a career profile which runs completely parallel to the process of collectivized accumulation itself. Beginning as an engineer in Petrobras, he was then recruited by the Grupo Ultra and spent most of his managerial career in that most successful of all tri-pés, Oxiteno.

Having set out UNIPAR and Ultra as contrasting cases, it is perhaps worthwhile to note that there are also similarities in their histories. First, Ultra, like UNIPAR, has its origins in a family fortune and the ultimate ownership of the group is still in the hands of Pery Igel, son of the founder. Second, the Ultra group, like UNIPAR, was originally involved in Petroquimica Uniao, and eventually sold all of its equity to Petroquisa. The crucial difference seems to have been Igel's ability to put control of the petrochemical undertakings of the group into the hands of others who fit better into the process of collectivized capital accumulation, namely Beltrao and Cunha. The recent history of the UNIPAR group lends support for this interpretation. Paulo Geyer, like Pery Igel, is no longer directly involved in the operational management of the group. Its affairs are increasingly managed by men (e.g., Michel Hartveld) with technocratic training and by a management built up primarily in the context of joint ventures with the state and the multinationals. Perhaps coincidentally, but at least concurrently, UNIPAR finally managed to enter into a joint venture with Petroquisa in the Camaçari pole by purchasing a substantial interest in DETEN, a producer of synthetic detergents. In addition, one of UNIPAR's original Sao Paulo tri-pés, Poliolefinas, won the bid to produce half of the low density polyethylene in the Polosul.

UNIPAR and Ultra will probably both end up among the most powerful groups in the petrochemical industry. But, more important in terms of the present analysis, is the fact that they will probably end up being run by "professional" managers who value operational autonomy from their stockholders and who are well-suited to working with their technocratically oriented counterparts within the state apparatus. Participation in the process of collectively organized accumulation in the poles is only one of the factors leading in the direction of this convergence, but it is an important one.

An exhaustive examination of the evolution of other local capital groups in relation to their nonparticipation in the poles might produce a more sophisticated thesis regarding the pole's effects on local groups. However, an impressionistic review of a few of the more salient cases suggests that, in general, the UNIPAR/Ultra contrast would be supported. A more individualistic, "classic bourgeoisie" sort of orientation does not lend

itself to successful involvement in the kinds of collective project of accumulation that the poles represent.
The most fiercely independent of all the local groups,
Votorantim,(33) has remained completely aloof from the
petrochemical industry despite previous investments in
allied areas. Those entrepreneurs that have dropped out
of tri-pés, Euvaldo Luz for example, seem to have been
of the more individualistic, traditional type while those
family groups who have maintained or increased their involvement, for example the Mariani group, seem to have
leadership that is comfortable with a more collaborative,
technocratic orientation. Almost unquestionably, the
institutional effects of integrated complexes extend
beyond the tri-pés, influencing the general character of
local capital groups.

CAMAÇARI AND THE PROBLEM OF INTEGRATION

The collectivization of capital accumulation has had
consequences both for the internal structure of newly
created firms and for the nature of the local capital
groups involved in petrochemicals. Not surprisingly it
seems also to have had consequences for the ability of
firms to act collectively in political terms. ABIQUIM,
the chemical industry association, is in the process of
trying to build a political presence on the order of
ABDIB, the very vocal and reputedly very powerful association of capital goods producers. ABIQUIM is currently
mounting a campaign, with the support of every major
group from UNIPAR to Petroquisa, to convince CIP to cal-
culate allowable return on investment on the basis of
replacement cost of capital rather than on historical
cost corrected for inflation. If successful, the campaign would have the effect of raising petrochemical
prices as well as increasing the profitability and cashflows of all the firms involved and would have to be considered a major lobbying victory. The onset of ABIQUIM's
new activism coincided with the election of a new slate
of officers headed, as one might expect from this discussion, by Paulo Cunha.
The revitalization of ABIQUIM is indirectly related
to the changes which arose from the poles. Before Camaçari, ABIQUIM tended to be dominated by the Paulista multinational corporations and was much more reticent to engage in ambitious political projects. Out of Camaçari
have come a group of firms and managers who are confident
of their ability to work together and also confident that
they represent a politically legitimate nationalist project of accumulation. Given the extent to which political
rules determine the profitability and economic strength
of different economic sectors in Brazil, the capacity for
political integration that is emerging in ABIQUIM is an

accomplishment at least as important as the poles' other institutional effects.

This discussion of the petrochemical industry has had what some might consider a curious focus, not just on social and organizational factors but on the problem of integration in particular. This is not simply because technical and economic relations between petrochemical companies make questions of integration interesting. It is because the problem of integration within the dominant class is fundamental to Brazilian dependent development in general.

While development economists of a neo-classical bent, along with Marxists of the more orthodox variety, have tended to ignore problems of the integration of the owning class, students of the empirical behavior of capitalist societies have continually been impressed by the variety of integrating mechanisms which bind together corporations. For dependent developing countries like Brazil, the problem of integration is especially critical for two reasons. First, industrial capital remains more thoroughly in the hands of individual families and entrepreneurs. The means of production are not just private property but also personal property. The personal nature of the relation between owners and firms makes transfer and agglomeration difficult. Ties between firms parallel the ties between owners, a set of linkages which are not necessarily the most conductive to capitalist accumulation.

Second, international actors in the dependent developing economy have an equally adverse effect on the integration of the owning class, but for the opposite reason. While the links between local firms may be too personalistic, the multinationals suffer from the lack of deeply rooted personalistic ties to the owners of other firms in the economy. Multinational corporation managers have only shallow social ties to complement the various impersonal bonds based on the firm's economic interaction with other firms.(34) In addition, commitments by multinational managers on the local scene can be kept only contingently, subject to the decisions of superiors in foreign headquarters. Finally, of course, the global operations and identities of international firms gives them an economic flexibility and a political vulnerability that separates them decisively from local firms and creates a major cleavage at the core of the capitalist class.

Overcoming the cleavage between local and international capital in particular, and the problem of integration in general, is central to constructing the social basis for capitalist accumulation in the context of dependent development. It is because integrated petrochemical complexes speak to this problem that their importance goes beyond increasing domestic output of domestic

plastics and chemicals. The poles' collectivizing schema
of capitalist accumulation has succeeded in creating
firms which are local and which also operate on a more
modern, impersonal, managerial capitalist basis. In doing so, this schema has increased the capacity of these
firms for collective action, both economic and political,
and has managed to incorporate the skills and resources
of the multinational corporations without allowing their
participation to have a detrimental impact on the integrative capacity of the firms in which they are owners.

Perhaps most important of all, new opportunities have
been created for the integration of state managers into
an essentially private corporate network. Intensive collaborative ties have been developed between owners of
private capital, local and foreign, and those parts of
the state apparatus most concerned with capital accumulation. With this accomplishment, the collaboration developed through Camaçari goes beyond the level of integration found in the more traditional capitalist centers,
such as the United States. The effective integration of
state firms and private capital, in combination with the
pole's other social/organizational effects, may be taken
to represent a kind of "leap-frog" of institutional development which could result in Brazilian capitalism
being considered organizationally more advanced than that
of some of its mentors.

PRESENT COSTS AND FUTURE BENEFITS

In June of 1979, Tio C. Chen, brought to Brazil from
Columbia University by the Brazilian Society of Consulting Engineers, pronounced Camaçari "the greatest ec-
ological crime of the twentieth century."(35) Whether
or not Chen's accusation is well founded, it raised the
question of perspective. The development of the petrochemical industry has been examined here from the perspective of elites intent on fostering the accumulation
of capital. Other perspectives in which the priorities
are ordered differently have not been considered. Because an "insiders" perspective has been taken, the poles
seem to be the most rational, if not the only rational,
way to proceed, not just from the point of view of capital and the state, but from the point of view of the
society as a whole.

At this point it would seem appropriate to return to
João Cunha. Practically buried in his accusation that
the poles represented a conspiracy to sell out to the
multinationals was another kind of questioning. "I denounce and question the priority of this investment of
billions of dollars..." said Cunha,(36) continuing with
the accusation that because local costs were high, the
end result of increasing local production would result in

raising prices for petrochemical products and that therefore the real loser would be Brazilian consumer. A "Chicago school" economist might easily have made the same
argument on the basis of a strict interpretation of the
theory of comparative advantage. Antônio Ermírio de
Morães, the exemplar of the kind of local bourgeoisie
that was not included in the poles, questioned the economic rationality of the poles in essentially similar
terms, saying that they represented an attempt to "produce at all cost" rather than the rational exploitation
of national resources.(37)

The rationale of the poles' creators is essentially
"developmentalist." The accumulation of capital and the
concomitant construction of a more differentiated local
productive apparatus is the primary aim. Developmentalist projects like Camaçari can be attacked from several
different points of view. Chen represents one, Antônio
Ermírio de Morães represents another, and João Cunha represents a curious amalgam of the two. The first critical
perspective focuses on nonmarket, noncapitalist social
goals. Preserving the natural environment is one such
goal, but a more critical one in contemporary Brazil is
improving the distributional characteristics of the country's development pattern. The second basis for criticizing developmentalist projects is an "efficiency" argument in purely market terms, with international comparison usually providing the criterion of efficiency in the
absence of "real" market prices internally. Antônio
Ermírio de Morães is making essentially this kind of critique. Developmental projects should be given priority
according to their efficiency (i.e., their cost characteristics in market terms) and "inefficient" projects
should be eschewed.

The "efficiency critique" and the "alternate goals"
critique may be combined by arguing that any departures
from efficiency should be explicitly aimed at furthering
social goals. Thus, João Cunha (and probably Antônio
Ermírio de Morães) could argue that the consequences of
inefficient (high cost in international terms) production
in the poles are negative in distributional terms, increasing the profits of a few firms while increasing the
cost of living for most of the population. These critiques are debatable, but they are not without foundation. The ideal development project for Brazil would be
capital saving and labor intensive, use local raw materials, and produce goods at costs at or below their cost
of production in other countries. Basic petrochemicals
have none of these characteristics.

Basic petrochemicals is one of the most capital intensive of all modern industries. COPEC's own estimates
for the cost of job creation in the central pole run
about $300,000 per job,(38) and the investment per job

for the cracker in the Polosul runs over $500,000. Neither of these estimates involves the allocation of necessary infrastructure investment. It is not until the third or fourth generation plants, such as those producing synthetic fibers, that these figures begin to drop below $100,000 per job. If the aim were to invest several billion dollars in order to generate new jobs, the petrochemical industry would be at the bottom of the list.

For a nonoil producing country, there is of course an additional problem. In the production of basic petrochemical feedstocks, the raw material, naphtha in this case, accounts for between 50 to 70 percent of the cost of production.(39) The other significant cost factors are capital, which in Brazil is also an imported input to a significant degree, and energy, again largely derived from imported petroleum. Petrochemicals are then not only capital intensive but relatively import intensive.

Production of petrochemicals tends to be a high cost endeavor in Brazil. Though Petrobras keeps the nominal cost of naphtha for petrochemical uses at U.S. levels, which is to say below European and Japanese prices, the real opportunity cost of feedstock in Brazil is clearly higher than it would be in a petroleum producing country. (Indeed one might argue that, for the Saudi Arabians who have been flaring off ethane and methane, the opportunity cost of the feedstocks for ethylene would be zero.) Brazil is also a "high cost producer" in terms of the second most important cost, capital costs. Candal(40) estimates that capital costs in petrochemicals in Brazil are between 30 to 90 percent higher than comparable investments in the United States. And finally, of course, the arguments on petroleum based feedstocks also apply to petroleum based energy costs.(41)

Petrochemical development has spoken dramatically to one kind of distributional goal - regional decentralization. Not only has it resulted in massive industrial investments in a relatively backward region, but it has also created powerful corporate organizations with roots in the region. When the management of COPENE look beyond the consolidation of Camaçari and consider the possible destinies of their future cashflows, two possibilities are obvious. One is what happened to Petroquimica Uniao, whose dividends are close to 100 percent of its profits. This gives Petroquisa and the UNIPAR group funds to invest but limits the entrepreneurial opportunities available to Petroquimica Uniao's management. The other possibility, much more exciting for an entrepreneurially oriented manager, would be the creation of some new industrial endeavor and the only place that COPENE is likely to be allowed to undertake such a venture is the Northeast. COPENE is thus beginning to see itself as a firm

with a "calling for the Northeast" and is beginning to
see the acclimitation of its management and skilled workers to life in Bahia as an important "comparative advantage" over possible competitors for the right to undertake new ventures in the Northeast.

Even with respect to the goal of regional decentralization, however, the consequences of Camaçari must be
considered mixed. The beneficiaries of its development,
even in the Northeast, are relatively few in number. The
important employment generating effects of Camaçari await
the creation of the "fourth generation" firms, the trans-
formers and producers of final products, and so far the
development of these firms has been painfully slow. The
danger still exists that Camaçari might become a sort of
export enclave, sending its basic and intermediate products to the factories of Sao Paulo. This would benefit
a few workers, but the effect on Salvador would be mainly
to drive up the cost of real estate and the effect on
most of the population of the Northeast would be nil.

If the petrochemical industry addressed noneconomic
social goals, the achievement of these goals could be
balanced against its relative cost inefficiency. Given
the ambiguity of its social consequences, the question
"Should Camaçari have been built at all?" cannot be dis-
missed. The question is not whether Brazil should have
a chemical industry, or even whether Brazil should become
involved in the petrochemical industry; it would be ab-
surd to contemplate one of the ten largest capitalist
economies in the world going without a chemical industry.
The question is how far it makes sense to push backwards
integration when the raw material towards which that
backwards integration is heading is absent.

The alternative strategy would be to import basic and
intermediate petrochemicals instead of importing the petroleum required to make them and to begin the chain of
the petrochemical industry from there. This would have
the advantage of allowing a greater concentration of investments in more labor intensive downstream industries,
or perhaps in other basic industries using local raw materials. It would also enable Brazil, in principle, to
take advantage of the low cost production of other countries and thereby lower the cost of the final demand consumer goods that are the ultimate "petrochemical product." If Brazil could increase the international compet-
itiveness of its labor intensive plastic auto parts and
polyester suits by importing capital intensive basic
petrochemicals rather then producing them locally, the
tradeoff would seem beneficial. The attractiveness of
such a possibility is further enhanced by the fact that,
because of the marginal cost pricing of exports, the international prices of commodity petrochemicals are often
below developed country domestic prices by as much as 20
to 50 percent.(42)

The counter argument is that relying on external
sources of petrochemical products would put Brazil at the
mercy of the international market and would thereby run
counter to "national security." Given existing and prob-
able future dependence on imported petroleum, a "national
security" argument would seem hard to support - importing
ethylene glycol hardly puts a country in a qualitatively
worse position than importing petroleum. A more plausible modified version of the argument involves the issue
of forward linkages. It is argued that the international
market in commodity petrochemicals is too thin to be
relied on as fluctuations and rapid changes in the availability of supplies produce a level of uncertainty that
impedes the development of downstream industries. While
empirically sound, this argument assumes away the possibility of institutional innovation. What would be required would be a variety of long-term contracts for supplies from a diverse set of sources, presumably managed
in some centralized way as Petrobras now manages petroleum imports.

To argue against going the full import substitution
route in petrochemicals is to argue against almost half
a century of economic tradition in Latin America and
thereby to run the risk of being called either a romantic
or a reactionary. Nonetheless, the position at least
merits debate. A similiar position seems to have been
taken by Japan after 1973. The data on ethylene production in Table 5.2 give an indication of Japan's post-1973
policy. Between 1978 and 1982 Japan will put in virtually
no new ethylene capacity. Indeed, if one examines growth
of chemical production overall, the difference in Japanese strategy pre-1973 and post-1973 is striking. In the
decade prior to 1973, Japan's industry was the fastest
growing in the developed world, growing at almost double
the rate of the North American industry. In the four
years following the oil crisis, Japan's industry was the
slowest growing in the developed world, growing at about
one-third the North American rate.(43) Brazilian policy
makers must have at least had some second thoughts when
they noticed that the Japanese stopped building petrochemical complexes at about the same time Brazil was
beginning.

Even if Brazil's integrated petrochemical complexes
were "irrational" from the point of view of overall social goals, wastefully using resources that would have
brought more benefits to the people of Brazil had they
been otherwise employed, the complexes would still have
made sense from the perspectives of their creators because alternative patterns of development would not have
entailed the same institution building. The kind of collectivized accumulation that is possible in basic and
intermediate petrochemicals is not possible downstream.
Without integrating back to basic petrochemicals, there

would have been neither the tri-pés, not the close collaboration between semi-autonomous state managers and
private capital.

For the men who created Camaçari, the value of the
institutions created along with it is unquestionable.
Others must remain more agnostic. The corporate structures that have been created are technocratically efficient, but they are also unabashedly capitalist. Their
fundamental logic is one of making profits. Managers
measure their own efficiency in terms of profits: their
personal positions and career prospects depend on profits. Since profits in turn are dependent on the politics
of official loans and incentives, tarifs, and price controls, the quest for profitability is a political quest
as well as a technocratic one. For those in control of
the profits generated there is no issue; for those who
wonder where the surplus might have gone otherwise, the
question remains.

Does the development that has occurred in the petrochemical industry make sense only in terms of the self-
interested goals of those involved or is it a victory for
development conceived in larger social terms? Based on
the present situation in Brazil and the international industry, one can debate the question but not answer it.
The rationality of the petrochemical industry can only
be evaluated once certain predictions about the future
evolution of the industry are accepted. Some future scenarios vindicate the poles' creators as visionary entrepreneurial heros whose self-interest coincided with the
needs of their fellow citizens. Others turn them into
skillful manipulators of the system who managed to shape
events to their own gain at the expense of their fellow
citizens.

One of the central elements in the "visionary entrepreneurial hero" scenario is the high degree of flexibility of the institutional mechanisms that have been
created. Take, for example, the possibility of gradually
moving to ethanol as a basis for olefin production. If
projected increases in alcohol production based on sugar
cane are used, not for burning in private automobiles
but to provide ethanol for the production of ethylene,
then Camaçari and the Polosul may be one day viewed simply as the necessary institutional foundations for a
shift to sugarbased olefins.

Ethanol as a source of ethylene is attractive not
just because the raw material is a labor intensive local
product. It also offers the prospect of technological
leadership. Petrobras is currently rumored to have developed a process for producing ethylene from ethanol
that is cost competitive with existing naphtha-based
processes and has the additional advantage of involving
smaller scale units (60,000 tons/yr. rather than 400,000
tons/yr.) as well as being adiabatic and therefore using

relatively little energy. The small scale of the process would allow more geographic decentralization and closer fits between growth in capacity and demand. Since ethylene from ethanol technologies is not of particular interest to the major oil companies, or for that matter to developed countries without Brazil's agricultural potential, the possibility of Petrobras gaining international technological leadership in this area does not seem farfetched. With technological leadership would come the possibility of exporting capital goods to other nonoil producing less-developed countries interested in developing production of chemicals and plastics in smaller steps while exploiting their agricultural resources at the same time. In this scenario, Camaçari and the Polosul are the result of wily strategies designed to create downstream demand, train workers and managers in the skills necessary to run process-technology industries, and create the overall institutional base without which the ethanol would have been wastefully burned in cars. The petrochemical complexes will have been an essential, if slightly diversionary, springboard toward leadership in ethanol-based ethylene production.

The obverse scenario is also, unfortunately, too plausible to be ignored. In this scenario, ethanol remains a minor sideline while the petrochemical juggernaut rolls along. In 1984 a fourth petrochemical pole is announced, despite the fact that no significant local oil deposits have been discovered, and Brazil's petroleum bill remains a major albatross dragging down the overall rate of development. The decision to embark on the fourth pole is the result primarily of the tremendous political strength of an alliance between regional political elites and the collectivized corporate machinery that has developed around the petrochemical poles. The tripés, generating tremendous cashflows based in part on excessive prices which have resulted from five years of well-organized lobbying, need room for expansion. Another $3 billion is invested in basic petrochemicals, despite slower growth in demand having increased the possibility for overcapacity.

This scenario can be made even more extreme by adding a few plausible assumptions about trends in the international industry. Assume that massive new Middle Eastern projects in basic petrochemicals are coming on stream, projects with minimal raw material costs in countries with virtually no domestic markets. The countries involved are willing to export their products at prices that cover only variable costs, an economic sacrifice they see as relatively minor in relation to the institution building that can accompany such projects. At the same time, in the developed countries, plants built by Exxon and Union Carbide are beginning to come on stream

122

using Carbide's major breakthrough in polyethylene technology and therefore able to produce polyethylene at substantially lower costs. Overall, basic and intermediate
petrochemicals, thermoplastic resins, and the entire
chain of products that flow from them are available on
the international market at prices that are fractions of
the cost of locally produced Brazilian equivalents. Brazil is paying the price for having allowed the direction
of its industrial development to be too much shaped by
the requirements of capitalist institution building; its
people are paying for the past profits of the tri-pés.

These ventures into futurology resolve nothing, but
they do make clearer the range of potential outcomes that
can be projected from current developments in the Brazilian petrochemical industry. They also make very clear
the limitations of any social science evaluation of Brazil's integrated petrochemical poles. We can delineate
what has been accomplished technologically and economically. We can lay out the social organizational roots
of these accomplishments as well as their immediate institutional consequences. But when it comes to making a
judgment as to the rationality or irrationality of the
complexes in overall social terms, the best that we can
do is to ask to come back to that question in 1984.

NOTES

1. This paper is based on fieldwork conducted in
Brazil in the spring of 1979. It does not take into account changes that have occurred since then, either in
the international industry or in Brazil. The time and
generous cooperation of dozens of managers and executives
is gratefully acknowledged. They are not thanked individually here to avoid implicating them in my own interpretations of the industry.

2. Without undercutting this claim, it should be
put in perspective. Camaçari is not the largest complex
in the world in terms of total capacity; other complexes
have multiple naphtha crackers, each bigger than the one
at Camaçari. It is the largest single investment because
other complexes have been constructed by stages and because few such massive complexes have been built since
the prices of equipment and engineering skyrocketed after
1973.

3. The number of plants may vary slightly on different counts, depending, for example, on whether the
maintenance central (CEMAN) is counted as a plant separate from COPENE and whether the White-Martins Oxygen and
Nitrogen supply facility is counted as one of the units
in the pole. I have counted neither.

4. These figures for investment are in historical
(circa 1974) dollars and do not include state financed
investments infrastructure.

5.   Ethylene is often used as a summary measure for petrochemical capacity. It is not only the most important single basic petrochemical product (in terms of volume), but its production from naphtha entails the co-production of propylene which is the second most important petrochemical product (by volume). Ethylene and propylene are both olefins, gaseous at normal temperatures. Aromatics, the other major division of basic petrochemicals, are heavier, liquid at normal temperatures, and therefore transportable. They include benzene, toluence, and xylenes.

6.   "Petrochemical Project Planned in Argentina," Oil and Gas Journal 58, no. 36 (September 1960): 108.

7.   "Survey: Chemicals," The Economist, 7 April 1979, pp. 3-30.

8.   Ibid., p. 23.

9.   Peter Evans, Dependent Development: The Alliance of Multinational, State and Local Capital in Brazil (Princeton: Princeton University Press, 1979); Ivo de Souza Riberio, "A Participação da Petroquisa no Desenvolvimento da Indústria Petroquímica no Brazil," unpublished paper, 1969; Albert Hahn, "The Brazilian Synthetic Polymer Industry," Petrochemical Series, no. 1 (New York: United Nations (UNIDO), 1969).

10.   Albert Hirschman, The Strategy of Economic Development (New Haven: Yale University Press, 1958).

11.   Albert Hirshman, Development Projects Observed (Washington: Brookings Institution, 1967).

12.   Robert Moss, "The Moving Frontier: A Survey of Brazil," The Economist, September 1972, pp. 11-73.

13.   Otto Perroni, "A Ação de Petroquisa na Implantação do Polo Petroquímico do Nordeste," Petroquisa, 1972.

14.   Otto Perroni, "Complexos Petroquimicos" and "Uma Tentativa de Quantificação das Economias Internas no Complexo do Camaçari." Papers presented at the Primeiro Congresso Brasileiro de Petroquímica, Rio de Janeiro, 8-12 November 1976.

15.   The same kind of local political entrepreneurship that occurred in Bahia was central to the origins of the Polosul. Local Rio Grande do Sul technocrats and politicians spent years developing plans for the pole and convincing federal officials that it should be located in the South.

16.   Arthur Candal, "Problemas e Perspectivas de Comércio Exterior para o Setor de Petroquímica." Paper presented at the Fundação Centro de Estudos do Comércio Exterior, Rio de Janeiro, 12 October 1978.

17.   Ibid., p. 22.

18.   S.A. CLAN, Desenvolvimento da Indústria Petroquímica no Estado de Bahia (Bahia: Conselho de Desenvolvimento do Reconcavo, 1969): Vol. 1, p. 4.

19.   Perroni, "Complexos Petroquímicos," p. 54.

124

20.   J. Tavares Araujo and Vera Dick, "Governo, Em-presas Multinationais a Empresas Nacionais: O Caso da Indústria Petroquímica," _Pesquisa e Planejamento Econó-mica_ 4, no. 3 (1974):   629-654.

21.   The number of firms involved in the Polosul is much smaller than the number at Camaçari, even though the central cracker is larger, because there is no provision for the processing of aromatics in the Polosul.

22.   There are eight downstream firms in all, but only six of them are newly constituted; the other two, Oxiteno and Poliolefinas, are subsidiaries of previously existing tri-pés.   Consequently Petroquisas' share of these ventures is an historical given.

23.   João Cunha, _Estado de São Paulo_, 22 August 1978, p. 29.

24.   Polibrasil was formed prior to Camaçari (though in its earliest stages it had been intended for the Northeast).   It was approved by the CDI for São Paulo in 1972.   Polipropileno S.A. was one of the later additions to Camaçari and was approved by the CDI in 1974.

25.   Francisco Sercovich, "State-Owned Enterprises and Dynamic Comparative Advantages in the World Petro-chemical Industry: The Case of Commodity Olefins in Bra-zil," Development Discussion Paper, no. 96 (Cambridge: Harvard Institute for International Development, 1980).

26.   "A Longa História do Propileno Nacional," _Diri-gente Industrial_ 19, no. 1 (1978):   8-17.

27.   The lack of overlap described here applies only to major thermoplastic resins.   If production of any product in conjunction with one of the poles were con-sidered, Rhodia, for example, is in all three poles.   It is only in the major thermoplastic resins that such care has been taken to avoid allowing multiple participation by multinational corporations.

28.   Evans, _Dependent Development_, pp. 231-235.

29.   "A Difícil Escalada Rumo a Expansão na Petro-química," _Exame_, 8 March 1978, pp. 20-26.

30.   "A Longa História," _Dirigente_, p. 10.

31.   "Beltrão, Como Consolidar a Grande Empresa Na-cional," _Tendência_, August 1976, pp. 4-9.

32.   _Exame_, 1978, p. 22.

33.   Evans, _Dependent Development_, pp. 154-155.

34.   Ibid., pp. 158-162.

35.   _Estado de São Paulo_, 13 June 1979, p. 18.

36.   Joao Cunha, _Estado de São Paulo_, 22 August 1978, p. 29.

37.   _Estado de São Paulo_, 13 June 1979, p. 18; 20 May 1979, p. 13.

38.   Cost per job estimates depend on how the jobs associated with CEMAN, the central maintenance unit, are allocated. $300,000 results in allocating roughly half of CEMANS personnel to COPENE, assuming the rest are used to help maintain downstream plants.

39. U.S. International Trade Commission, Summary of Trade and Tariff Information: Synthetic Plastics Materials (Washington: USPGO, 1977) TSUS items 405.25 and 445.05-445.75.

40. Candal, "Problemas e Perspectivas," p. 38.

41. Partly in response to this problem, the utilities central in the Polosul was redesigned at considerable expense to burn coal.

42. Candal, "Problemas e Perspectivas," p. 4.

43. "Survey Chemicals," The Economist, April 7, 1979 pp. 3-30.

6
The Exchange and Absorption of Technology in Brazilian Industry

Francisco Colman Sercovich

INTRODUCTION

Brazil suffers from the severe handicap of being heavily dependent on imported energy, particularly oil, as shown in Table 6.1.

Clearly, although energy vulnerability is expected to decrease during the next few years through increased hydropower, the alcohol program, and a $1.5 billion drilling program which calls for 500 new exploration and extension wells to be drilled in promising offshore areas by early 1980s, it will do so only very slowly. As a consequence, reliance on international debt finance will almost certainly become even heavier than it is today. This is epitomized by a single indicator, the Brazilian gross external debt, which today amounts to over $55 billion. Assuming a moderate rate of growth of about 6 percent per annum, this debt is expected to become three times as large by 1987.(1) For social reasons, especially the need to create 1.5 million new jobs every year just to avoid mounting unemployment, recessionary policies to cope with the subsequent balance of payments problem cannot be used. Because of these factors, industrialization in Brazil must proceed along export-oriented lines.(2) This approach, of course, has been pursued for a number of years and is based on: (1) heavily rewarding export-oriented activities, (2) promoting import-substituting activities when they are likely to end up exporting, and (3) penalizing inward-looking activities.

Bearing all this in mind, it would make very little sense indeed to look at the process of technological change under way in the Brazilian economy as a phenomenon of purely domestic projections - as one not linked to the development of a dynamic export capability. This chapter focuses on this necessary, but also deliberate, strategic link; a link between endogenous technological learning

127

128

Table 6.1.
Brazil: Commercial Energy Balance (in thousand b/d oil equivalent)

	1974	1978	1982*
Consumption	1240	1655	2100
Domestic Production	595	770	1100
Oil	183	200	320
Hydro	381	505	660
Coal	31	40	50
Nuclear	0	0	20
Alcohol	0	25	50
Net Imports	645	885	1000
Oil	626	845	960
Coal	19	40	40

*projected

Source: National Foreign Assessment Centre, Washington, USA, 1979

and development of export capabilities that takes place largely via the building of organized domestic design skills.

The impact of this kind of development on the world market is not negligible. Mention must be made of the fact that Brazil, together with a handful of other newly industrializing countries (NIC) will account, in terms of energy imports, for the equivalent of around 20 percent of total OPEC exports by 1985. It is already one of the four major engineering and technology suppliers to Middle East countries.(3)

From this vantage point we can see that Brazil is increasingly performing the role of a world technology recycler by absorbing advanced country's know-how and technical skills, putting them to work in the Brazilian milieu, adding know-how derived from Brazilian experiences and R&D efforts, adapting these skills, and finally exporting them with varying degrees of domestic innovative additions, mainly to less developed Third World countries in agreement with what can be called the "infant-in-the-kindergarden" type of approach (already used by the French in Algeria and other former French colonies, and by the Japanese in South Asia during the 1950s and 1960s).(4)

Although it is true that technology recycling is also taking place in other Latin American countries such as Argentina and Mexico, nowhere in the region has it been given such a deliberate and planned status as in Brazil. (5) Clearly, to those acquainted with the Japanese experience, this round of events will not sound at all unfamiliar. Quite apart, however, from historical and institutional differences and those having to do with degree of lateness in industrialization, exposure to transnational corporations, and availability of skilled manpower, there are also two other important differences. Brazil is a naturally resource-rich country while Japan is naturally resource poor. Direct state participation in production plays an important role in Brazil while it performs none at all in Japan. Put another way, these circumstances indicate that the obstacles against pursuing an "outward looking" development strategy are much more formidable in the Brazilian case than they have been in the Japanese.

BRAZILIAN EXPORT POSITION

Brazil is, by far, the most substantial Latin American exporter of manufactured goods. It accounted for more than 40 percent of total manufacturing exports by Latin American in 1977 - once "maquila" (border assembly) exports from Mexico are excluded.(6) While manufacturing exports accounted for only 3.5 percent of total Brazilian exports in 1963, they now account for about 50 percent, with a 38 percent annual rate of growth between 1963 and 1978 and a 25 percent growth rate between 1973 and 1978. Expected annual rate of growth of manufacturing exports for the next few years is 50 percent. It will probably reach $8 billion in 1980 and is planned to amount to $40 billion by 1987, when manufacturing exports are expected to account for nearly 60 percent of total exports. No doubt these figures sound rather impressive and may be a bit too optimistic. Nonetheless, they allude to a dynamic trend that, beyond the pluses and minuses of sharp statistics, is undoubtedly there.

Total landed value of package deals involved in mainly large scale engineering projects and turnkey plants abroad is estimated to have accounted for some $3.5 billion since 1977. Among the large number of projects involved, mention should be made of the turnkey railroad system from Baghdad to Aksahat in Iraq, the expansion of the Guri dam in Venezuela, the Safwa-AlJubail Freeway in Saudi Arabia, and a housing nuclei in Algeria. These operations provide outlets for a wide variety of technology inputs and industrial products, some of which are manufactured by Brazilian subsidiaries of multinational enterprises. As a matter of fact, these enterprises are also involved in package deal exports such as an LNP plant to Algeria, a food processing plant to Chile, hydroelectricity facilities to Nigeria and El Salvador, and so forth. At present Brazil shares fourth place in the Middle East $300 billion a year contract market with France. South Korea leads this market and the USA occupies twelfth place.

How far and how much of the above-mentioned $3.5 billion is actually dollar flow to Brazil is hard to assess for a number of reasons. First, the association between tangible and intangible exports is not easily found because those exports are listed separately without indication of whether they are linked or not. Second, several of the major Brazilian export organizations involved in this kind of business are already operating as true multinationals, undertaking procurement whenever it best fits their proposals and enjoying the advantages of tax-havens. Third, an overvalued cruzeiro and a substantial gap between the official and "parallel" exchange markets certainly does not help to make things more transparent.

However one thing is certain: thanks to this growth in intangible exports, Brazil today is half-way to balancing its "technological balance of payments" (i.e., that part of the balance of payments having to do exclusively with inflows and outflows of technological know-how, technical services, engineering services, payments for patents and licences, and the like). According to the Banco do Brasil, in 1978 the value of outflows of this kind accounted for some $220 million, about 40 percent of the value of inflows. Insofar as this is not just a partial event but the result of a secular trend in the development of Brazil as a technology and service exporter, the fact acquires particular importance.

From a Brazilian point of view, large engineering projects and industrial turnkey plant exports are playing a role in generating a flow of "captive" industrial exports analogous to that of interaffiliate trade links in the case of advanced industrial country-based multinationals. This export channel is likely to become increasingly important during the next couple of decades. However, this natural trend toward "coupling" technology, service, and tangible (capital good) exports from the same origin is going to suffer the offsetting influence of a circumstance already referred to, i.e., the rapid process of multinationalisation of large Brazilian contractors and trading organizations. (This includes state-owned organizations such as Interbras, which channels a good deal of total Brazilian service exports.)

Starting from scratch in 1976, Interbras reached a turnover of $835 million in 1978. It is, among the forty or so trading companies that have sprung up in Brazil

during the last few years, the single most important one.
It was in charge of marketing and subsidizing around 40
percent of total Brazilian exports of large engineering
projects in 1978. Currently it has approximately twenty
new proposals under consideration in twenty nations with
twenty-three Brazilian companies. Contracts already underway include a manioc root mill in Nigeria, hotels in
Iraq, a fishing port in Uruguay, a turnkey anydrous alcohol distillery and a sewage system improvement venture
in Costa Rica, improvements for Funchal airport in Made-
ira, two ceramic factories in Nigeria, a petrochemical
supply base in Ecuador, and electric isolation tests for
dynamos at the Salto Grande hydroelectric plant on the
Argentine-Uruguay border. Interbras is also participating in the large railway project in Iraq referred to
above.

Together with COBEC, the only government authorized
warehouse operated in Brazil, Interbras is reported to
have been allotted about half of the entire subsidized
credit line devoted by the Central Bank to financing
business by trading companies. Brazilian trading companies benefit from institutional barriers to entry imposed
on their foreign-based peers. In effect, the latter do
not have access either to the credit line just mentioned,
nor to tax credits and exemptions enjoyed by Brazilian
trading companies. It is quite likely that this was at
least part of the reason why attempts to establish wholly-owned Brazilian trading subsidiaries in Japan have
failed so far and the joint-venture path is now being
used instead. In addition, Interbras also channels private and governmental financing programs to the producers and consolidates tax incentives to goods and services exported into single packages, charging a commission
of roughly 5 percent off the top for these services only
if the project is landed. There is no obligation for
Brazilian contractors to do business abroad via Interbras, although there may be clear advantages for them in
doing so.

The role of trading organizations in the expansion
of service exports should not be overlooked - and the
Brazilians recognize this. The trading companies have
special advantages, particularly in dealing with large
export contracts, thanks to their risk-sharing schemes
and the capacity to put together the wide range of inputs
- capital, technology, management, finance, etc., - as
well as the various organizations normally required.
Another critical advantage they enjoy lies in their capacity to gather, store, retrieve, and use information on
a worldwide basis.(7)

Backed by local trading and government incentives,
Brazilian companies are emerging as major contenders in
a business sector so far controlled by firms from developed countries: the export of large scale engineering

projects. In their endeavours they are now suffering stiff competition in the field of international project bidding from countries such as Pakistan, India, Yugoslavia, and South Korea. They are usually at a cost disadvantage vis-à-vis these countries because of higher freight and personnel travel costs. They have, however, a number of nonprice advantages, and this is an important feature in a market where price does not necessarily play a decisive role in the bidding process. The main nonprice advantages enjoyed by Brazilian engineering and contracting companies are: (1) the tradition of work under very tough environmental conditions and in large projects (Transamazonia highway, Brasília, dams),(2) skills at rapidly training unskilled people on a massive scale, and (3) "special" trade links, i.e., the use, particularly by Interbras, of its leverage as a heavy oil importer from a handful of countries.

The recent success of Mendez Jr. in winning the Iraqui turnkey railway contract is a case in point. Allegedly, the Brazilian "empreiteiro" was not the lowest bidder. A consortium of Indian contractors claimed to be at least $100 million lower (total value of the contract was over $1.2 billion). The Indians felt that the real reason the Brazilians won the tender was their country's debt position with Iraq. This alone would certainly not have been enough, but there can be little doubt that it helped a great deal, together with the active presence in Iraq of Braspetro, Petrobras' petroleum prospecting subsidiary which discovered major oil resources there.

Table 6.2 provides an overall picture of the sectoral and geographical breakdown of Brazilian technology and service exports. Among the over ninety-five cases that we managed to identify, fifty-eight (61 percent) concern infrastructural works, twenty-five (roughly 26 percent) involve industrial facilities, and the remainder are training and preinvestment studies. The main advantages enjoyed by Brazilian companies lie in the fields of civil engineering - largely roads and dams - and rather simple industrial plants - largely those related to processing of raw materials. In other words, service and technology exports expansion is by no means taking place across the board. On the contrary, it seems to be related to certain sectors of economic activity where, for different reasons and at various stages of Brazilian development, emphasis was once focused. For example, we can cite the Kubitschek period in regard to civil engineering and the post-1973 period in connection with biomass technology and engineering. The uneveness of Brazilian technological development is demonstrated by the sharp contrast between patterns of technological absorption in, for example, petrochemicals, on the one hand, and in nuclear technology on the other. While in the first case one comes across the most advanced technological program that we know of, that concerning the olefin plant for the third petrochemical hub (8), the second case involves an approach which has been receiving intense criticism on the grounds that it lacks a strategy aimed at technological absorption.(9)

TOWARDS AN INTERPRETATION: THE INFANT INDUSTRY ARGUMENT AND DYNAMIC COMPARATIVE ADVANTAGES

If we look at the profile of Brazilian technology and service exports, one thing becomes apparent: cases range from those involving a very slow and gradual knowledge and skills accretion, i.e., civil engineering, to those involving substantial steps forward based on research and development programs, i.e., those related to ethanol-based technology. Underlying these important differences, one common element is always present: a learning process. This learning process may not have been the key reason why foreign contracts were awarded to Brazilian companies, but certainly it has been a necessary condition. As other countries are going through similar kinds of experience, and as the existence of a learning process is the key to the infant industry argument, an examination of this argument may help to conceptualize what we observe or, rather, what we observe may help us to enhance the explanatory value of the argument.

The development of an intuitively sound rationale for the infant industry argument appears to be in less than satisfactory shape. What the argument essentially contends is that subsidies or tariffs are justified when there is an underinvestment in knowledge acquisition so that actual learning is lower than potential learning. And this applies equally to import competing and to export-oriented industries because, irrespective of where the output is sold, whether abroad or at home, there will be a better allocation of resources at worldwide scale - assuming malleability, etc. So it is perfectly plausible, and even desirable, to apply the infant industry argument in the case of export-oriented industries - which fits Brazilian needs. Put this way, there does not seem to be any problem with the argument and, thus restated, the Mill-Bastable infant industry dogma has won its place as one of the two exceptions allowed to free-trade principles, (the other being the optimum tariff argument).

The trouble begins when an attempt is made to develop the practical implications of the argument. The problem lies in the unsatisfactory degree of specification as to the nature of both what is being learnt and the process of learning itself. The necessary mediations between the basic, abstract contention of the argument and its formulation as a guide for policy are largely missing.

In the first place, it is not clear at all whether the argument refers only to routine production experience

Table 6.2
Structure and Destination of Brazilian Consulting, Engineering, and Industrial Plant Exports, 1973-1979 (in number of contracts)

	Infrastructural Works	Feasibility and Other Preinvestment Studies	Industrial Plants	Training	Total
Nonneighbor Oil Exporting Countries (7)	19	4	6	1	30
Neighbor Oil Exporting Countries (2)	9	-	5	-	14
Total Oil Exporting Countries (9)	28	4	11	1	44
Other Neighbor Countries (8)	22	5	12	-	39
Other Nonneighbor Countries (9)	8	2	2	-	12
Total Nonoil Exporting Countries (17)	30	7	14	-	51
Total (26 Countries)	58	11	25	1	95

135

Note: – Nonneighbor oil exporting countries include: Saudi Arabia, Algeria, Iraq, Nigeria, Iran, Libya and China.

       – Neighbor oil exporting countries include: Venezuela and Ecuador.

       – Other neighbor countries include: Bolivia, Colombia, Costa Rica, Dominican Republic, Chile, Peru, Paraguay and Uruguay.

       – Other nonneighbor countries include: Mauritania, Tanzania, Portugal, Mozambique, Ivory Coast, Angola, Egypt, Syria and Sudan.

       Interbras was involved in at least thirty-eight of these operations (including the most substantial ones) producing finance and supplying marketing services.

Source: Interbras, Engineering and Consulting Companies and Brazilians Index, no. 18 (1979).

("learning by doing" proper) or to something else as well, such as learning by spending. Second, however this question is decided, it appears that the argument involves thinking in terms of a given, or "frozen," stock of knowledge which is "there" to be learnt and mastered (either just "by doing," and/or "by spending"), so that the period of protection (or subsidy) would cease when, after a certain known period, the knowledge has been acquired.

This way of dealing with the argument (no others have been put forward in terms of how and what is learnt so far as I know) seems misleading. To think in terms of a given stock of knowledge which is "there" to be learnt involves assuming that, for any given industrial activity, there is a single, universal activity; that there is a single, universal learning curve. Thus those who have started earlier would suffer the handicap of being closer to the plateau of the curve, while those who are given the chance to enter the industry under the protection of subsidies, because of their incipient stage of knowledge, could learn at a much faster rhythm until eventually they also reached the plateau of the curve and then could do without any further protection. As John Stuart Mill put it:

> The superiority of one country over another in one branch of production often only arises from having begun it sooner. There may be no inherent advantage on one part, or disadvantage on the other, but only a present superiority of acquired skill and experience. A country which has this skill and experience yet to acquire, may in other respects be better adapted to the production than those which were earlier in the field.... Nothing has a greater tendency to promote improvements in any branch of production than its trial under a new set of conditions. But it cannot be expected that individuals should, at their own risk, or to their certain loss, introduce a new manufacture, and bear the burden of carrying it on until the producers have been educated up to the level of those with whom these processes are traditional...."(10) (emphasis added)

Clearly, although involving a dynamic justification, this is definitely a static approach. Only rarely do advanced industrial countries and developing countries move along the same learning curve and no one knows when the plateau will be reached - if ever. Every successive generation of industrial plant (and recall that advanced industrial countries are still the largest market for plant design and construction) involves beginning a new learning curve fed by learning accruing to both plant engineering and design engineering teams through their experience with previous plant designs. Although these two sources of increased knowledge usually do not give rise to sharp discontinuity in learning paths, they certainly offset decreasing returns to learning which occur when the life-span of only one plant generation is considered. Certainly, as a result of research and development efforts, sharp discontinuities can also occur with fairly well known technologies, giving rise to new areas of increasing returns to learning.

As a result of the previous discussion it can be inferred that not only it is a mistake to think in terms of a single stock of knowledge to be mastered along a single learning curve, but also that, even if we assume that there is a single, universal learning curve, it does not guarantee convergence in knowledge and experience between the developing and the developed country. The latter may, for instance, enjoy a larger market for plant construction and design and thus have access to a permanently wider and deeper range of technological experience, despite being at a higher level along the learning curve. Therefore it is very difficult, if not self-defeating, to attempt to justify the infant industry argument on the basis of single learning curves for, if we constrain ourselves to considering only routine learning by doing, everybody learns, and only under very special circumstances is convergence certain to occur, even provided that learning proceeds at a higher rhythm in the developing than in the developed country.

Fortunately, doing is not the only source of learning and we can proceed to a more rewarding way of approaching and justifying the infant industry argument. For this purpose, let us distinguish among three kinds of learning: (1) by-product learning, (2) adaptive learning, and (3) post-localized learning. By-product learning is simply the standard learning by doing acquired in an almost compulsive way, not at all by intent, whenever a productive activity is performed. This is kind of learning which is acquired irrespective of whether anything special is done to further it. Adaptive learning entails some degree of intentionality, although it may sometimes be difficult to distinguish it from by-product learning. The difference is that, while by-product learning involves learning the production manual, adaptive learning entails improving on it. It goes beyond a mere passive knowledge acquisition to include certain ad-hoc activities aimed at improving operational conditions. Both kinds of learning are similar in that they have rapidly decreasing returns. They refer to short-time horizons and to single-plant experiences, while they differ in that only from adaptive learning can one expect improvements on the original technology which may eventually be

of some use beyond the single plant where the learning
is occurring. Finally, post-localized learning involves
not just learning the production manual and improving on
it, but also learning to rewrite it and, eventually,
writing a new one. It has a much longer time horizon
than the previous two types of learning, it refers not
to single plants but to sequences of plants, and it involves the development of a key capability: process design skills. (This can be adapted to the case of learning
in the field of infrastructural works.)

One can expect, a priori, that the larger the content
of post-localized learning in the experience of a given
productive activity, the greater the chance it will become capable of generating tradable intangible packages
for export packages which are related to the development
of a genuine dynamic comparative advantage. Conversely,
whatever technology exports may develop will tend to be
more erratic the lower the content of post-localized
learning involved. These are just hypotheses, but evidence from Brazil seems to support them. Brazil is most
successful as an exporter of intangibles in two sectors
which have received heavy support by the government in
order to integrate their development: civil engineering
and raw material processing. In both of these cases the
whole technological cycle, from design to erection to
training and operation, has been exhausted domestically,
and in both of them national firms occupy dominating
positions in the domestic market.

These learning processes are also the rationale behind the concept of obsolescing bargain.(11) We can also
hypothesize in this connection that the larger the content of post-localized, planned learning in the technology absorption process, the greater are the chances that
traditional patterns of obsolescing bargain will be su-
perseded. It is likely that Brazil will prove to be the
test case par excellance to test these hypotheses as it
must export competitively in order to develop. From what
we have seen above, we may tentatively conclude that
technology is being utilized in such a manner as to make
Brazil competitive internationally in a number of very
critical sectors.

NOTES

1.   See Wharton Econometric Forecasting Associates
Inc., "Study on the Brazilian Balance of Payments," February 1980. A further element which, from the Brazilian
standpoint, makes it difficult to handle this problem is
that a very large amount of current foreign indebtedness
is in the hands of private international banks whose
lending capacity to Brazil has already been saturated.
Direct petrodollar recycling via IMF is being considered
as one of the new ways to deal with the problem.

2.   This prediction is based on the so-called "outward looking development model." This model should be
clearly distinguished from the "economic abertura" approach pursued in Argentina, Chile, and Uruguay. The
latter involves letting foreign competitors enter the
domestic market by tariff reductions in the expectation
that enhanced competition will force the domestic industries to become more efficient and eventually, provided
that they survive, to become exporters. The former model
reverses this sequence by planning to increase efficiency
through first entering foreign markets and then, eventually, opening up the domestic market to foreign competition. The contrast between these models is shown dramatically by the daily complaints heard in Argentina about
the penetration of allegedly subsidized Brazilian products, ranging from eggs to steel products, as a result
of recently agreed upon closer economic ties between both
countries.
3.   See F.C. Sercovitch, Energy and Technology Balance in a New Bargaining Framework, II Conferencia Inter-
nacional sobre America Latina y la Economia Mundial.
(Buenos Aires: OEC/Instituto Torcuato Di Tella, 1980).
4.   See F.C. Sercovitch, State-Owned Enterprises and
Dynamic Comparative Advantages in the World Petrochemical
Industry - The Case of Commodity Olefins in Brazil (Cambridge: Harvard Institute of International Development,
1980).
5.   Indeed, in some respects Brazilian strategy,
with modifications, can be said to be moving closer to
that of other typical NICs, such as South Korea, than to
that of other Latin American countries, particularly
since 1976 when domestic growth slowed down severely.
Witness, for instance, Brazil's closeness to South Korea's leadership in the Mideast market for large contracts. The Foreign Ministry (Itamaraty) has organized
an efficient information network to help Brazilian companies identify business opportunities and, particularly,
large contracts abroad. Engineering firms have also organized themselves, through CONESE (Council for Service
Exports) in order to encourage the Government to enact
legislation. (So far this has been available mainly to
support manufacturing exports.) The President of Brazil
became directly involved in negotiations aimed at modifying the contract concerning expansion of the Guri dam by
sending a letter to President Herrera Campins calling for
the ideals of regional integration as the appropriate
framework to avoid solving the problem in favor of third-
party interests.
6.   Border exports from Mexico to the USA account
for about half of total Mexican manufacturing export.

7.   It is well known that Japanese trading companies
excel in this field. They operate as gigantic and ubi-
quitous information vacuum cleaners. To give just an indication of their abilities in this respect, the nine
largest Japanese trading companies process more than
120,000 incoming and outgoing messages every day. Their
daily output of written material amounts to the equivalent of 6,000 pages the size of the New York Times. Certainly Brazilian traders are only learning the business
(with active support from the Itamaraty), but they appear
to be doing it well.

8.   See Sercovitch, State-Owned Enterprises and
Dynamic Comparative Advantages.

9.   See, for example, criticisms put forward by Joaquim F. de Carvalho, former Director of Nuclen (Nuclebras
Engenharia S.A.), in Journal do Brasil, 14 September
1980, especially the section beginning on p. 5.

10.   See John Stuart Mill, The Principles of Political Economy with Some of Their Application to Social
Philosophy (New York: A. M. Kelley, Bookseller, 1965),
p. 92.

11. See Raymond Vernon, Sovereignty at Bay. The Multinational Spread of US Enterprises (New York: Basic
Books, 1971) and Storm over the Multinationals, The Real
Issues (Cambridge: Harvard University Press, 1977).
The concept of "obsolescing bargain" basically refers to
the changing bargaining balance between firms and industries in countries with different degrees of development
as a result of declining barriers to entry over time with
respect to ownership, control and management in specific
productive activities.

7
State Entrepreneurship, Energy Policy, and the Political Order in Brazil

Kenneth Paul Erickson

OPEC's price revolution during the 1970s has posed fundamental challenges to the Brazilian development model, leading - indeed, forcing - the nation's policy makers to reorder national priorities. Seeking to defend the threatened national economy, they have served as entrepreneurs, creating or transforming enterprises, institutions, and processes in order to replace foreign oil with domestic oil and substitute fuels, to conserve energy, and to expand exports of goods and services to pay for ever more costly oil imports. This chapter describes and discusses the entrepreneurial dimension of Brazil's energy policies since the first oil shock in 1973. It concludes by pointing out that success in economic terms may carry with it serious consequences in social and political terms.

INTRODUCTION

The Oil Shocks and Brazil's Energy Crisis

The architects of Brazil's sustained postwar economic boom sought to create a modern economy in many ways modeled upon that of the United States. Policies pursued from the late 1940s through the 1970s were highly successful, for economic output increased by an average of about 7 percent per year over more than three decades. This success was achieved at a cost, however, that was not apparent until the first oil shock, when crude oil prices quadrupled. Abundant supplies of cheap imported petroleum had simply been taken for granted as the nation erected an oil-fuelled industrial economy, built highways and protected domestic auto manufacture, and supplanted rail, coastal, and river shipping with truck transport. Oil consumption multiplied sixteen times from 1946 to 1974, while oil's share in Brazil's total energy use tripled from 13 to 39 percent. In 1974, 85 percent of that oil was imported.(2) Some analysts argue, moreover,

141

that these figures, which present primary energy consumption, understate Brazil's dependence upon oil and that
calculations based on effective end use of energy are
more indicative of the nation's real dependence upon the
product. Using the latter calculation, which reduces the
contribution of hydroelectricity and firewood, the nation's second and third leading energy sources, petroleum provides 60 percent of Brazil's effectively utilized
energy.(3)

Motivating the drive to industrialize was a desire
to reduce Brazil's dependence upon the world's dominant
capitalist industrial nations. By seeking to emulate the
United States, the world's most energy-inefficient economy,(4) Brazilian policy makers achieved their growth
goals but - after OPEC's price revolution - they found
they had merely transformed the nature of their dependency. Brazil is now the largest oil importer in the Third
World, and its foreign oil bill for 1980 is projected to
top $10 billion, compared to only $573 million in 1972.
Soaring oil bills played a major part in hiking Brazil's
foreign debt from $12.5 billion in 1973 to $57 billion
by September 1980.(5) It is now the largest in the
world. Brazil owes this money not to the OPEC nations,
but to private banks and international lending agencies
dominated by the capitalist industrial nations. The direction of its dependence therefore remains unchanged.
Not only does Brazil's petroleum-based development model
pose grave financial risks, but, since the nation imports
over three-quarters of its oil, it jeopardizes the very
security of the nation's economy. As we will see below,
the precariousness of its supply lines has already been
demonstrated three times in less than a decade.

Entrepreneurship by the State

Joseph Schumpeter, in his classic The Theory of Economic Development, described entrepreneurs as those who
innovate economically - who carry out new combinations of
the means of production. Most industrial capitalists are
not entrepreneurs, he noted, for they merely run their
businesses in routine ways. Schumpeter pointed out, however, that one need not be an industrialist to be an entrepreneur, and he cited cases of financiers or "promot-
ers" who carry out the new combinations referred to
above.(6) An examination of the policies, practices, and
results of Brazil's technocratic economic policy makers
reveals that they, too, possess and exercise entrepreneurial skills; skills that are nowhere more evident than
in the energy sector.(7)

Technocratic policy makers may apply their entrepreneurial abilities either directly or indirectly. Direct-

ly, they are creators and managers of public sector companies such as Petrobras, the national oil company, Eletrobras and its affiliates in electricity generation, and mining and manufacturing companies in iron and steel, chemicals, aircraft, weapons, and many other fields. Indirectly, they guide – through incentives, penalties, and regulations – the development of new industries and activities in the private sector. As an illustration, consider the history of the Brazilian automobile industry, an industry which ultimately increased Brazil's dependence on oil. Transnational auto firms began manufacturing in Brazil in 1958 because of public policy. Economic technocrats forbade the mere final assembly of imported parts and set a timetable gradually raising the share of domestic components in the vehicles. By the late 1970s, with annual output around one million vehicles, Brazil had become the world's tenth largest auto producer. Well over 90 percent of the components are manufactured locally. This dramatic expansion in vehicle output did not happen by chance or because of "impersonal market forces." Indeed, this would have been impossible in a society whose per capita income averaged $300 in 1960 and $400 in 1970. Rather, it was a result of public policy. In the years that followed the military coup of 1964, the government implemented a policy of income concentration, in effect taking money out of the pockets of the poor and transferring it to the rich. In a relatively poor country, policy makers thus assured a market for heavy consumer durables such as cars. Motorists also benefited in the 1950s and 1960s from a government subsidy that held down gasoline prices and from an intensive highway program that increased the mileage of paved roads more than 20 times between 1955 and 1974.(8) The recent efforts to develop a fuel-alcohol program and to substitute coal for fuel oil in industry, discussed below, are clear cases of indirect entrepreneurship. The following sections examine both direct and indirect forms of state entrepreneurship in Brazilian energy development.

DIRECT STATE ENTREPRENEURSHIP: THE PUBLIC SECTOR

Nationalism and the Creation of Energy Corporations

Brazil's sustained rapid economic growth dates back at least to Getúlio Vargas' authoritarian rule between 1930 and 1945. In the "Revolution of 1930," Vargas and a group of self-styled modernizing nation-builders overthrew the weak, decentralized "Old Republic" and replaced it with a strong, centralized, interventionist state. Through restructured political insitutions, they shifted the favors and support of public policy from the planter oligarchy to the nascent industrial bourgeoisie. The interventionist state has systematically fostered industrialization ever since.

The resultant economic expansion and urbanization dramatically increased the need for commercial fuels, and to meet this need state policy makers and technocrats fashioned entrepreneurial roles for themselves. This is most clearly apparent in the energy sectors that surged forward after the war. In petroleum, Petrobras, the state oil monopoly, was created in 1954; and in electricity, in 1962 technocrats created Eletrobras, a holding company that coordinated the expanding state and federal hydroelectric generating agencies.

Brazilian nationalism played a major role in the creation and policies of both organizations. Indeed, nationalist sentiment was so strong that Brazil nationalized its oil before any of it had been discovered. As early as the teens and twenties, Brazilian administrative policies effectively discouraged foreign oil companies from exploring or refining in Brazil, although they were allowed to import and market their refined products. Decree-laws issued by Vargas in the 1930s made official their exclusion from exploration or refining. Only later, in 1939, was oil discovered in Brazil. The monopoly role which Congress gave to Petrobras in 1954 was, of course, the logical conclusion to this process.

Important in forming public opinion throughout these decades was a widespread belief that Brazil possessed vast reserves of crude petroleum which the major international oil companies knew about but conspired to keep secret. In this way, it was believed, the companies perpetuated a tight market situation in order to sustain a high price for products from Venezuela and the Middle East. It was the fault of the foreign oil companies, therefore, that Brazil remained an oil importer.(9) No compelling evidence was ever marshalled to support the charge; indeed, many years of drilling by Petrobras have turned up only modest finds rather than the bonanza predicted. Nonetheless, there are good reasons to disagree with the oil companies' claim that the charge was totally implausible. Documents exist to show, for example, that the foreign concessionaires in Iraq instructed their crews to drill "shallow holes on locations where there was no danger of striking oil," and, in the case of an unintended find, to plug the well and keep its existence secret.(10)

The state took over the electric power sector more gradually but no less definitively. Foreign concerns dominated commercial electric power in Brazil from the turn of the century until the 1950s and 1960s when public agencies developed a major role in hydro generation. These agencies soon overshadowed the foreign companies and then progressively bought them out. The government

took over the final foreign-owned company in 1978.(11)
As in petroleum politics, strong nationalist feelings
conditioned the options available to both the foreign
companies and the state officials. During the democratic
period from 1946 to 1964, the voters' almost universal
antipathy for the foreign power companies made it not
only distasteful but nearly impossible for politicians
to approve rate increases. The companies therefore
slowed and ultimately stopped investment in new generating projects, since the lagging rates would not provide
sufficient revenues to recoup their capital along with
the desired return on it. Politicians and planners in
the industrializing Southeast, which consumed well over
half of the nation's electricity, feared that a worsening
electricity crunch would strangle their booming economies. They responded in the 1950s by creating several
state (and one federal) hydroelectric generating companies whose giant dam complexes began to come on line in
the 1960s. These agencies then sold their power wholesale to the foreign utilities for distribution and the
industrial boom continued. The new generating agencies
attracted very able teams of entrepreneurial technocrats
who successfully executed their agencies' specific projects and then devoted the rest of their careers and their
accumulated experience to the state power sector.(12)
     Institutionally, in 1962 Congress took the final step
by creating Eletrobras to coordinate electric power development in Brazil. This holding company supervises the
regional generating agencies and sets plans for the sector. Eletrobras, like Petrobras, is a legacy of Vargas
and the Revolution of 1930. In 1934 Vargas laid the legislative foundations for the later restructuring of the
electric power sector, and he submitted a bill to create
Eletrobras in 1954, though it did not pass Congress for
eight years.(13)

Petrobras and Domestic Petroleum Policy

     Petrobras was founded only after long and bitter de-
bate in which an articulate minority of Brazilians opposed the creation of a state monopoly. Immediately,
however, the new corporation justified its proponents'
faith by dramatically increasing domestic production of
crude petroleum. Annual output increased nearly fifteen
times between 1955 and 1960, from 5,500 to 81,000 barrels
per day. These years of success fed the illusory belief
that Brazil would soon become self-sufficient in oil, although the latter figure represented only about 40 percent of the petroleum consumed in the nation.(14) Output
doubled again by 1970, to 167,000 barrels per day, but
overall economic expansion and surging car and truck output in the 1960s caused consumption to rise more rapidly
than production. The 1970 output now represented 34

percent of consumption. Domestic production changed little through the 1970s while national consumption more
than doubled so that in the mid to late 1970s Petrobras'
contribution to the total barely topped 15 percent.(15)

This dependency on imports, of course, was not alarming as long as oil remained cheap and plentiful on the
world market - a situation Petrobras officials expected
to continue indefinitely, as Ernesto Geisel, then president of the oil monopoly, testified to a congressional
committee in the late 1960s.(16) Relying on this projec-
tion, Petrobras continued business as usual, searching
for oil at home while buying ever-increasing quantities
of foreign crude to refine in Brazil.

The oil crisis was therefore totally unexpected, and
it forced Geisel, now President of the Republic, to order
major policy shifts. As a result, Petrobras sharply increased domestic exploration, with a new emphasis on offshore areas; in a dramatic break with the past, it invited foreign oil companies to explore in Brazilian territory, and it began drilling for oil on contract in
other countries.

Offshore exploration soon brought discoveries. In
1974 Petrobras announced a major find in the Campos basin
off Rio de Janeiro state, and subsequent exploratory
drilling in the basin indicates an estimated reserve of
1 billion barrels. Petrobras has made significant
strikes offshore in the North as well. The Campos basin
finds in 1974 led euphoric officials, such as Planning
Minister Mario Henrique Simonsen, to predict production
of one million barrels per day by 1980, which would have
made the country self-sufficient in oil. Even the more
guarded estimates, however, failed to take into account
the lengthy period needed to adapt and prove out novel
deep-water technologies, not to speak of coping with
suppliers' delays and accidents. Only in late 1979 did
production exceed the levels of the early 1970s.(17) By
the mid-1980s Petrobras will produce at least 370,000
barrels per day, but it is unlikely to reach the 500,000
barrels per day targeted by President Figueiredo. Even
at the higher figure, moreover, output would not satisfy
half the nation's petroleum needs.(18)

The oil price pinch also led Brazil, in a major foreign policy departure in 1976, to invite foreign companies to explore for oil on "risk contract." This is the
first time that foreign companies have been allowed to
prospect on Brazilian territory since the 1920s. The
"risk" contracts force the foreign companies to take
specified economic risks. This distinguishes them from
the old-time concession contracts of the Middle East and
elsewhere which gave the concessionaires long-term oil
rights in major portions of a country's territory. The
companies could then either work their concession or

"bank" it, as suited their private interests. The Brazilian contracts, whose terms are probably the stiffest in the world, require a company to begin drilling by a fixed date, usually a year or less from signing, and to spend a stipulated minimum dollar-figure while drilling a minimum number of wells. If oil is not discovered in a fixed time period, the contract area reverts to Petrobras, thereby preventing the companies from hiding or postponing discoveries. If a contractee strikes oil in commercial quantities, it prepares the well for production and then turns it over to Petrobras, in return for which it will recover all its expenses plus a previously negotiated but confidential percentage of the revenues. (19) This share may come to 35 percent of production, according to one report.(20)

None of the seventeen contractees from the first two rounds of bidding (1976 to 1978) struck oil in commercially viable quantities, leading to an apparent decline in interest by the transnational companies. Therefore in 1979, in the third round, Petrobras sought to rekindle interest by offering onshore blocks for the first time. (21) Finally, in a fourth round in late 1979 and 1980, Petrobras went further by opening bidding for the first time to domestic private and state enterprises. One Sao Paulo state consortium won a contract and in mid-1980 was drilling in the western portion of that state.(22)

Tracing the gradual evolution in the terms of the risk contracts, we can see that Brazil's serious balance of payments problems have led the nation's petroleum policy makers to whittle away at the monopoly role assigned to Petrobras by the Congress. The law establishing Petrobras very specifically mandated that exploration, production, refining, and the maritime transport of crude petroleum "constitute a monopoly of the Union (Federal Government)."(23) The initial concept of risk contracts restricted contractees to performing exploration and services for Petrobras in offshore areas, that is, in areas where the transnational giants enjoy leads in advanced deep-water technology. The foreign companies already possess the necessary equipment for this type of work. The advantage to Brazil, therefore, was that drilling could start almost immediately. Soon, however, the contract areas moved onshore where Petrobras itself possesses the necessary technology and experience, and afterward other Brazilian firms were permitted to share in Petrobras' domain. Finally, "to gain greater cooperation from private initiative in the search for oil," President Figueiredo and Minister of Mines and Energy César Cals agreed in December 1979 to permit contractees not only to explore but also to produce the oil they find, and to receive part of their compensation in oil. They proposed, moreover, to restrict Petrobras to the areas in which it is currently exploring and to open all other areas to the private sector.(24)

The implications of these latest policy changes are far reaching. Almost certainly, one or more of the contractees will some day strike oil, particulary since the areas open to them are to be expanded. Their success will quite likely damage Petrobras. The state company, despite its recent successes in the Campos basin, came under criticism during the late 1970s for being in some degree responsible for Brazil's dependence on foreign oil. To these specific charges must be added an amorphous suspicion or malaise regarding state corporations, a feeling which is a by-product of more generalized distrust and antagonism toward the authoritarian state. Such antagonism is openly expressed in the present period of political opening. Once one of the contractees finds oil in this climate of criticism and suspicion, not only Petrobras as a corporation but the very concept of state monopoly is likely to be further undermined.

When Petrobras and President Geisel announced the risk contract concept in 1976, public debate on the topic was impossible because of the press censorship of the era. The first risk contracts seemed, moreover, to be tightly controlled service contracts through which Petrobras could execute its monopoly role, and not necessarily a dilution of that role. The later erosion of the monopoly has come in a more liberalized political era in which censorship has been lifted, and the issue is now beginning to be debated.(25) So far, however, the debates have not reached a broad audience, and the issue has not yet become a matter of passionately felt national urgency, as was the original Petrobras debate in the late 1940s and early 1950s.

Petrobras, in its creation and initial activities, is an example of entrepreneurship. The rapid rise in crude oil production in the late 1950s resulted from new combinations of the means of production in Brazil. From the 1960s into the early 1970s, however, Petrobras' domestic operations ceased to be entrepreneurial as its officials merely managed the company in a routine manner. The oil crisis forced Petrobras to intensify its domestic exploration efforts, so that the 1 million feet of exploratory well drilled in 1977 was 2.5 times the amount drilled in 1973. Of this total, 48 percent was drilled offshore, compared with 35 percent in 1973. The 325 offshore wells included in Petrobras $1.2 billion exploration program for 1978 through 1981 compare with only 250 drilled on the continental shelf in the preceding 10 years.(26) By expanding exploration into deep waters offshore in the early 1970s, Petrobras officials took a risk and did create new combinations of the means of production. The risks paid off with the Campos basin

finds beginning in 1974. The decision to open exploration and production to other companies, both domestic and
foreign, surely creates new combinations and hence is entrepreneurial. The key imponderable in this regard is
whether Brazil will be able to control the transnationals
and prevent the political abuses of which they have been
guilty elsewhere.(27)

Electric Power Policy: Hydro and Nuclear

Brazil's most abundant domestic energy resource is
hydroelectricity. By 1976, hydropower supplied 92 percent of the nation's electricity, and this accounted for
24 percent of all primary energy consumed in Brazil.(28)
The oil crisis has spurred policy-makers to accelerate
the development of hydroelectricity. An Eletrobras study
projects the tripling of installed hydroelectric capacity
between 1978 and 1995, from 22,000 to 69,000 megawatts.
The share of electricity in total primary energy consumption is expected to rise from 27 to 35 percent. Brazil's
potential hydroelectric capacity is estimated at 209,000
megawatts (compared with 158,000 for all western Europe),
so the sector has considerable room for expansion. Brazil will even be able to convert some of this hydroelectric energy into hard foreign currency, once it completes
some new aluminum and iron and steel projects whose energy-intensive products will be exported.(29) The constant expansion of the hydroelectric sector is the result
of direct entrepreneurial activity by officials of the
interventionist state. Indeed, one analysis of power
generation is subtitled "Entrepreneurship in the Public
Sector."(30)
Eletrobras' strategy through 1995 contains a new element, that of indirect entrepreneurship, for it recom-
mends a policy departure which would allow private enterprises or rural communities to build dams on low or me-
dium-head sites in order to supply their own power needs.
These sites are too small to be worthwhile for the public
sector. Eletrobras would require concessionaires to install low cost standardized equipment, to build facilities that would fully utilize the power potential of the
waterway, and to sell any surplus electricity to the regional grid.(31) So far no implementing guidelines have
been adopted and no private or local groups have offered
to build such facilities, probably because of uncertainty
about the terms of resale for the surplus and because of
risks inherent in untried institutional relationships.
Permitting other parties to build small or medium
dams does not pose a threat to Eletrobras comparable to
the threat posed to Petrobras by the risk contracts.
Self-generation is an old concept in Brazil. In 1952,
for example, self-generating units produced 15 percent
of Brazil's electric power.(32) Many self-generators are

manufacturing plants that generate electricity along with the heat or steam needed for their industrial processes, a technique that is highly energy efficient. Because they produce this electricity for their own use and not for resale to third parties, they merely relieve some of the demand pressure on the grid without undermining the distribution monopoly of Eletrobras' regional affiliates. Since electricity distribution constitutes a natural monopoly, there will be no ultimate challenge to Eletrobras' role in setting the direction for the sector; Eletrobras already possesses the necessary technology, so the self-generators would simply carry out the holding company's standardized plans. Given the fixed power potential of each dam site, construction of a generating facility offers a completely predictable return. In the electric power sector, therefore, there can be nothing like the potential bonanza that could, in the oil sector, turn a risk contractee into a major producer and a potential threat to the state monopoly. Finally, the self-generators would not export a share of their production, as would the risk contractees.

To supplement hydroelectricity, which in the mid-1970s many Brazilians erroneously believed to be nearly fully exploited, and to extend national autonomy in applied technology, the Brazilian government announced a mammoth nuclear power program in 1975. Based on a controversial accord with West Germany - an accord which the United States tried unsuccessfully to block - this program aimed to bring Brazil into the club of nuclear nations and to guarantee abundant electricity for continued rapid growth. The government set up a national holding company, Nuclebras, for all nuclear power activities, and its officials optimistically predicted that sixty-three reactors would supply half the nation's electricity by 2000 and that Brazil would become a major exporter of nuclear technology and equipment. Influenced by such predictions, many Brazilians greeted the accord as an important step in national emancipation from the world's dominant industrial nations and from the grip of the OPEC cartel.

By 1979, however, nearly all relevant domestic groups had concluded, on the basis of compelling evidence, that the nuclear program will not serve either their group interests or the national interest. The public debate over nuclear power in Brazil has not turned on reactor safety and radiation danger, as it has in the industrial nations. The major issues have been cost, decisional competence, and the real extent of technology transfer. Nuclear electricity was shown to be at least twice as expensive as hydroelectricity in Brazil, engendering opposition from industrialists and economic planners.(33) Brazilian capital goods producers complained that the best contracts went to German firms because, astonishingly, Brazilian negotiators of the accord had put into German hands the controlling votes on the project's executive bodies. When documents proving this were leaked to the press in 1979, broad nationalist support rallied against the accord.(34) Brazilian scientists argued that the deal would almost certainly retard rather than accelerate efforts to reduce Brazil's scientific and technological dependency on foreign nations because it amounted to buying a "black box" of ready-made technology, rather than developing indigenous capabilities in nuclear science. One prominent nuclear physicist argued that if the government had not decided in 1967 to concentrate research funds on light-water, enriched-uranium technology, "we would already have a functioning 30-megawatt prototype power reactor, using heavy-water, natural-uranium technology."(35)

By late 1979, it appeared that Brazil would have to cut its losses, either by building no more than the two reactors firmly contracted for, or by revising the accord so that future reactors could be built on terms more favorable to Brazil. The outspoken civilian opposition then quieted down, confident that such strong protest from so many quarters had won the day.

It hadn't. After six months of apparent inaction by public officials, President Figueiredo ironically chose World Environment Day in June 1980 to expropriate 239 square kilometers of São Paulo coastline as the site for the third and fourth German reactors. Federal negotiators had used the interim to secretly inform the São Paulo state government and the state's Energy Company of São Paulo (CESP) that CESP was going to build and run the two new reactors. Federal officials sweetened what might have been a bitter pill for CESP to swallow by promising subsidies to hold CESP's construction costs on the reactors to the total the company would have spent on hydroelectric projects of the same capacity. They also promised to sell to CESP, on very favorable terms, the old São Paulo Light properties currently owned by Eletrobras. These include a large distribution network to which CESP had been selling power wholesale, two generating facilities, and waterways and dams with which it can now create a pumped-storage generating system near São Paulo. With the entire nuclear and Light package, CESP will be the largest electric utility in Latin America.(36)

Not only did the government officials prepare the deal in complete secrecy, but the "security community" (a euphemism referring to the vast network - some 250,000 strong - of commissar-like military and police agents assigned to each important agency of all civilian ministries, as well as to state and many local government agencies) prepared contingency measures against the civilian opposition. A report was leaked to the press demonstrating that security agents had meticulously monitored all antinuclear activity and built up a dossier on the participants. Incredibly, the document claimed that a carefully orchestrated conspiracy had been mounted against the accord by a broad group of interests, most notable among them the governments of the United States and the Soviet Union as well as the Brazilian Jewish community. The document claimed that Jews sought to impede Brazil's progress because of the government's pro-Arab foreign policy.(37)

The evolution of Brazil's nuclear energy policy gives rise to several observations on politics in authoritarian Brazil, on nuclear-energy policy-making in general, and on state entrepreneurship. First, the nuclear program is clearly favored by the military establishment, and military officers possess institutional resources that can outweigh a massive civilian consensus, the recent political opening notwithstanding. Not only has the President of the Republic been a military officer for the last sixteen years, but the military control a security apparatus that reaches into every executive agency in the country. One colonel serving as Secretary of Coordination and Planning in the Rio Grande do Sul state government best expressed the military view of the nuclear power program: "I wish to emphasize that a nuclear program is fundamentally, and almost exclusively, a matter of national security. The harnessing of energy from a nuclear reactor is secondary."(38)

Before one concludes that military authoritarianism led to an outcome unique to Brazil, however, one should consider the Brazilian case in comparative perspective. A recent study of nuclear energy development in the United States and France, two liberal democracies, found a pattern similar to the Brazilian one. In these countries, too, the inherent risks in the technology, its security implications, and the messianic faith of the nuclear science community in the rightness of nuclear power created and reinforced closed decisional processes that evaded thorough scientific and economic scrutiny. (39) While evidence from around the world demonstrates that nuclear generation compares extremely unfavorably with hydroelectricity in countries where hydro potential is abundant, most nuclear programs have been initiated more for concerns of world power or national grandeur than to produce cheap power. Brazil, thus, is no exception.

Finally, the nuclear program gets a negative evaluation when one rates it on entrepreneurship. Or course, to establish nuclear generating facilities is to create new combinations of the means of production, and this is the essence of entrepreneurship. But Schumpeter assumed that the competitive pressures of the market system would winnow out those innovations that failed to prove cost-effective, a condition that does not hold for Brazilian nuclear power. All the available evidence indicates that nuclear generation of electricity in Brazil today costs at least twice as much as hydroelectricity. The Brazilian taxpayers, therefore, will have to float an otherwise sinking innovation. Such a subsidy is the condition under which CESP was assigned its two reactors. Moreover, entrepreneurship involves "getting a new thing done," in Schumpeter's words, and this implies a minimal level of effiency.(40) The design deficiencies, unsuitable site location, sloppy construction, and lax safety standards at Angra dos Reis, the site chosen for a U.S.-built Westinghouse reactor (Angra I) and for the first two reactors from Germany (Angra II and III) hardly seem to qualify under this aspect of entrepreneurship.

The site is only twenty-five kilometers from a geological fault where three minor tremors have occurred in less than two decades. Mudslides from adjacent hills pose a danger in rainy months. With the exception of the bedrock supporting Angra I, the site's soil is sandy and requires expensive pilings to bear heavy buildings. No other reactors anywhere in the world have been placed on comparable soil. The absence of a well thought out safety program is illustrated by the Laurel-and-Hardy-like details of a serious fire at Angra I in October 1977: "...the fire began at lunchtime in a storage room. The keys to it were with the man in charge, who was out having lunch on the beach. The fire department was called and arrived on the scene in a few minutes, but the pumper trucks carried no water. Instead of taking water from a large storage tank only 500 meters away, the firemen preferred to go 5 kilometers to get it. There were hydrants at the reactor site, but the firemen had not brought the necessary tools to open their valves." The government investigation, later leaked to the press, revealed that seventy-one fires had occurred at the site in a five month period in 1977. After the fire, moreover, the political police coerced engineers on the project to sign a document attesting to the adequacy of safety measures there. The engineers were told they would lose their jobs if they refused to sign.(41) The delays in completion of Angra I, now more than three years behind schedule, the inability even to start construction on Angra II, and the still delayed final siting of Angra III are all owing to these problems.

State Entrepreneurship and Foreign Energy Supplies

Despite many programs to increase domestic energy output, it is clear that for the foreseeable future Brazil will not become self-sufficient in energy production. Foreign sources will continue to supply a large segment of the nation's energy demand. The Brazilian government has therefore developed a multi-faceted international energy policy whose principal components include: (1) intensive, pragmatic diplomatic activity, particularly through bilateral negotiations, to insure that the flow of oil will not be cut off and that cooperative projects with neighboring countries will increase Brazil's supplies of other forms of energy, particularly hydroelectric power and natural gas, (2) direct exploration and production by Petrobras in foreign countries, on risk contract, (3) aggressive promotion of Brazilian exports around the world so that Brazil can pay for energy imports or can directly swap Brazilian products for oil and coal, (4) reversal of Brazil's long-standing refusal to allow foreign companies to search for oil on Brazilian territory, as described above, and (5) development of nuclear power through the agreement with West Germany.

Because Brazil depends on foreign sources for more than three-quarters of its oil, a cutoff in imports would mean a truly catastrophic paralysis of the entire economy. Cutoffs have been threatened three times since 1973, and vulnerable Brazilian foreign policy makers have adjusted policy to comply with the demands of Arab suppliers on at least two of those occasions. In January 1974, the Brazilian foreign minister responded to the threat of embargo by tilting official Mideast policy toward the Arabs; up to that time Brazil had consciously pursued a neutral approach to Israel and the Arab countries. In 1979, the Iranian revolution provided the second occasion of an oil cutoff. Iran was then Brazil's biggest supplier, and the collapse of Iranian exports following the overthrow of the Shah soon reduced Brazil's normal three month stock of crude oil to little more than one month's. While negotiating for increased Iraqi deliveries to make up the shortfall, Brazil recognized the Palestine Liberation Organization as the legitimate representative of the Palestinian people. Iraq then stepped in to supply 400,000 to 500,000 barrels per day, or about half of Brazil's oil imports.(42) The third supply cutoff, during the Iran-Iraq conflict in the Fall of 1980, comes at press time for this book, so it is too soon to tell if Brazil will have to make additional foreign policy concessions to secure replacement supplies. At a recent meeting of the Group of 77 developing countries, Brazilian representives made an outspoken argument for the restructuring of present world trading and financial institutions and processes. Brazil's position on this issue should favorably predispose most OPEC nations toward it as it negotiates new supply contracts.(43)

Of longer-term importance than Brazil's activity in traditional diplomatic arenas are its innovative and agressive departures in economic diplomacy. Brazil's new

economic diplomacy has shifted an important share of responsibility in foreign policy-making away from the Ministry of Foreign Relations, most of whose high-level officials have little training in economics, to other
institutions. Most notable among these are the Ministry
of Mines and Energy, under whose supervision fall four
giant state companies (Petrobras, Eletrobras, Nuclebras,
and the Vale do Rio Doce Company, whose iron ore is sometimes bartered directly for energy supplies), Petrobras
itself, the Ministry of Industry and Commerce, and the
Ministry of Finance.(44)

At first Petrobras directly performed some of the new
tasks in the international energy and economic arena, but
as the dimensions of these tasks ballooned, policymakers
responded by creating new institutions designed expressly
for them. With 10 percent Gross Domestic Product (GDP)
growth rates after 1968 causing national oil consumption
to soar, Petrobras officials decided to seek contracts
to explore and produce oil in foreign countries. To this
end they created a Petrobras subsidiary, Braspetro, in
1972. Braspetro's contracts generally involve joint ventures with transnational majors, independents, or host
country national companies, and they earmark for Braspetro a portion of the crude discovered and produced, usually at a rate below the world market price. Braspetro
has contracted to explore in at least eleven countries,
and it has made significant strikes in Colombia, Algeria,
and Iraq.

To promote Brazilian exports around the world, officials of the agencies cited above, as well as the President of the Republic, serve aggressively as international
sales representatives. For example, when President João
Batista Figueiredo paid a state visit to Caracas in November 1979, his party included one hundred Brazilian
private businessmen. The deals discussed, if consum-
mated, could amount to between $2 and $3 billion.(45)

Petrobras, as Brazil's largest single importer, first
sought to market Brazilian goods abroad in order to generate foreign currency to pay for the crude it buys. In
1976 it created Interbras, a new subsidiary to carry out
this function. Interbras is a trading company that pro-
motes and sells Brazilian manufactures and commodities
and sometimes exchanges them directly for energy resources. In conjunction with officials from the Ministry
of Industry and Commerce, Interbras officials travel the
globe in pursuit of major deals.

Brazil, now at middle-level economic development, has
a wide variety of goods and services needed by many of
the oil-producing states. Possessing good water resources for agriculture, for example, it can supply sugar, coffee, soybeans, cotton, and other foods and fibers

to the arid nations of the Middle East. Brazilian agricultural planners have been sensitive to market opportunities, as when they turned their country from an occasional importer of soybean products in the 1960s to a
major exporter, second only to the United States, in the
1970s. The government inaugurated in 1979 has promised
to foster the expansion of export agriculture.

During the sustained economic growth of the postwar
decades, Brazilian architects and civil construction
firms gained a wealth of experience in designing and
building residential, commercial, and industrial establishments, as well as highways, airports, power dams,
irrigation systems, and the like. This experience in an
"underdeveloped" milieu with tropical and subtropical
conditions provides the Brazilians with a selling point
when negotiating with nonindustrialized oil producers.
One survey for 1979 forecast $3 billion in Brazilian
service exports, mainly from construction contracts, with
the possibility that these would rise to $5 billion by
1982.(46)

Finally, because Brazil's level of industrialization
is several steps ahead of that of the OPEC countries, it
can offer diverse products such as shoes and textiles,
simple instruments and machine tools, automobiles and
airplanes. Embraer, Brazil's main aircraft manufacturer,
also an entrepreneurial corporation in the public sector,
began exporting in 1975 with $5 million in sales abroad;
it boosted exports to $38 million in 1978 and expects to
expand them sharply in the future. It found its first
customers in Latin America, Africa, and the Middle East,
but by 1980 it had sold its Bandeirante to commercial
charter and commuter lines in the United States and the
United Kingdom, and the French Air Force had bought
fifty-four of its Xingu planes.(47)

Since the Brazilian military are seeking major-power
status, it is not surprising that the nation has developed the largest armaments industry in the Third World.
Brazilian weapons salesmen aggressively pursue export
contracts around the world, with particular emphasis on
the Middle East. The Brazilian weapons sales catalogue,
as of 1979, included fighter and transport planes, armored combat vehicles, light tanks, boats, surface-to-air
missiles, rocket launchers, mortars, cannons, lazer-di-
rected targeting devices, machine guns, automatic pistols
and rifles, grenades, ammunition, and communication
equipment. Brazil is the largest manufacturer of wheeled
combat vehicles in the non-Communist world, and foreign
sales of these received a substantial boost when Brazilian designed and produced Urutu and Cascavel vehicles
operated by Libyan soldiers significantly outperformed
Egypt's Soviet-made armored vehicles in the Egyptian-
Libyan border conflict in June 1977. Libya had purchased
about 125 of the vehicles earlier that year, at more than

$500,000 each.(48) The Iran-Iraq conflict of 1980 is likely to increase demand for the armored vehicles, which are produced by Engesa, an engineering firm backed by the state's recently created Board for the Arms Industry, Imbel. To increase the speed and reliability of delivery of these vehicles and other industrial exports, government officials in mid-1980 adopted new regulations to eliminate Varig Airlines' monopoly in international air exports. This allowed Engesa, several other industrial exporters, and Transbrasil Airlines to form jointly a new all-cargo airline, Aerobrasil, to ship their products abroad.(49)

Let us now look at some specific examples of Brazilian sales and barter deals. The Middle East is one focal point for Interbras efforts because the region drains such a great share of Brazil's foreign exchange. In 1974, for example, Brazil made $2.4 billion worth of purchases from Middle Eastern countries, while selling them only $331 million, or 7 percent.(50) One of the prime targets of Interbras negotiators, at least until the overthrow of the Shah, was Iran. In 1977 the two nations signed a five year, $6.5 billion trade agreement that moved Iran back into top-supplier position by increasing Brazil's oil purchases from 75,000 to 275,000 barrels per day, or to almost one-third of Brazil's then 800,000 barrel per day import appetite. More significant than the amount of this agreement was the stipulation that the Iranian government buy products from Brazil worth at least 30 percent of the value of its oil sales. Iran did not fulfill its commitment, however, for the Shah's fascination with the most sophisticated gadgetry and his close affinity for the United States caused his government to order from the United States or Western Europe, even when ordering goods which Brazil could supply. (51) Barter deals in the Middle East include a 1978 agreement by Brazil and Algeria to exchange 24,000 Brazilian made Volkswagens for $62 million in crude oil. Brazilian officials have actively pursued Nigeria and Angola, Black Africa's two major oil producers, seeking contracts in industry and agriculture, along with increased deliveries of crude. (52)

Toward the socialist nations, the Brazilian military regime maintained correct, low-level ties in the 1960s. As economic diplomacy came to overshadow traditional diplomatic concerns in the 1970s, however, the government actively expanded relations with them. Indeed, in 1972 the Minister of Finance announced that next on the agenda of Brazil's export drive would be "the conquest of communist markets." Braspetro, and later Interbras, were conceived as means to this end.(53) To be sure, Brazil's large state agencies help smooth the way, for they are the type of organizations that negotiators from the socialist world are used to dealing with. During the Arab

158

oil embargo, the Soviets sold Petrobras 30 million barrels of diesel fuel. This opened the door to significantly expanded trade between the two countries, mainly
Soviet oil for Brazilian coffee, other commodities, and
manufactures such as textiles and shoes. When the Iran-
Iraq conflict cut Brazil's supplies in 1980, the Soviets
offered 24,000 barrels a day at least through the end of
the year.(54) Brazil has also established beneficial
trade relations with Poland. In 1976 the two signed a
five year, $3.2 billion agreement to exchange Brazilian
iron ore for Polish coal. Brazil has expanded trade with
China, exchanging iron ore, iron and steel products, and
hydroelectric construction contracts for Chinese oil.(55)
    To summarize, when Petrobras' domestic activities de-
veloped entrepreneurial elan in the 1970s, its international activities did likewise. Exploring abroad meant
creating new combinations of the means of production, and
the risks paid off with significant finds. Indeed, the
Majnoon field that Braspetro discovered in Iraq is a giant, containing estimated reserves of 7 billion barrels
of crude oil, with a potential output of 750,000 barrels
per day.(56) In the light of Brazil's acute foreign exchange shortage and of Iraqi nationalism, which led to
the takeover of all other foreign oil operations in Iraq
and which seemed liable to endanger future Braspetro operations there, in early 1980 Brazilian negotiators sold
their share of the field to Iraq. The Majnoon strike
thus will not produce the long run benefits of partnership, but it did relieve some short run pressure on the
balance of payments, and it served as the basis for
Iraq's stepped-up deliveries to Brazil when Iran's output
collapsed in 1979. The establishment of Interbras likewise constituted entrepreneurial institution-building.
Not only do its officials seek and gain new markets, but
it offers important marketing support for other entrepreneurial activities of the Brazilian state, particularly in the weapons and aircraft industries.

Creating Infrastructure: Transportation Policy and Energy Conservation

    After the first oil shock, the government committed
itself to revitalizing rail and maritime freight-hauling.
(57) One-third of the $1.2 billion Energy Mobilization
Fund is now earmarked for the Program for Alternate
Transportation, and rail-freight statistics already show
marked improvements. Although the share of freight handled by the railroads dropped from 23 percent in 1952 to
17 percent in the late 1960s and early 1970s, it had
rebounded to 20 percent by 1975 and government planners
hoped to raise it above 30 percent by 1980. Large sums
are allocated for improved signal systems and new rolling
stock so that the freight capacity of the main line

linking the Southeast and South will rise from 25 to 45 million tons per year. Two new electrified routes will be completed in the Southeast and South, the "Steel Line" between major steel producing and consuming centers and the "Soy Line" from southern agricultural-export areas to the port of Paranágua. In mid-1979 the national railroad ordered 1,800 new cars, including tank cars to carry alcohol and hopper cars to carry coal and charcoal. The transportation program will upgrade mass transit in the major urban areas. Existing commuter rail lines in Rio and São Paulo will be improved, the subway systems of those cities will be extended, and electrified streetcar and trolleybus systems will be installed or expanded in six cities. In São Paulo, for example, this program is creating a 270 kilometer trolleybus system, with 1,200 vehicles. This is one case where hydroelectricity can replace petroleum in transportation.

Finally, the Ministry of Transportation is investing to improve maritime transport, particularly along the coast where most of Brazil's major cities lie. In the postwar period, truckers took an even greater share of the nation's freight haulage from ships than from trains. Maritime shipping carried 25 percent of Brazil's freight in 1952, but only 10 percent in 1970. By 1975 this had risen only marginally, to 11 percent. The reequipping of the nation's merchant fleet, which rose from 344 vessels in 1970 to 1,031 in 1979, the creation of coal-handling facilities in most major ports, and the establishment of container facilities to speed and cheapen switching from one mode (ship, rail, road) to another should enable maritime transport to reverse its decline. This is crucial for Brazilian efforts to conserve fuels, since ships use only half the energy of trains and one-sixth the energy of trucks to transport the same load of freight a given distance.

Early results augur well for these investments. For example, in 1977 Portobras, the revitalized Brazilian port authority, completed a 15 kilometer rail spur from the main railroad line to the river port of Estrela in Rio Grande do Sul, constructed new loading equipment, warehouses, and silos in the port, and dredged a channel in Taquari River. The newly-outfitted port immediately attracted cargo by rail from the soy-growing areas of the southern interior for the 400 kilometer trip via inland waterway to the Atlantic port of Rio Grande. In 1980, its third year of operation, it is expected to handle one million tons of freight.(58)

INDIRECT STATE ENTREPRENEURSHIP: ENERGY DEVELOPMENT IN THE PRIVATE SECTOR

Alcohol Production

Since Brazil will not be able to produce enough petroleum to meet its liquid-fuel needs, policy makers and scientists have turned to alcohol as an alternative. In late 1975, President Geisel established a National Alcohol Program to produce anhydrous ethanol for mixing with gasoline. In 1979, President Figueiredo expanded the national commitment to alcohol, projecting that by 1985 Brazil would produce 10.7 billion liters per year. This can substitute for 170,000 barrels per day of crude petroleum, or roughly the equivalent of Brazilian domestic oil production in the 1970s.(59) Alcohol output rose from 664 million liters during the 1976-1977 harvest year to an estimated 3.8 billion liters in 1979-1980, significantly exceeding the 2.5 billion liter target proposed by Geisel in 1975. Figueiredo's expanded alcohol program went beyond gasohol by setting a target of 1.7 million all-alcohol cars by 1985. By October 1980, nearly 2,000 service stations, mainly in the cities, had alcohol pumps, and alcohol-powered cars were in such demand that buyers had to wait thirty to forty days for delivery.(60)

Indirect entrepreneurship - stimulating the private sector to produce more fuel - in some ways poses more challenges than direct entrepreneurship. In the case of both state monopolies - in petroleum and in electricity - state activities have been restricted to production and distribution of an energy resource. The state monopoly companies have owned, and thus exercised complete control over, the means of production, and they have operated with the assurance that effective demand existed for their product. In the case of the alcohol program, state technocrats must call forth synchronized output from five different branches of the private sector: farming, distilling, retail fuel distribution, capital goods production, and vehicle manufacturing. Planters must increase sugar cane output to meet the national targets, capital goods suppliers must produce distillery equipment and the distillers install it at the same pace, service-station owners must put in alcohol pumps, and the auto industry must produce enough all-alcohol vehicles to use the fuel, but not enough to cause shortages.

There are great risks to government credibility and national confidence in any crash program whose interdependent parts could easily fail to mesh properly, but so far official policies and a good measure of luck have kept the program close to target. Although planters did not expand their cane cultivation as rapidly as planned, low international sugar prices in the late 1970s led Brazil to reduce sugar sales on the world market, converting a greater proportion of the crop into alcohol. Indeed, the price had fallen so low by 1979 that the Institute of Sugar and Alcohol was paying Brazilian growers the support price of $280 per ton for sugar which it then sold abroad for $185, making alcohol production surely the preferable alternative.(61) High world sugar prices in 1980 started debates over the desirability of increased sugar exports, something which might put the squeeze on alcohol output. This, of course, could cause grave problems for distillers, producers of distilling equipment, and owners of alcohol-powered cars. When the Iran-Iraq conflict cut Brazilian oil imports, however, the government reaffirmed official commitment to the alcohol program by halting sugar exports.(62)

For the Brazilian economy, the all-alcohol cars save in two ways: they replace imported oil and, because they can run on hydrated ethanol, they cut the cost of fuel-alcohol production. Hydrated ethanol costs nearly 20 percent less to manufacture than anhydrous ethanol. Hydrated ethanol cannot be used in gasohol, however, because in the presence of gasoline the 5 percent water in solution with it will precipitate out and collect in the fuel tank.

The development of alcohol-powered cars is a result of policies designed to reduce the nation's technological dependence. The government has financed alcohol-combustion research at the Air Force Research Center since 1974 and, as a result, the technical norms to be met by the multinational auto firms producing the cars are norms devised in Brazil. When the alcohol engines began coming off the assembly line in late 1979, they were the first automotive engines produced in Brazil for which a royalty did not have to be paid to a foreign parent company.(63)

Policy makers of the entrepreneurial state negotiated with representatives of the auto industry, winning agreement to the production target of 1.7 million all-alcohol cars by 1985. Since all-alcohol engines are new to Brazil, public policy provides incentives to speed their acceptance. The sales tax, annual highway use tax, and fuel price at the pump are lower, and financing terms are easier than for gasoline models.(64)

There can be no question about the entrepreneurial role of state officials in the alcohol program. They restructured markets and created new combinations of the means of production in five different but interdependent branches of economic activity in the private sector. To this end, they funded research and development leading to the commercial adoption of a new technology.

Coal Production

Coal has been selected to take the place of fuel oil, the main energy source used in Brazil's rapidly expanding

162

industrial sector. After the second oil shock, the government proposed a program to increase annual coal production from 10 million to 35 million tons by 1985. Brazil's southern states have sizeable coal reserves, estimated at 22 billion tons, although this is relatively low-grade coal with a high ash content.

The task for public policy, therefore, is to get Brazilian industries to accept the coal. In September 1979 officials took a major step to achieve this goal. The Ministers of Industry and Commerce, of Mines and Energy, and of Transportation signed an agreement with the presidents of the "sindicatos" (associations) of cement firms and of coal mining firms to begin substituting coal for fuel oil in the cement industry, an industry which consumes at least 20 percent of the fuel oil used in Brazil. By 1984, the cement industry should burn 5.6 million tons of coal, saving the nation 2.8 million tons of fuel oil. To this end the signatories agreed to perform the following tasks: the coal industry will raise its output to meet the target, the cement industry will progressively increase its coal consumption according to an agreed-upon timetable, and, during the transition, government subsidies will neutralize fuel-price differences among firms in the sector, the Ministry of Mines and Energy will install coal depots in five cities and improve existing depots in six other places, and the Ministry of Transports will improve eight ports, enhance the navigability of three rivers in Rio Grande do Sul, build feeder rail spurs to the coal fields, and upgrade the rail lines between coal mining areas in the South and major cement-producing areas of the Southeast.(65) These plans to create new transportation facilities for the coal are very ambitious and costly. In the 1980s climate of financial austerity, it will take an extraordinary amount of political will to avoid significant delays.

ENERGY POLICY AND THE POLITICAL ORDER IN BRAZIL

Entrepreneurial Technocrats and the Bourgeoisie

State technocrats have played entrepreneurial roles in Brazil at least since Vargas' rule in the 1930s. As the preceding sections demonstrate, perhaps the best recent examples of state entrepreneurship can be found in policies, institutions, and initiatives to develop or secure energy resources. Consider the set of acronyms identifying public commitment to new tasks: Petrobras, Interbras, Braspetro, Eletrobras, Nuclebras, Portobras, Embraer, Imbel, and many others. Not only do Brazilian state technocrats innovate directly, through the productive organizations they control, but they also innovate indirectly. That is, by selectively applying carrot-and-stick measures such as credit, tax, and tariff policies,

import permits, and regulatory requirements and restrictions, they have coaxed or coerced innovation out of the
private sector. The fuel-alcohol and coal programs each
involve a web of complex policies emanating from at least
three ministries, policies ambitiously designed to elicit
new behavior from three or more branches of the economy.

Federal and state agencies have initiated and sustained the development of new technologies. Programs to
harness the photosynthetic energy of plants, to produce
shale oil commercially, to develop fusion energy, and
even to design and export aircraft and weapons systems
have resulted from initiatives by state agencies.(66)
Support from the state has thus helped Brazilian scientists and engineers move onto technologically uncharted
terrain where they are developing the new technologies
themselves, rather than importing them from already industrialized nations.

What is the relationship between the Brazilian bourgeoisie and the entrepreneurial technocrats? It is clear
that the technocrats not only control powerful means of
production themselves, but they shape the rules for the
private sector as well. In setting the direction for the
national economy, state policy makers have easily overshadowed the Brazilian bourgeoisie in a pattern of domination consistent with the nation's historical experience. Indeed, one analyst argues persuasively that the
state has dominated class and interest groups not just
since the Revolution of 1930 but throughout Brazilian
history.(67) This by no means implies that state dominance conflicts with the general interests of Brazil's
industrial and commercial bourgeoisie, despite the conflicts that arise with specific groups over specific policies. In a penetrating analysis of the relationship
among state, multinational, and local private capital in
Brazil's recent industrial expansion, one scholar demonstrates that the local bourgeoisie needs the support of
the state and that the shared interests of the two in the
preservation and expansion of the system far outweigh
their conflicts over specifics.(68) After all, with 7
percent annual GDP growth rates and an industrial growth
rate averaging more than 8 percent, the bourgeoisie has
unquestionably multiplied its wealth.

The case highlights an insight from Schumpeter's later work. Implicit in his early discussion of entrepreneurship was the notion that entrepreneurs come from the
world of private business and thus are pathbreakers of
and for the bourgeoisie. This notion reflects a frequently expressed interpretation of the socio-political
changes that accompany the process of industrialization,
namely that the ascendant bourgeoisie takes control of
its nation and sets the direction not only of its economy
but of its political system as well. Schumpeter, in his
later work, rejected that interpretation. In reflecting

on the class role of the bourgeoisie, he observed: "But without protection by some nonbourgeois group, the bourgeoisie is politically helpless and unable not only to lead its nation but even to take care of its particular class interest. Which amounts to saying it needs a master."(69) In the case of industrial policy in general and energy policy in particular, entrepreneurial technocrats of Brazil's interventionist state have played the role of master, creating conditions under which the bourgeoisie could enrich itself. In this way they have very effectively looked after the bourgeoisie's class interest. To borrow words from Barrington Moore, Jr., the Brazilian industrialists have "exchanged the right to rule for the right to make money."(70) Thus for Brazil, more obviously than for many other nations, there is a relevant insight in Marx's assertion that the state is the executive committee for the bourgeoisie.(71)

Energy Entrepreneurship, Political Authoritarianism, and Social Welfare

The state has certainly been entrepreneurial in the cases covered here, but what are the implications of this type of energy entrepreneurship for most Brazilians and for the future political order? Though not the focus of the present study, it should be acknowledged that the past decade's economic expansion has occurred at great social cost. Numerous studies point to the nation's increasingly inegalitarian income distribution, sharply rising rates of infant mortality, outbreaks of epidemic disease, increasing industrial accident figures, and other depressing social indicators.(72)

On the international level, Brazil's dependency remains. Brazilian policy makers created a diversified industrial economy in order to reduce Brazil's dependence on foreign countries but, ironically, they followed the model of the United States, a model requiring abundant supplies of cheap energy, particularly petroleum. The United States, at the time it built its industrial economy and for many decades thereafter, was self-sufficient in petroleum. Brazil never was, a factor that did not concern policy makers until 1973, since inexhaustible cheap petroleum seemed readily available from foreign sources. Not only did the era of cheap oil end abruptly in 1973, but so did the assurance of supply, no matter what the price. Public policy had concentrated Brazil's sources of oil supply in one of the most consistently volatile regions of the postwar world, the Middle East. In this way not only the policy makers but all Brazil's citizens have found themselves at the mercy of forces over which they have no control at all, as the Arab oil embargo of 1973, the Iranian revolution of 1979, and the Iran-Iraq war of 1980 all demonstrated.

To criticize Brazil's entrepreneurial policy makers for creating an oil-dependent economy is not to single them out as uniquely shortsighted. Throughout the post-war period, economists, geologists, and policy makers from all the industrialized nations underestimated the speed at which energy demand would grow and at which petroleum would replace other fuels such as coal, while they overestimated the rate at which petroleum reserves and production would expand.(73) The problem lies in the energy-intensive model adopted by both planners and the public, not only in Brazil but virtually everywhere. In the most creative and insightful analysis of contemporary energy policy yet to appear, Leon Lindberg convincingly argues that this model has grave implications for social welfare, individual liberty, and the political order. For Brazil, where the well-being of the poor has already declined in recent times, his analysis leads one to predict that future entrepreneurial successes by the energy technocrats will further erode the standard of living and reduce the rights of citizenship for the majority.

Lindberg points out that the policy makers have consistently developed supply-oriented energy policies, that is, policies designed to meet demand rather than conservation-oriented policies designed to manage and limit demand. Writing the summary chapters of a seven nation research project that included several years of business-as-usual behavior by policy makers after the oil shock of 1973, he observed: "Projections of demand, and the increasing growth rate of demand are still treated essentially as the givens of policy, not as objects of policy."(74)

National energy policy-making systems thus did not show themselves capable of self-correction, even after the first oil shock. For this reason Lindberg prefers the term "energy syndrome" to "energy crisis." In medical terms, "crisis" refers to the turning point in a disease, a transformation which leads either to recovery or death. "Syndrome" implies no such turning point but is rather "a group of symptoms that occur together and that describe a system malfunction." Among the supply oriented symptoms Lindberg highlights are "an interacting set of political, institutional, and structural obstacles that constrain the search for alternative policies."(75)

One factor constraining the search for alternative policies is the peculiar decision making dynamic of large scale bureaucracies, a dynamic that accounts for their success. They take complex problems and break them down into their component parts, each of which is analyzed and solved in a separate, specialized sub-unit. Although the problem under consideration may be complex and involve sharp value tradeoffs, as is the case with energy policy, problem solvers and decision makers working on each of its component aspects typically deal with only one value. For them, the tradeoffs are not apparent or at least not their responsibility.(76)

To illustrate, combustion and materials specialists working on the design of alcohol engines would have no part in the decision to plant cane and distill alcohol from it. Their job satisfaction would derive from establishing engine specifications and testing components to make alcohol-powered cars a reality. They would not have to be responsible for the fact that the alcohol program has raised food prices by pushing food crops off the best land near São Paulo, nor for the fact that refinery effluents have seriously aggravated water pollution.(77)

At the top level of the bureaucracy, where one might expect recognition of the blind spots arising from this bureaucratic dynamic and comprehensive treatment of the value conflicts ignored there, the tradeoffs are seldom clearly considered. "There is a tendency in such a system for private or sectoral values to prevail over or to constrain general or public values. Private or sectoral payoffs are simpler, narrower in scope, and more immediate. Higher-level payoffs to 'society' involve complicated social effects hard to predict, explain, or even observe."(78)

Officials holding peak positions in the top-level organizations, argues Lindberg, possess a value structure that favors big, complex, supply oriented solutions to energy problems. Members of the "industrial technocracy" are "the preeminent carriers of a cultural orientation that embodies a manipulative and anthropocentric attitude toward man and nature (and natural resources), the elevation of efficiency and productivity as prime values, and an uncritical faith in the technical fix as the solvent of all problems."(79) The evolution and characteristics of Brazilian energy policy are surely consistent with Lindberg's general observations. The nation's entrepreneurial technocrats take pride in thinking big.

The pattern of interest organization in Brazil reinforces this bias for bigness and supports outcomes favorable to private or sectoral groups. For two key sectors, petroleum and electricity, state technocrats control the means of production and articulate sectoral interests. In sectors where the technocrats do not exercise direct control, the corporative nature of interest representation in Brazil provides for officially recognized "sindicatos" that speak for the interest of the sector and give it a voice in policy making bodies. In this system, big organizations have far greater access to the technocrats than small ones, and individuals and "society" have none at all. As one advocate for conversion of manioc, rather than sugar cane, into alcohol put it, "...manioc is being forgotten in the discussion of energy sources, because, unlike sugar, it lacks a godfather...."(80)

Manioc, a crop traditionally planted by poor peasants on small plots, cannot compete politically with the "sugar sheiks" who control large plantations and wield great political power. As initially proposed, the alcohol program was to create jobs that would redistribute income downward in poor rural areas. In practice it has created relatively few truly new jobs and has concentrated in fewer hands ever larger tracts of land in rural São Paulo where most of the cane is grown. Meanwhile, experimentation with manioc cultivation and fermentation are continuing. If the technocracy should favor manioc in the future, past experience should lead us to expect official support for mechanization on large landholdings, dispossessing peasants and creating a corps of "manioc sheiks" alongside the "sugar sheiks." Manioc would then have its own godfather.

In the modern bureaucracies of Brazil, as elsewhere, complex problems are treated by separate specialized subunits in a way that obscures the tradeoffs. Until the oil shock of 1979, even the major programs such as oil, electricity, alcohol, and coal were developed and managed without close coordination and explicit recognition of the tradeoffs among them. It took an externally imposed crisis situation, one so serious that it threatened the very survival of the system, for decision makers finally to treat once discrete energy policies as parts of a whole. With the nation's usual crude oil stocks down from three months' to less than one month's supply, and the redoubled OPEC price schedule endangering Brazil's credit on the world market, policy makers finally acknowledged the tradeoffs that investment in one energy resource meant for the development of the others.

The externally imposed crisis was so grave, said President Figueiredo in an address to the nation, that the government had no alternative but to take "war economy" measures. He "appealed to the patriotism" of his technocratic ministers "to contain their entrepreneurial drive" during this reordering of national priorities. For the first time the president advocated real, rather than hortatory, conservation measures.(81)

The newly created National Energy Council set out to check further growth in oil consumption. Its members were completely at sea with so novel a concept as conservation, particularly since many argued that conservation and growth were incompatible. Planning Minister Mario Henrique Simonsen, for example, wrote that "...the only effective rationing is through stagnation (or semistagnation)."(82) Council members therefore skirted the thorny problem of enforcing conservation on productive sectors of the economy and chose instead to focus on individual use of passenger cars. They mandated measures that had been tried successfully before, such as raising gasoline prices and closing filling stations at night and

on weekends. These, however, could have only a relatively small impact on petroleum consumption because the
"easy" conservation had already been achieved. For example, because real gasoline prices had doubled since 1974,
the amount consumed per car had dropped by more than 40
percent since then.(83)

The substantial rise in petroleum imports during the
late 1970s was due not to gasoline consumption but to
rising fuel oil and diesel fuel use in industry and commercial transportation, the sectors dear to the heart of
the industrial technocracy. If oil imports were to be
reduced a bit and then frozen, as the president had ordered, policies would have to enforce conservation upon
these privileged sectors. In mid-July, the Council
therefore tried monthly delivery quotas. It soon abandoned them, when the economic chaos they caused promised
to be as economically and politically damaging as the
stagnation Simonsen had evoked. In little more than a
month, fuel-short factories began to shut down, har-
vesting equipment stood idle, and the roads were lined
with out-of-gas trucks.(84) After the failure of the
delivery quotas, the government had no alternative but
to try price rationing.

Two factors facilitated the shift to price rationing
in August. First, Simonsen lost his leverage to oppose
fuel price rises when he was ousted in a cabinet shake
up. Second, advocates of conservation via the price
mechanism made a convincing case for their approach. Indeed, their data showed that Simonsen himself, through
subsidized fuel oil prices designed to help industry, had
contributed significantly to the soaring oil imports after 1974. This subsidy had distorted Brazil's energy
price structure to the point that imported oil was much
cheaper than domestically produced energy resources,
causing a shift away from the latter and toward fuel oil.
Firewood in 1979 cost twice as much as fuel oil for the
same caloric output, steam coal cost two and one-half
times as much, and hydroelectricity (at the low, industrial rate) cost nearly six times as much. Fuel oil sold
for a lower price in Brazil than in all but the oil-ex-
porting countries.(85) In August the government raised
diesel and fuel oil prices by 50 percent, halting the
growth of oil imports. Further measures, such as the
expansion of fuel alcohol and the banning after 1980 of
petroleum derivatives in crop drying, should enable the
economy to grow over the short run, even with imports
frozen.

The technocracy could not ignore economic tradeoffs
that endangered the security of Brazil's energy supplies
and the nation's access to international capital markets.
After all, these threats directly challenged the viability of the economy that the technocrats guide and, hence,
their very raison d'être. Domestic social and political

tradeoffs, however, do not force themselves upon the consciousness of the policy makers in the same way. Thus they continue to be ignored. These costs are not imposed personally upon the technocrats, but rather upon Brazil's poor majority. They do not even occur in the domain for which the technocrats accept responsibility, specifically the most modern sectors of the economy. By narrowly circumscribing their area of competence, Brazilian technocratic policy makers can avoid confronting the evidence that, on social and political grounds, the model they have created is basically flawed. In the same spirit, the alcohol program is a perfect example of a supply-oriented policy designed to prove that times have not changed and that with significant though not fundamental modifications the Brazilian economic model remains viable.

The flaw in the model is one much more apparent to political or social analysts concerned with the well being of the majority than to technocrats concerned principally with economic output statistics. The roots of the flaw lie in the economic imperative of the energy syndrome, which drives technocrats to confront the energy squeeze by investing ever greater sums in order to guarantee to the economy the energy supplies to which it has become accustomed. Such investments require a tradeoff in the form of constraints on consumption. This implies a worsening standard of living for poor and middle income people, because it is those least able to defend their interests whose consumption will be sacrificed. They can be expected to protest over their declining consumption and to oppose the system that inflicts such sacrifices upon them. To protect the system from such challenges, those ruling it will tighten repressive controls, eroding or denying the rights of citizenship to the protesting sectors. The repression could ultimately aggravate tensions to the point that the system could break down politically. In parallel fashion, the spiralling energy investments could soak up so much capital that the economic system itself would stagnate and break down.

In energy, the investments are gargantuan. One Brazilian econometric study estimated the capital costs and foreign exchange requirements of three possible scenarios from 1981 through 1995. The most plausible scenario pegs capital investments in electricity and fuels at $170 billion over the fifteen years. Energy investments represent 11.5 percent of gross capital formation between 1981 and 1985, rising to 16.6 percent between 1991 and 1995. (86) Indeed, if the Brazilian energy sector manages to implement its investment plans, by 1985 it will be absorbing 8 percent of the nation's gross domestic product, compared to a historical rate of 2 percent.(87)

The projected foreign exchange costs for imported energy come to $121 billion for the fifteen year period.

These energy imports will consume 30 percent of the value of exports between 1981 and 1985. The ratio falls to 15 percent for the 1991-1995 period, owing to a projected dramatic rise in the volume of nonenergy exports. The drain on Brazil will undoubtedly be worse than forecast in the study, however, because it used a crude oil cost of $18 per barrel, while international oil prices had risen to more than $33 by late 1980.(88)

Both the cost of imported fuel and the investment figures represent production by Brazilians which will not be consumed by them. These sums will go to buy either energy or the capital facilities that will produce energy at a later date. The Brazilians who will consume the energy, however, are not likely to be the same ones who sacrificed their consumption, for the producers and consumers come from different classes. Lindberg explains the dynamic: "Individual consumers will pay higher prices for energy and other goods; welfare programs will be eroded and tax policies will be manipulated to provide direct and indirect subsidies to increase energy production; ...inflationary forces will be controlled by deflating the economy and accepting higher levels of unemployment (or lower wages)...."(89) Employment is further threatened because energy entrepreneurs must compete for financing in the same capital market with manufacturers, builders, and other employers. Better able to pay the highest interest rates, the energy projects will drive up the cost of borrowed money for everyone. They will thus absorb capital that would otherwise have gone to different borrowers, most of whom are likely to be small businesses that employ relatively high amounts of labor for a given unit of capital. Many of these small businesses will not only be unable to expand but will close down, throwing their present labor force out of work.

High capital investment in energy resources will not compensate the unemployed by creating a fund of stable jobs, though it will create some initially, during construction. Once basic facilities have been built, the production of electricity, oil, and gas employ relatively few people per unit of output. Coal production traditionally employs more, though this should not be overestimated for Brazil where the coal expansion plans involve highly mechanized strip mining. Only the alcohol program is labor intensive, and its architects are seeking to mechanize as much as possible. The Brazilian authors of the econometric study cited above therefore describe the future in terms very similar to Lindberg's: "The enormous volume of resources committed to the energy sector will certainly result in the sacrifice of other industrial and agricultural sectors and in the reduction of funds for health, education, housing, and urban infrastructure."(90)

Such a situation surely has ominous implications for
the Brazilian political order. The magnitude of sacrifice demanded by the energy syndrome is unlikely to be
forthcoming voluntarily in a representative regime under
the rule of law. Brazil, of course, has had neither a
representative regime nor the rule of law since 1964.
Nevertheless, the present military rulers have initiated
a political opening that is inching in that direction,
even if it presently falls far short of the "democratization" that most wish it to be. The energy syndrome,
if unchecked, is likely to abort the political liberalization and may well make the future political order even
more repressive than during the worst years of the early
1970s.

One way out of the impasse, of course, would be to
reduce fundamentally the amount of energy required by the
economy for each unit of ouput. This would not necessarily require slowing economic growth, but it would mean
restructuring it so that a different mix of goods and
services would be produced. Consider, for instance, the
impact of radically slowing the growth of output of passenger cars. One study compared three scenarios for the
auto fleet in Brazil from 1980 to 2000, using different
growth rates: (1) the recent historical growth rate of
16 percent slowly declining to 8 percent, (2) a steady
growth of 6.3 percent, and (3) a steady growth of 3.3
percent. In the year 2000, the combined demand for gasoline and alcohol would come to 74, 49, and 30 tons of
petroleum equivalent, respectively.(91) Not only would
the demand for motor fuel be sharply lower with the lower
growth rates, but the savings in construction of highways, parking facilities, and the like would then pay for
more mass transit to move the urban population in the
absence of cars, as well as for other public services and
investments.

Along these lines, one Brazilian economist suggests
that private cars be banned from main thoroughfares so
that busses can ply them without being held up in the
ever slower traffic jams caused by the exploding auto
population. Busses, by traveling their routes faster,
would greatly increase their capacity to handle passengers, and the expanded ridership would travel more hap-
pily since travel time could be greatly reduced: "Without paving another square meter, without building another
kilometer of subway, and without a single new bus, it
would be possible perhaps to double the flow of passengers on mass transit."(92) Such radical and long-range
perspectives are surely alien to the value structure of
today's industrial technocracy.

These observations by Brazilian economists are consistent with the insights of a Swedish analyst, who noted
that private consumption is more energy intensive than
public consumption and that "Future energy demand will

increase much more rapidly if we let private consumption increase quickly."(93) In Brazil, the government that is calling for sacrifices to reduce energy consumption could take the long view expressed above. It is already investing in rail and bus transit in urban areas, but busses can only be attractive if the private cars clogging the arteries are removed so the busses can proceed. If the government desired to face the energy squeeze by favoring more energy efficient public consumption, one early step probably would be to severely restrict the use of private cars in cities on workdays. This, however, would create a context directly threatening to the auto industry. Indeed, it would reverse the thrust of recent policies, for we have already noted that the alcohol program represents an effort to preserve for the auto industry the economic model of the bygone era of cheap energy. Brazil, thanks to its industrial technocracy, is now a prisoner of its past sucesses.

NOTES

1.   This chapter draws heavily on data I generated for my lengthier discussion of the patterns of energy supply and consumption in Brazil, "The Energy Profile of Brazil," in Kenneth R. Stunkel, ed., National Energy Profiles (New York: Praeger, forthcoming January 1981). I am grateful to Praeger Publishers for permission to include some passages of that study in the present chapter. I am also grateful to the Research Foundation of the City University of New York for support through a PSC-BHE Research Award that enabled me to visit Brazil in June and July 1980. That visit enabled me to gather some of the data that appear here and to exchange ideas with Brazilian scholars currently working on energy policy. The faculty seminar of the Energy Policy Studies Program at Hunter College, CUNY, the Technocracy Seminar sponsored by the Center for Inter-American Relations, and the "Brazilian Model Revisited" seminar of the Center for Developing-Area Studies at McGill University provided valuable critical forums to present and sharpen concepts and data which appear here. I am deeply indebted to the following colleagues whose perceptive critiques of an early draft enabled me to recast materials, sharpen my focus, and eliminate error: Thomas Bruneau, T. Owen Carroll, Daniel R. Gross, Marcos Gianetti da Fonseca, Thomas A. Sladek, Mark Sonnenblick, and Franklin Tugwell. Of course, neither these constructive critics nor the CUNY Research Foundation bear any responsibility for the interpretation and materials that I have chosen to present here.
2.   Erickson, "Energy Profile"; 1946 data from J.A. Wilberg, "Consumo Brasileiro de Energia," Energia Elétrica 27 (1974), as quoted in José Goldemberg, "Política

Energética," in Henrique Rattner, ed., <u>Brasil 1990: Ca-minhos Alternativos do Desenvolvimento</u> (Sao Paulo: Bra-siliense, 1979), p. 178.

3. Frederico Magalhaes Gomes and João Lizardo R.H. de Araujo, <u>O Papel dos Combustiveis no Balanço Energético Brasileiro</u> (Rio de Janeiro: COPPE/UFRJ, 1980), pp. 2-6.

4. For comparative analysis demonstrating that the United States is the world's most energy-inefficient economy, see Kenneth Paul Erickson, "The Political Economy of Energy Consumption in Industrial Societies," in Robert M. Lawrence and Martin O. Heisler, eds., <u>International Energy Policy</u> (Lexington, Mass.: Lexington Books, 1980), pp. 113-143.

5. <u>International Financial Statistics</u> 32 (July 1979): 80-81; <u>New York Times</u>, 3 October 1980, p. D3.

6. Joseph A. Schumpeter, <u>The Theory of Economic Development</u> (New York: Oxford University Press, 1961), pp. 74-94; first published, 1909.

7. See, for example, the superb analysis of state entrepreneurship in Peter Evans, <u>Dependent Development: the Alliance of Multinational, State, and Local Capital in Brazil</u> (Princeton: Princeton University Press, 1979), pp. 213-273.

8. On income concentration via public policy and the impact on the working class, see Kenneth Paul Erickson and Patrick V. Peppe, "Dependent Capitalist Development, U.S. Foreign Policy, and Repression of the Working Class in Chile and Brazil," <u>Latin American Perspectives</u> 3 (Winter 1976): 19-44; data on highways from <u>Anuário Estatistico do Brasil, 1956</u> (Instituto Brasileiro de Geografia e Estatistica, 1957), p. 171, and (1977), p. 573.

9. Peter Seaborn Smith, <u>Oil and Politics in Modern Brazil</u> (Toronto: Macmillan of Canada, 1976), pp. 1-102.

10. John M. Blair, <u>The Control of Oil</u> (New York: Pantheon, 1976), pp. 81-85; quote from the general manager of the Iraq Petroleum Comany, Ibid., p. 82.

11. The Economist Intelligence Unit, <u>Quarterly Economic Review for Brazil</u>, 1978, p. 21.

12. Judith Tendler, <u>Electric Power in Brazil: Entrepreneurship in the Public Sector</u> (Cambridge: Harvard University Press, 1968), pp. 1-42 and passim.

13. Jean-Marie Martin, <u>Processus d'industrialisation et développement energétique du Brésil</u> (Paris: Institut des Hautes Etudes d'Amérique Latine, 1966), pp. 274-275, 284-285.

14. Instituto Brasileiro de Geografia e Estatística, <u>O Brasil em Numeros</u> (Rio de Janeiro: Instituto Brasileiro de Geografia e Estatistica, 1966), p. 64; Smith, <u>Oil and Politics</u>, pp. 131, 135.

15. <u>Anuário Estatístico do Brasil, 1972</u> (Instituto Brasileiro de Geografia e Estatistica, 1973), p. 202; Frank Niering, Jr. "Brazil: Offshore Search at Crucial Stage," <u>Petroleum Economist</u>, June 1978, p. 232.

174

16.   Latin America Economic Report, 20 July 1979, p. 220.

17.   Erickson, "Energy Profile."

18.   Jornal do Brasil, 5 July 1979, p. 17; Folha de São Paulo, 22 July 1979, 12 June 1980, p. 21.

19.   Petroleum Economist, January 1977, pp. 29-30.

20.   Adilson de Oliveira, João Lizardo R.H. de Araújo, and Luiz Pinguelli Rosa, "Impasse Atual e Perspectivas a Longo Prazo da Política Energética no Brasil," Encontros com a Civilização Brasileira 23 (May 1980): 25.

21.   Erickson, "Energy Profile."

22.   Folha de São Paulo, 19 June 1980, p. 19.

23.   Brazilian Federal Government Law No. 2004, 3 October 1953.

24.   Text of Cals' telex on this topic, with commentary, reproduced in A Brecha: Jornal da Associação Profissional de Geólogos do Estado do Rio de Janeiro, May 1980, pp. 6-8.

25.   The issue of A Brecha, May 1980, cited above contributes to the debate, as did several panels at the 1980 meeting of the Sociedade Brasileira pelo Progresso da Ciência.

26.   Frank Niering, Jr., "Brazil: Offshore Search," p. 234.

27.   For examples of abuses, see Blair, Control of Oil, pp. 25-120.

28.   Anuário Estatístico do Brasil, 1978 (Rio de Janeiro: Instituto Brasileiro de Geografia e Estatistica, 1979), p. 498.

29.   Latin America Regional Reports: Brazil, 9 November 1979, p. 4; Eletrobrás, Plano de atendimento aos requisitos de energia eletrica até 1995 (Brasilia: Eletrobras, September 1979), p. 6 annex and passim.

30.   Tendler, Electric Power in Brazil.

31.   Eletrobrás, Plano de atendimento, pp. 2.5 and 2.6.

32.   O Brasil em Números: Apéndice do Anuário Estatístico do Brasil, 1960 (Brazil: Instituto Brasileiro de Geografia e Estatistica, 1961), pp. 58-59.

33.   O Estado de São Paulo, 8 April 1979, pp. 7-9.

34.   O Estado de São Paulo, 23 August 1979, pp. 6, 21; 25 August 1979, p. 5; 9 September 1979, p. 21; 20 September 1979, p. 6; 29 September 1979, p. 6.

35.   Jornal do Brasil (Rio de Janeiro), 10 May 1979. See also José Goldemberg, Energia Nuclear no Brasil: as Origens das Decisões (Sao Paulo: Editora Hucitec, 1978).

36.   Isto E, 11 June 1980, pp. 12-19.

37.   Text of security document in Folha de São Paulo, 6 June 1980, p. 5; for the descriptions of the security community see Veja, 25 June 1980, pp. 20-25, and Isto É, 25 June 1980, pp. 15-17.

38. Evaluation of Projeto de lei no. 16/80, annexed to memo from Colonel Eduardo Emílio Maurell Muller, Secretário de Coordenação e Planejamento, to the Chefe da Casa Civil of the Rio Grande do Sul governor (Of. SCP/ 138-80, Porto Alegre, 1 April 1980).

39. Irvin C. Bupp and Jean-Claude Derian, Light Water: How the Nuclear Dream Dissolved (New York: Basic Books, 1978).

40. Joseph A. Schumpeter, "The Creative Response in Economic History," Journal of Economic History 7 (November 1947): 153.

41. Details on the Angra problems in Isto É, 27 September 1978, pp. 80-83, quote pp. 81-82; Norman Gall, "Nuclear Setbacks," Forbes, 27 November 1978, pp. 104-110; Der Spiegel, 19 September 1978; O Estado de São Paulo, 13 April 1979, p. 7; 17 April 1979, p. 5.

42. These cases and others in this subsection are discussed in greater detail in Erickson, "Energy Profile." Iraqi supply figures from Petrobrás News as reported in Latin America Weekly Report, 3 October 1980, p. 7.

43. Latin America Weekly Report, 26 September 1980, p. 9.

44. Ronald M. Schneider, Brazil: Foreign Policy of a Future World Power (Boulder: Westview, 1976), pp. 107-125.

45. Latin America Weekly Report, 16 November 1979, p. 29.

46. The Economist Intelligence Unit, Quarterly Economic Review for Brazil 1 (1979): 20.

47. O Estado de São Paulo, 27 May 1979, p. 56; Latin America Economic Report, 4 May 1979, p.3; 13 July 1979, p. 1; Latin America Regional Reports: Brazil, 12 September 1980, p. 4.

48. O Estado de São Paulo, 27 May 1979, pp. 6-8; Latin America Political Report, 4 March 1977, p. 66; Latin America Regional Reports: Brazil, 9 November 1979, p. 3; Clovis Brigagao, "Brazil's Military Industry: A Discussion of Recent Developments," LARU Working Papers 27 (December 1979): 22-41.

49. Folha de São Paulo, 15 June 1980, pp. 6 and 34.

50. Anuario Estatístico do Brasil, 1976 (Rio de Janeiro: Instituto Brasileiro de Geografia e Estatistica, 1977), pp. 246, 264.

51. Petroleum Economist, June 1978, p. 235; Platt's Oilgram News, 25 September 1978, p. 3; O Estado de São Paulo, 22 August 1979.

52. Erickson, "Energy Profile."

53. Stanley E. Hilton, "Brazil's Bilateral Relations," manuscript, January 1976, pp. V6-V18; quote p. V11; Jornal do Brasil, February 1976, pp. 1, 23.

54. New York Times, 3 October 1980, p. D3.

55. Erickson, "Energy Profile."

56. Petroleum Economist, October 1978, p. 442; Platt's Oilgram News, 23 May 1979, pp. 3-4; O Estado de São Paulo, 22 September 1979, p. 26.

57. Data on rail and maritime transport from Conjuntura Econômica, April 1978, pp. 88-91; May 1978, pp. 67-70; May 1979, p. 65; August 1979, p. 71-72; The Economist Intelligence Unit, Quarterly Economic Review for Brazil 4 (1974): 8; O Estado de São Paulo, 5 April 1979, p. 35; Latin America Economic Report, 19 October 1979, p. 327.

58. Folha de São Paulo, 19 June 1980, p. 17; 20 June 1980, p. 22.

59. Jornal do Brasil, 5 July 1979, p. 17.

60. O Estado de São Paulo, 12 October 1980, p. 156.

61. O Globo (Rio de Janeiro), 13 May 1979, p. 36; O Estado de São Paulo, 22 August 1979, p. 24; 24 August 1979, p. 26.

62. Latin America Weekly Report, 10 October 1980, p. 10.

63. Latin American Economic Report, 29 June 1979, p. 99; 14 September 1979, p. 286; O Estado de São Paulo, 2 August 1979, p. 34; O Globo, 28 August 1979, p. 25.

64. O Estado de São Paulo, 29 August 1979; 12 October 1980, p. 156; Latin America Economic Report, 12 October 1979, p. 315.

65. O Estado de São Paulo, 20 September 1979, p. 35.

66. On shale oil and fusion energy, see Erickson, "Energy Profile."

67. Raymundo Faoro, Os Donos do Poder: Formação do Patronato Político Brasileiro (Porto Alegre: Globo, 1958); on the domination of state economic policy makers over bourgeois interest groups, see Nathaniel H. Leff, Economic Policy-Making and Development in Brazil, 1947-1964 (New York: Wiley, 1968), pp. 32-34, 50, 73-74, and passim; on state domination of working-class organizations, see Kenneth Paul Erickson, The Brazilian Corporative State and Working-Class Politics (Berkeley: University of California Press, 1977).

68. Evans, Dependent Development, pp. 41-43, 270, 287.

69. Joseph A. Schumpeter, Capitalism, Socialism, and Democracy, 3rd ed. (New York: Harper, 1950), p. 138.

70. Barrington Moore, Jr., Social Origins of Dictatorship and Democracy: Lord and Peasant in the Making of the Modern World (Boston: Beacon, 1966), p. 437.

71. Karl Marx and Friedrich Engels, "Manifesto of the Communist Party," in Saul K. Padover, ed., Karl Marx on Revolution (New York: McGraw-Hill, 1971), p. 82.

72. Sylvia Ann Hewlett, The Cruel Dilemmas of Development: Twentieth-Century Brazil (New York: Basic Books, 1980), pp. 163-184; Erickson and Peppe, "Dependent Capitalist Development"; Erickson, Brazilian Corporative State, pp. 160-168.

73. Joel Darmstadter and Hans H. Landsberg, "The Economic Background," in Raymond Vernon, ed., The Oil Crisis (New York: Norton, 1976), pp. 15-37, and Blair, Control of Oil, pp. 4-15.

74. Leon N. Lindberg, ed., The Energy Syndrome: Comparing National Responses to the Energy Crisis (Lexington, Mass.: Lexington Books, 1977), p. 328, italics his. The seven countries are the United States, Canada, Great Britain, France, Sweden, Hungary, and India.

75. Lindberg, ed., Energy Syndrome, p. xi.

76. Lindberg, ed., Energy Syndrome, pp. 338-343; Lindberg relies heavily here on John Steinbrunner, The Cybernetic Theory of Decisions (Princeton: Princeton University Press, 1974).

77. On the social and environmental costs of the alcohol program, see Erickson, "Energy Profile."

78. Lindberg, ed., Energy Syndrome, p. 342, citing Steinbrunner, Cybernetic Theory, p. 146.

79. Lindberg, ed., Energy Syndrome, p. 339.

80. O Globo, 10 September 1979, p. 15.

81. Text of speech in Jornal do Brasil, 5 July 1979, p. 17; greater detail on the conservation measures in Erickson, "Energy Profile."

82. Jornal do Brasil, 7 July 1979, p. 13.

83. Joelmir Beting in Folha de Sao Paulo, 22 July 1979.

84. O Globo, 21 July 1979; Folha de São Paulo, 24 August 1979.

·85. M.F. Thompson Motta in O Estado de São Paulo, 17 June 1979; Joelmir Beting in Folha de São Paulo, 22 July 1979.

86. Adilson de Oliveira, Luiz Pinguelli Rosa, and Joao Lizardo R.H. de Araujo, Energia no Brasil nos Proximos 20 Anos: Três Cenários Alternativos (Rio de Janeiro: COPPE/UFRJ, 1980), pp. 99, 105.

87. Oliveira, Araújo, and Rosa, "Impasse Atual," p. 20.

88. Oliveira, Rosa, and Araújo, Energia no Brasil, pp. 86, 105.

89. Lindberg, ed., Energy Syndrome, p. 350.

90. Oliveira, Araújo, and Rosa, "Impasse Atual," pp. 23-24.

91. Oliveira, Rosa, and Araújo, Energia no Brasil, pp. 45-49.

92. Carlos Lessa, "A Questão Energética," Encontros com a Civilizacão Brasileira 23 (May 1980): 15.

93. Mans Lonnroth, "Swedish Energy Policy: Technology in the Political Process," in Lindberg, ed., Energy Syndrome, pp. 261-262.

8
Brazilian Foreign Policy: Options in the 1980s

Riordan Roett

INTRODUCTION

Those who wistfully seek a return to the halcyon days of Brazil-United States relations often blame the current sad state of the bilateral tie on specific policies or individuals, such as President Carter and his human rights policy. Others argue that the drift in the relationship is due to the rupture of military ties or point to a variety of other reasons. Perhaps this is the moment to again examine the nature of the complex relations between the two states. I will argue in this chapter that the current world economic malaise has crystallized a trend obscured for decades: that there is as much divergence as there is convergence in the relationship between these two countries. As Brazil attempts to cope with a rapidly deteriorating international economic and financial situation, the United States is of limited help in resolving short and medium term problems of policy. Less because of antipathy than because of necessity, Brazil has begun an historical shift in its diplomatic and political linkages. The United States will grow increasingly peripheral, although far from irrelevant, in the decades ahead as Brazil seeks new options and alliances to deal with real problems of development. The international realities of the 1980s no longer permit Brazil the luxury of a "special relationship." The advent of the Carter Administration merely coincided with the new realities that Brazil must face internationally. The agreement of February 1976 between Secretary of State Kissinger and Foreign Minister Silveira, which appeared to give special importance to Brazil, was not the beginning of something - it was the end. The long journey from dependent and submissive ally to an increasingly aggressive hemispheric partner had closed. While the next phase of Brazil's development may be more hazardous than its postwar growth, it is clear that Brazil will "be on its own."

179

180

THE POSTWAR PERIOD IN PERSPECTIVE

A false sense of bonhomie in the relationship is easily understood if one focuses only on the diplomatic and security aspects. The Brazilians enthusiastically supported the creation of the Inter-American defense and security system following World War II. The ties between the Armed Forces of the two countries were very strong and the United States military mission in Brazil was instrumental in the establishment of the Higher War College (Escola Superior de Guerra) in 1949. In 1954, Brazil joined the United States in calling for a consultative meeting under the terms of the Rio Treaty to deal with the alleged communist subversion in Guatemala. A statistical voting analysis of the period 1945-1954 ranked Brazil second only to Nicaragua in its voting support in the United Nations for North American positions; United States Cold War diplomacy was not questioned in Brazil. In 1965 Brazil provided the commanding officer for the OAS peace-keeping force sent to the Dominican Republic.

However, if one delves deeper and examines the relationship on key economic growth and development issues, the record is different. Brazil's weakness in the postwar period precluded any greater assertion of its economic growth goals; prior to 1960, the United States remained uninterested. The Joint Brazil-United States Economic Development Commission is a relevant case in point. The body began its work in July 1951 and submitted its final report in December 1953. Begun in an aura of enthusiasm, it ended without the promised United States financing for a series of recommended development projects. In 1958 President Juscelino Kubitschek's imaginative suggestion of Operação Pan Americana fell on deaf ears in Washington (Kubitschek proposed a United States-Latin America long-term multilateral program of economic development). In the great debate in Brazil in 1958-1959 over a stabilization program, the United States withheld approval of a $300 million loan until the Kubitschek government accepted the "shock treatment" terms established by the International Monetary Fund (IMF). In June 1959, Kubitschek dramatically broke off negotiations with the IMF; Brazil did not receive the United States loan. The Brazilian political left triumphantly used the IMF episode to demonstrate the disinterest of the United States in Brazil's economic problems. That argument emerged again in 1962 surrounding the possible application of the Hickenlooper Amendment, a rider to the 1962 Foreign Aid Bill obligating the United States to suspend aid to any country that confiscated United States property without the payment of just compensation. Brazil's efforts to settle the claim of the American and Foreign Power Company again raised the allegation that the United States

was only interested in the welfare of its private investors and not in the welfare of Brazilians.

With the overthrow of President João Goulart on 31
March 1964, the growing fissure between the two countries
was hidden by the policies of the new government: from
1964 to 1967 the two countries had an intense and special
relationship under President Humberto Castello Branco.
United States program loans and American private capital
were readily available to support both the stabilization
and the recovery plans of Brazil. Castello Branco supported United States foreign policy initiatives without
question. Ironically, the strong economic ties between
the two states - both public and private - created the
circumstances which allowed Brazil to increasingly identify its self-interests with a wider range of international actors. The 1964-1967 period generated the conditions required to take best advantage of the world
economic boom in the late 1960s and early 1970s. Brazilian growth rates soared to averages of between 10 and
12 percent. Brazilian exports in the 1968-1973 period
achieved an annual average growth rate of 27 percent.
The export profile diversified dramatically; manufactures
grew and commodity sales included an increasing number of
crops. That growing economic confidence permitted the
governments succeeding Castello Branco to assert Brazilian foreign policy interests that were opposed to the
stated policy of the United States.

Former Foreign Minister and Brazilian Ambassador to
the United States, João Augusto de Araújo Castro, in
addressing the Higher War College in 1971, asserted that
the great powers could not freeze the international system and that Brazil had a legitimate and increasing role
to play in world affairs. In 1968 Brazil refused to sign
the Treaty on Non-Proliferation of Nuclear Weapons (NPT)
as in 1967 it had rejected American pressure to sign the
Tlatelolco Treaty prohibiting nuclear weapons in Latin
America. President Medici unilaterally declared Brazil's
claim to a 200 mile territorial sea in the early 1970s.
Brazil strongly and publicly endorsed the 1969 "Consensus
of Viña del Mar," adopted at a meeting of the Economic
Commission for Latin America (ECLA) in May 1969 and presented to the Nixon administration. The document called
for a series of trade and development policy changes in
the Americas. The United States chose not to respond
substantively.

In spite of this tangible evidence to the contrary,
the United States assumed that Brazil and the United
States were in agreement. On various occasions President
Nixon indicated his recognition of the importance of Brazil. Secretary of State William Rogers visited Brasilia
in 1973 and announced that there were no problems to be
discussed. American private investment remained high and
was increasing in all areas of the Brazilian economy.

The superficialities of the benign relationship ended abruptly with the 1973-1974 petroleum crisis.

1974 AND CHANGE

In July 1974 the United States informed Brazil that it could not guarantee the processing of nuclear fuel for Brazilian reactors - reactors that were being built by Westinghouse, an American company. What had been a guarantee was shifted to "conditional" status.(1) The contracts for fueling Brazil's second and third reactors were affected. In the same year, countervailing duties emerged as an important economic issue between the two countries and late in 1974 United States shoe manufacturers demanded that the government act to prohibit growing imports of Brazilian shoes.

The autonomous trend in Brazilian international relations accelerated under the impact of the energy crisis. The largest developing country importer of crude oil, Brazil buys more than 80 percent of its petroleum on the world market. The search for alternative sources of energy in the mid-1970s focused heavily on nuclear energy. The failure of the United States to understand the technological and political connotations of its decision further convinced Brazilian policymakers of the need to seek alternative suppliers. In June 1975 the Brazilian government concluded a controversial agreement with the West German government. The agreement, an umbrella document, provided for a large number of commercial contracts between the two countries. Germany received a promise of secure uranium supplies, a heavy components facility was to be built in Brazil with German technology, and Nuclebras undertook to construct a pilot fuel-element fabrication plant. The much discussed uranium enrichment facility was scheduled to be built in Brazil during the following five year period. Nuclebras, assisted by a consortium of German companies, was responsible for the construction of the reprocessing plant.

Brazilian action in the energy field was paralleled by controversial policies in the international political arena.(2) In the United Nations, Brazil voted in favor of a resolution condemning Zionism. Cynics quickly pointed to Brazil's heavy dependence on the Middle East for its petroleum imports. In its expanding African foreign policy, Brazil recognized the Marxist government of Angola in November 1975. Both the Zionist resolution vote and the Angola move were contrary to clearly stated United States policy preferences.

The brief interlude of the Kissinger-Silveira special relationship agreement, signed in Brasília in February 1976, ended abruptly with the defeat of President Gerald Ford in November 1976. Candidate Jimmy Carter had already singled out Brazil as an international violator of his standards of human rights and had criticized Brazil's nuclear proliferation as dangerous and unnecessary. Vice President-elect Mondale, in a preinauguration trip to Western Europe, publicly tried to break the West German-Brazil agreement on nuclear technology. Both countries angrily rejected his interference. In March 1977 the Brazilians rescinded the twenty-five year old mutual defense agreement with the United States when the first human rights report was issued by the Administration in response to prior Congressional legislation.

The reality of the situation was soon clear, even to the Carter Administration. Its efforts to force Brazilian compliance with its new human rights policy had failed and attempts by Washington to break the nuclear agreement with West Germany were not successful - although by the early 1980s nuclear power would have a far lower priority among Brazilian energy alternatives. Growing controversy over Brazilian trade practices further exacerbated tension between the two countries.

Brazil had determined, following the 1973-1974 petroleum shock, that its continued survival required immediate and effective action in two areas: energy and foreign markets. The latter were needed to expand Brazilian exports still further to earn the foreign exchange needed to purchase increasingly expensive crude oil. Tied to combustion energy, Brazil's continued economic development, and many argued its political stability, required guaranteed oil supplies. But neither energy nor trade were areas in which the United States could - or would - help. In a period of relative decline in United States world power, and given the obvious United States energy dependence, Brazil accelerated its search for options. Perceiving growing pressures in the United States of a protectionist nature, new markets and new trade partners were essential.

THE RETURN TO THE HEMISPHERE

Following the 1973-1974 petroleum shock, and given the deteriorating relationship with the United States following 1976-1977, an early judgment by Brazilian policy makers was that Brazil's foreign policy in the hemisphere must be realigned.(3) Traditionally, in the framework of close United States-Brazil ties, Brazil had maintained a very low profile in South America. United States policy had traditionally favored Brazil in the geopolitics of the Southern Cone. Now Brazil slowly but deliberately moved to carve out a space for itself in the dynamics of Latin American international relations. Mexico's petroleum reserves, and the increasing assertion of Mexican interests in the hemisphere, made that country a logical area of diplomatic activity. President Geisel visited Mexico prior to leaving office and, in the summer

of 1980, President Lopez Portillo returned the vist.
Both countries agreed on a number of areas of cooperation; important in the agreement was the increase of
Mexican crude oil exported to Brazil. In an historic
turn about, Argentine President Videla and President Figueiredo of Brazil exchanged visits in 1980 and signed a
series of agreements in the areas of trade, nuclear technology, and investment; Argentine natural gas may soon
become available to Brazil. The remaining differences
between the two countries over the hydroelectric power
plants along the Parana River were resolved, thus guaranteeing Brazil unfettered access to the crucial resources
of Itaipu and other hydroelectric plants for the Southeast industrial complex centered around Sao Paulo. Relations with the Andean countries have improved, particularly with Venezuela and Peru. Venezuela, in mid-1980,
approved the Brazilian initiated Amazon Pact which will
lead to the development of that region by all countries
bordering on the Amazon Valley. Pointedly, nonhemi-
spheric actors were excluded.
     Suspicion remains, of course, about Brazilian inten-
tions in many areas of Spanish America. But, by and
large, there is a new realization among the nation-states
of the hemisphere of both the need and the desirability
of closer collaboration. Diplomatic, economic, and international cooperation is a pattern which is slowly but
irrevocably emerging in the inter-state relations of
Latin America. Putting aside the historically different
situation in the Caribbean and Central America, where
Mexico, Venezuela, Cuba, and the United States will play
the principal roles, the dynamics of the South American
continent and its relations with Mexico will remain a
high priority for Brazilian international relations in
the coming decades. Brazil's goals are complementary to
those of its neighbors. The economic, technological, and
resource advantages to all concerned are clear. As the
United States increasingly focuses on the short-term security problems in the Caribbean basin, the affairs of
the continent diminish in importance - precisely the
state of affairs most favorable to the autonomy of the
South American states.

MILITARY POWER AND BRAZILIAN FOREIGN POLICY

     Does Brazil's new international activity presage a
heightened military presence on the continent - and eventually elsewhere? This is a question often posed, and
seldom answered responsibly.(4) Brazil has the largest
armed force in Latin America, about 270,000 men in uni-
form. The Brazilian military establishment is twice as
large as that of Argentina and stands seventeenth in the
world. Interestingly, Brazilian military expenditures
have risen in recent years - an increase of 32 percent

between 1967 and 1975. But, given the impressive growth of the Brazilian economy in that period, defense expenditures represent a decreasing proportion of both Gross National Product and central government expenditures. The Arms Control and Disarmament Agency (ACDA) reports that military expenditures have dropped from 2.2 percent of GNP in 1967 to 1.3 percent in 1976. Defense expenditures, as a percent of central government spending, declined from 18.1 percent in 1967 to 11.1 percent in 1976.

Brazilian military modernization efforts in recent years have been directed at updating a badly outdated armed force and taking steps to protect Brazilian trade. Brazil has a coastline of 4,655 miles. The expansion of the country's merchant marine and its rapidly growing export trade have increased the need for coastal security and shipping lane protection. The modernization of the military and the acquisition of sophisticated weapons coincides with Brazil's emerging hemispheric and world roles. With the restrictions placed by the U.S. Congress on the sale of new weapons to Brazil, an indigenous arms industry has taken root. By 1978 Brazil ranked eighth among aircraft manufacturers in the non-Communist world; it possesses the second largest ship building industry in the developing world. Brazil has become a major exporter of arms as well. In 1978 the country ranked fifth among Third World exporters. Of the top five, only Brazil and Israel exported items that were produced locally. In 1980 Brazilian arms exports should reach $500 million - a 100 percent increase over 1979.

On a world wide comparison, Brazil spends relatively little on defense. Ranking as the eighth largest economy in the Western World and the tenth in the entire world, Brazil was in twenty-seventh position in 1978 in level of defense spending. In 1976, Brazil ranked one hundredth in the world in level of military spending as a percent of GNP. Brazil's navy ranks seventh globally, it has the fifteeth largest airforce, and the world's nineteenth ranking army - but these figures obscure deficits in both manpower training and modernity of equipment. To date, and for the foreseeable future, Brazilian military modernization will focus on territorial defense, counterinsurgency, and coastal and sea lane patrol. Its diplomatic offensive in Latin America and elsewhere in the world is overwhelmingly economic in thrust. Military support plays little, if any, significant role. Brazil has too much to gain from a nonbellicose consolidation of its new diplomacy to risk those achievements with a resort to aggressive behavior.

BRAZILIAN GOALS IN THE 1980s

Brazil's international efforts in the 1980s, and beyond, will concentrate on three areas of priority: first, the urgent need to decrease national dependence on imported crude oil and to identify reasonable alternatives, domestic and foreign, second, the search for new markets for Brazil's exports - and the earning of much needed foreign exchange - will be a constant in the country's policy and, third, the necessity for short-term international financing, private and public, to support the country's growing international debt, directly linked to the petroleum import dependence.

These three priorities imply a stark recognition of the diminishing role of the United States government. In a period of economic recession and rising clamor among American producers, increased access to American markets for Brazilian products is unlikely. Brazil will need to diversify its markets. While United States private banks hold a large part of the foreign debt in Brazil, European private financial institutions play an important role in providing annual financing for Brazil's debt-servicing and borrowing needs. The upward trend in Japanese and West European direct private investment indicates the attractiveness of Brazil to those states.

The diversification of Brazil's trade and financial linkages accompanies a return to Latin America for resource alternatives. Regional cooperation is an imperative in the decades to come. Economic integration within the Latin America Free Trade Area, cooperation with Argentina in developing the River Plate basin, natural gas imports from Argentina, coal in Colombia, petroleum in Mexico and Venezuela, natural gas in Bolivia - all indicate new and important options. In return the Latin American countries will receive greater access to an increasingly sophisticated source of technology and of manufactured and semimanufactured goods, including armaments. Collaboration with Brazil, on terms of quality, is an important way of securing peaceful regional and hemispheric development in the years ahead and provides a very important way of increasing the region's global autonomy as a unit.

Energy

Clearly, the Achilles heel of Brazil's future growth is its dependence on imported petroleum.(5) Even prior to the Iraq-Iran war of September 1980, that dependence was profound; given the possible dislocations in world supplies following the conflict in the Middle East, the short-run may pose even greater threats to Brazil's growth objectives. Alone among major Latin American states, Brazil is heavily dependent on imported petroleum. In 1977 it accounted for 62 percent of the total petroleum imports of Latin America. The country is the ninth largest importer in the world, and the first in the developing world. Brazil represents 35 percent of Latin America's consumption of petroleum and petroleum derivatives.

About 44 percent of Brazil's energy needs are provided by oil and gas; the country currently imports between 80 and 85 percent of its petroleum needs. The 1980 petroleum bill will run between $11 and $12 billion, with Brazil exporting about $21.5 billion and importing approximately $22 to $23 billion. As important as these figures are, they do not reveal the full complexity - and dependence - of Brazil. In 1980 approximately 40 to 45 percent of total petroleum imports are scheduled to come from Iraq. Based on a December 1979 agreement between the two countries, Brazil will provide technology for Iraq and the latter will provide Brazil with a stable supply of petroleum. Following Iraq, Saudi Arabia and Kuwait are the most important suppliers of petroleum to Brazil, emphasizing the relationship with OPEC. To decrease the degree of dependence, Brazil's negotiations with Latin American states are important: President Lopez Portillo of Mexico agreed, in July 1980, to raise current petroleum sales from 20,000 bpd in 1980 to 50,000 bpd in 1981, and eventually to 100,000 bpd, or slightly more than 10 percent of the national need. Venezuela has agreed, as well, to increase exports to Brazil.

While Brazil has made impressive progress in reducing national consumption - from slightly less than 1 million bpd in 1979 to about 850,000 bpd in 1980 - the dependence remains. In the first eight months of 1980, national consumption fell by 1.1 percent, compared to the same period in 1979. The use of petroleum derivatives fell 31.3 percent in July 1980 as compared with the previous year. These important conservation measures do not change the overall profile: 7 million-plus vehicles consume more than 20 percent of all domestic and imported petroleum. Ninety-six percent of all passengers and 70 percent of cargo are transported by road in Brazil. Brazilian domestic production stands at slightly less than 200,000 bpd. Government targets, probably overly optimistic, predict the following energy profile by 1985:

        140,000 released through conservation efforts
        500,000 domestic production
        170,000 released through expanded coal use
        120,000 released through charcoal use
         25,000 shale oil
        170,000 alcohol
         60,000 conversion to hydroelectric usage
         15,000 other (including solar)

This would mean an increase of slighty over 1 million bpd.

In addition to petroleum, Brazil looks to a varietv
of other domestically produced alternative energy supplies. There is a $5 billion, fifteen year, plan to con-
vert sugar cane to alcohol. Targets indicate, by 1985,
sufficient raw material to produce 10 billion liters of
alcohol for fuel a year, enough to power 500,000 automobiles. By 1985 the massive Paraguayan-Brazilian joint
hydroelectric project at Itaipu will come on line and
supply about 35 percent of total primary energy; this
will reach 40 percent by the year 2000. Government goals
are to increase domestic coal production from 7 million
tons in 1979 to 35 million tons in 1985. Brazilian coal
reserves stand at an estimated 21.8 billion tons - 90
percent of the total known reserves of combustible fossil
fuel in the country. While of high ash content, which
requires preliminary treatment and limits its use in some
areas of production, coal is an important asset. With
new technology and extended production and productivity
levels, coal and coal derivatives will provide about 29
percent of total energy demand by 1985. Biomass, natural
gas, wood, nuclear, and solar energy will make modest
contributions to reducing Brazil's dependence on imported
petroleum.

The vigorous efforts by Brazil to freeze current imports at about 900,000 bpd, introduce rationing, increase
prices, and energetically support the National Alcohol
Program - Proalcool - are coordinated by the National Energy Commission, created in July 1979 and chaired by Vice
President Aureliano Chaves. This challenge is central to
Brazil's continued economic development - and key to the
resolution of outstanding social problems in the coming
decades.

Foreign Trade

If energy remains the Achilles heel of Brazilian development, many see foreign trade as the eventual salvation for Brazil's foreign exchange needs. Nineteen-
eighty export figures will exceed the $20 billion target
by $1-1.5 billion; the 1985 target is $40 billion per
year. Brazil's trade has diversified dramatically. In
1978, a poor year for agriculture, for the first time
manufactured goods amounted to more than 50 percent of
total foreign trade. Agricultural products, which play
an important role in Brazil's foreign exchange, are no
longer dominated by coffee production. Soybeans, citrus
concentrate, and frozen poultry are now prominent. Iron
ore has risen from 1 percent of exports in the mid-1960s
to 10 percent in the late 1970s. By the mid-1980s, Brazil will be a major exporter of bauxite, and, in the same
time period, may become a steel exporter.

While exports are vital, a corresponding reduction in
imports is essential to eliminate the current negative

trade balance. In 1980 it is expected that imports will exceed exports by $1 to $2 billion. The drive for self-sufficiency in manufacturing and the total elimination of agricultural imports are crucial. As mentioned, Brazil should achieve self-sufficiency in steel by 1985. Several major petrochemical plants, now under construction, will begin functioning by the early mid-1980s, reducing dependence in that important area. Exploration of known mineral deposits - uranium, copper, zinc, aluminium - are advanced. Fertilizer plants should soon satisfy internal demand.

An important element in the trade profile is a diversification of partners. Where the United States bought 44 percent of Brazil's exports in 1960, that figure fell to 15.4 percent in 1975, 17.7 percent in 1977, and 19.0 percent in 1979. Latin America increased its share in Brazilian exports from 7 percent in 1960 to 15 percent in 1979; the European countries accounted for 26.7 percent of Brazil's exports in 1960 and 37.4 percent in 1979. Japan, Spain, and Italy are also important buyers of Brazil's goods.

Imports pose a different set of issues. The import profile is far less diversified. The United States, Western Europe, especially West Germany, and Japan are the country's major suppliers, together providing nearly 50 percent of all imports. The United States provides nearly three times the imports of any other nation. In Latin America, Argentina provides about one-third of Brazil's imports in the region, followed by Chile and Mexico. Iraq and Saudi Arabia dominate the petroleum imports; in Asia, Japan dominates, followed by South Korea and Singapore.

Brazil's balance of trade problems are of the first importance. The drain on foreign reserves by the trade deficit is of highest priority. Thus the export promotion theme is essential to long-range economic health and the continued search for new markets for Brazilian goods will dominate government planners. While Brazil is moving away from the United States as a market for its exports, the U.S. remains dominant in imports, a potential source of conflict as the forces for diversification gain in strength.

Financing

Given Brazil's growing public and private debt, which will reach between $55 and $56 billion at the end of 1980, access to foreign capital is essential. Brazil, in the mid-1970s, was the largest recipient of export credits from the industrialized countries to the nonoil producing nations. Brazil was also the largest developing country recipient of direct overseas private investment - 12 percent of the total. U.S. firms represent

190

30.4 percent of the total foreign investment in Brazil,
2.2 times the level of West Germany and 3 times the level
of Japan. Brazil is one of the world's largest takers
of commercial bank loans. In 1977, it ranked fourth,
with U.S. banks the leading private lenders.

Brazil, in 1980, borrowed down on international reserves to finance its debt. Amortization will necessi-
tate payments of approximately $7 billion in 1980. 1980-
1982 are the years of greatest repayment burden since the
original 1973-1974 loans repayment schedule is heaviest.
The 1980 Iraq-Iran conflict raises the threat of higher
oil prices. While Brazil has oil reserves for about
three months, rising costs may have a severe impact in
early mid-1981, raising the issue of whether or not Brazil will have to resort to the International Monetary
Fund for stand-by support.(6) Brazil has refused to consider that option heretofore, but the realities of the
world economic situation, and changing conditions at the
Fund for nonoil producing countries, may moderate the
country's policy.

SUMMARY

Brazil faces a number of difficult options in 1980.
The heavy burden of its foreign debt has raised fears
among private bankers that they are over-exposed; next
year's deficit is expected to be $13 billion. U.S. banks
hold 60 percent of the total foreign debt. If new ways
are not found to recycle petrodollars, either through the
IMF or a new mechanism, it may be increasingly difficult
for Brazil to convince the private banks of its credit-
worthiness. The dramatic Middle East oil conflict has
forced Brazil to turn to the Soviet Union and in October
1980 Brazil agreed to buy 24,000 bpd from the Soviets.
Domestic gasoline, diesel oil, and fuel oil prices were
increased by the government. The gasoline increase was
the sixth in one year; the cost has tripled in one year
and stands at just under $3 a gallon.

These are real and short-term policy problems. In
the broader perspective, it must be remembered that Brazil's economic difficulties are of a global nature. As
a nonoil producer, Brazil's size, level of industrial development, and export needs make imported petroleum and
the resulting debt financing burden key challenges for
the government. These real questions should not obscure
the slow but steady and positive growth of Brazil's relevance in regional and global affairs. In Latin America,
the last five years have seen Brazil become a major actor
¬ and partner. Motivated in part by the desire to politically diversify its international and regional ties, and
in part in the hope of finding help in resolving its
pressing resource needs, the hemisphere looms large in
future international action.

As the triple threat of energy, exports, and debt financing continues to dominate the Brazilian agenda, its ties with the United States will continue to weaken, although never abate. The United States can be of little direct assistance in Brazil's search for energy alternatives, having done so poorly itself in responding to the post-1973 challenge. In the trade area, the United States faces trade deficits and political pressures for protection from American producers. In the financing area, it is the private banks that will make the final determination about Brazil's debt worthiness, not the government. Indeed, in an area in which United States government assistance would be useful, in the international lending agencies and the recycling of the petrodollars available for nonoil producing countries financing, Washington has shown few notable signs of leadership.

In part, then, while remaining dependent on United States imports, Brazil's efforts to decrease that dependence, combined with the broadening of its export markets, will continue in the 1980s. Energy alternatives are focused internally and on other neighbors. Financing will rest with other institutions or with private groups. Brazil's international relations are evolving. That evolution is fraught with new challenges and difficulties that moving away from the United States will not resolve. Nevertheless, the signs are clear, the path well marked: the old relationship has atrophied. A series of new relationships are in the process of being consolidated; that process, which will dominate the 1980s, will basically reorder the ties between the United States and Brazil and transform Brazil's global role by the 1990s. While not a world power, Brazil will exert influence in selected areas of policy concern. Compared to the major industrial powers, Brazil remains less developed.(7) When compared with the rest of the developing world, it looms larger. It is that intermediate status that colors its options. Brazil's success - or failure - will determine to some degree the fate of other Third World contenders for greater influence in the international system during the last decades of the 20th century.

NOTES

1. William W. Lowrance, "Nuclear Futures for Sale: To Brazil from West Germany, 1975," International Security I, no. 2, (Fall 1976) reviews the nuclear agreement controversy.

2. Ronald M. Schneider, Brazil: Foreign Policy of a Future World Power (Boulder: Westview Press, 1976), reviews the evolving nature of Brazil's international relations.

3.   See Wayne A. Selcher, <u>Brazil's Multilateral Re-</u>
<u>lations: Between First and Third Worlds</u> (Boulder: West-
view Press, 1978), chapter 8.
4.   For a recent discussion of this issue, see "U.S.
National Security Interests in Latin America: Projections Over Time," Final Report, prepared for the Office
of the Assistant Secretary of Defense, International Security Affairs, 1980.   (Dr. Margaret Daly Hayes, principal investigator).
5.   Antônio Aureliano Chaves de Mendonça, "The Brazilian Energy Question," Address presented at the lunch-
eonmeeting offered by Brazilinvest, Washington, D.C., 1
October 1980.
6.   See, for example, "Why Brazil Needs to Court the
IMF," <u>Business Week</u>, 29 September 1980, p. 101 and Eve-
rett G. Martin, "Brazil Seeks to Augment Heavy Debt,"
<u>Wall Street Journal</u>, 15 September 1980.
7.   It is well worth remembering that the gross data
about Brazil's size and importance can obscure important
shortcomings.   For example, while the value of Brazil's
foreign trade is greater than any other nonoil importer,
the country's total trade is equal to less than 2 percent
of the industrial countries' trade - less than 10 percent
of U.S. trade or 11 percent of West German trade.   Also,
while Brazil is the world's tenth largest economy, nearly
equivalent in size to Canada and Italy and two-thirds
that of the United Kingdom, it is only one-third as large
as West Germany, one-quarter as large as Japan, and only
8 percent the size of the United States economy.   See
Albert Fishlow, "Flying Down to Rio: Perspectives on
U.S.- Brazil Relations," <u>Foreign Affairs</u> 57, no. 2,
(Winter 1978-79).

9
Brazil in 1980:
The Emerging Political Model

Thomas G. Sanders

As the 1980s get underway, a definable political model seems to be emerging in Brazil. The process of transition from a military-authoritarian toward a civilian-democratic regime that has been evolving since 1974 took significant steps forward in 1979. Although it is always hazardous to predict the political future of any country, what is taking place now has a coherence that makes some sense and provides hints of how a democratic system might be institutionalized.

The slow pace of the Brazilian transition - which has already gone on for several years without any clear indication of its termination - has led some observers to doubt that the military guardians of the regime really intend to withdraw from power. Although antidemocratic factions in the Armed Forces, ongoing authoritarian features in the present system, or economic factors leading to a crisis could halt, frustrate, or reverse the process toward a democracy, such an outcome should not be assumed in advance. The transition from authoritarianism to democracy, though difficult, is an undeniable trend not only in Latin America, but also in southern Europe, which has many cultural and political similarities to Latin America.

Since 1974, authoritarian regimes in Portugal, Spain, and Greece have been replaced by genuine, if struggling, democratic systems. In South America, the Ecuadorian Armed Forces junta bowed out in 1979 while in 1980 Peruvian voters elected Fernando Belaunde Terry as president. Bolivia held elections in 1979 and 1980, but the Armed Forces in that chronically unstable country refused to honor the results. In Chile, the regime won a victory in a plebiscite for a new constitution, but at the price of suspected fraud and the most intense mobilization of the opposition in seven years. In Nicaragua and El Salvador, long-standing authoritarian systems have been overthrown and each has begun the difficult process of political reorganization.

Recent Brazilian political events fit into this international picture. The tendency of military governments to see themselves as caretakers rather than permanent regimes is illustrated in Brazil by the "moderating power" which the Armed Forces used to justify their intervention in 1964.(1) Although the military has found excuses to continue to remain in power, the first President after the coup, Marshal Humberto Castello Branco, clearly sympathized with the future reestablishment of a democratic system. The accession to office of President Ernesto Geisel in 1974 meant a return to power of the legalist, democratically-oriented "Castellistas." As the process has continued, civilian groups in Brazil have been virtually unanimous in favoring the return to a democracy.

The current political transition began in 1974 when President-elect Geisel carried out consultations with various civilian groups on a "decompression" or "distensao" of the tight authoritarian situation that he had inherited.(2) Although the government took the initial steps in enlarging the space for political activities, the opposition occupied that space with great effectiveness and pressured to expand it. Since 1975, the principal initiatives and pressures for further redemocratization have emanated from the opposition, but the government has demonstrated exceptional political skill in controlling the process and in coopting the proposals of the opposition. The transition, consequently, has not been caused by either government or opposition but rather by the relationship between these.

CHANGES IN BRAZIL'S POLITICAL CONTEXT SINCE 1974

We can best understand the political process and the emerging model by examining a series of interrelated developments since 1974 that have reduced the authoritarian features of the system and contributed to a more effective democratic functioning. There is no question that the political context of Brazil in 1980 is quite different from what it was in 1974. The new environment is a result of the following changes: (1) the elimination of the exceptional political restrictions that grew out of the crisis of 1968, (2) the expanded area for diversified political expression, (3) revision of the party system, (4) more significant elections, and (5) the formation and activities of pressure and interest groups. All of these features, taken together, constitute a coherent infrastructure for a model of redemocratization.

The Elimination of Exceptional Restrictions Resulting from the Crisis of 1968

On 13 December 1968, a confrontation between the Armed Forces and its civilian opponents resulted in a drastic crackdown. Congress, which had refused a military request to remove the political rights of a young Deputy, Márcio Moreira Alves, was closed, and President Arthur da Costa e Silva summarily removed the political rights of many of its members. The regime entered a period of exceptional repression and reduced political activity which was to last until 1974.(3)

The main symbol of the change was the Fifth Institutional Act (AI-5), decreed by the government, which allowed the President to close Congress and cancel the political rights of individuals considered hostile to the regime. AI-5 also permitted a waiver of the right of habeas corpus and prescription of the death penalty in certain cases of subversion. The government justified AI-5 as necessary to counter subversion, terrorism, and violence. Throughout 1968, civilian opponents of the regime, including politicians, students, workers, segments of the Catholic Church, and ordinary Brazilians, had intensified their political activities. In Congress, not only the opposition party, the Brazilian Democratic Movement, (MDB) but the progovernment National Renovating Alliance (Arena) had voted against proposals from President Costa e Silva. When the police and Armed Forces broke up demonstrations, arrested protesters, and occupied the University of Brasilia, officials of the courts and members of Congress criticized these actions.

Unfortunately for Brazil's future, opposition to the government was not restricted to peaceful tactics. Radical Marxist cells were also active and resorted to violence and terrorism. The Armed Forces interpreted the growing wave of opposition as a repudiation of their intervention in 1964 and an attempt to return to the preceding civilian populist administrations. The top officials considered even peaceful protest unacceptable at a time when eliminating the terrorist threat demanded national unity and consensus. They judged the civilian political class to be ingenuous in failing to perceive the necessity to directly confront this dangerous threat to national security and values.

In addition to the imposition of AI-5, the crackdown of 13 December was followed by an all-out war against the terrorists. Arbitrary arrests, incommunicado detentions, and interrogations under coercion, which were conducted during the coup of 1964 and sporadically thereafter, became standard practice in 1969.(4) In retaliation, the terrorists attracted worldwide publicity by kidnapping high level diplomatic personnel, including the ambassadors of Switzerland, Germany, and the United States in

Brazil, and holding them hostage until the Brazilian government freed selected political prisoners and expelled them from the country. Brazil's international image fell as security forces and terrorists engaged in a struggle which led to suffering for many innocent people. By mid-1970, however, harsh repression and the inability of the terrorists to attract sympathy from the population resulted in a victory for the government.

In the latter part of the administration of President Emílio Garrastazu Médici (1969-1974), the prospect of a "decompression" or "detente" was widely discussed. The terrorists had been defeated. In the congressional elections of 1970, the government party, Arena, had won decisively over an MDB which suffered the defeat of many of its most prominent leaders. The country was riding a wave of confidence as a result of economic growth which, after 1968, averaged over 10 percent annually although petroleum price increases and the international grain shortage augured the beginning of a new epoch of difficulties. In the government, prominent officials concerned about the negative image Brazil and the Armed Forces had developed due to government repression, concluded that it was time to initiate the process of democratic reinstitutionalization.

Ernesto Geisel came to the Presidency as a reflection of this mood. He was determined to end the excesses of the security apparatus, which had come to function as a virtual autonomous entity within the government. Cautious, conservative, and authoritarian, he wanted to bring about political change in what he described as a "slow, gradual, and sure" way. Although the opposition stressed that AI-5 should be abolished as soon as possible, Geisel regarded it as a means of keeping the process of change under control and of avoiding precipitous actions by the opposition, although he hoped that he would have to use it only rarely.

Although censorship declined and political activity increased, political participants still felt that they could not function freely because of the ongoing activities of the security forces. Reflecting the views of hardline elements in the Armed Forces, security officals opposed the increased political activities, spread rumors of destablilizing Communist activities, and then used these rumors as an excuse to continue harrassment, detentions, and interrogations under torture. Such violations of human rights and contradictions of the process of decompression were especially common in Sao Paulo, where the Information Center of the Second Army coordinated security operations.

The beginning of the end of these abuses was the Herzog incident. Late in October 1975, Vladimir Herzog, a journalist, was summoned to provide information on the alleged reorganization of the Communist Party in Sao

Paulo. Though he had previously been in good health, Herzog's body was shortly afterward returned to his family in a sealed coffin, which they were not allowed to open. Critical public opinion assumed, correctly, that he had died under torture and 8,000 persons attended an ecumenical service for him in the Sao Paulo Cathedral (Herzog was Jewish). Three months later Manuel Fiel Filho, a worker, suffered the same fate as Herzog.

These two murders were not part of the government script. Geisel was outraged and held the Commander of the Second Army, General Ednardo d'Ávila Mello, responsible, removing him from his position. Since Geisel's action constituted a direct challenge to hard-line military who sympathized with the security forces, he had to move with authority and deciseveness to avoid a coup. Military consensus supported the President as Commander-in-Chief, and the tendency of the security agencies to function unchecked was stopped. The President's decision thus terminated the most reprehensible type of human rights violations then current in Brazil - detentions, torture, and sometimes murder on the grounds of suspected subversion or of possessing knowledge about subversives.

Three years later, in 1978, a Brazilian court rendered a judgment on the Herzog incident which the newsmagazine Veja called "the most crucial change of substance ever registered in the development of the question of human rights in Brazil."(5) When Herzog's wife and children filed suit against the federal government, a young judge of the federal court in Sao Paulo, Marcio José de Moraes, held the government responsible for his imprisonment, torture, and death. While the problem had been resolved at one level by firing General Mello, the court case went further by emphasizing the legal principle that security officials of the government are responsible for the life and health of persons they interrogate. Detentions with violations of human rights had previously depended for their resolution on a combination of pressure by influential groups and persons and the willingness of government officials to respond to these actions. As a result of the Moraes decision, one of the three branches of the federal system guaranteed, in principle, that human rights were protected by the law and that violators would be punished.

AI-5 was abandoned by the Geisel administration on 1 January 1979. Although Geisel prided himself on using AI-5 with restraint, he had applied it to close Congress in April 1977 and to decree a package of measures designed to guarantee that the government would win the congressional elections of 1978. He had also used it to remove the political rights of several public figures, including José de Alencar Furtado, leader of the MDB in the Chamber of Deputies in 1977.

During its ten years of existence, AI-5 was used against 1,577 Brazilians, most of them public officials, including 6 federal Senators and 110 Deputies or their alternates. With the help of AI-5, the regime had removed many of the natural leaders of the opposition, especially the more critical ones, thus guaranteeing that the government would win a majority in key federal and state indirect elections. The provision of AI-5 limiting habeas corpus had enabled the security apparatus to arrest and interrogate suspects without fear of judicial intervention. This procedure, more than any other, led to the serious human rights violations that damaged Brazil's image after 1968 and placed a check on open political criticism and activity. Restraining the security forces and eliminating AI-5 have created in Brazil the open environment necessary for serious redemocratization. The opposition can now say and do what it wants without fear of arbitrary and extra-legal restraints.

The question naturally arises whether the government might, in a crisis, revive these measures. In an authoritarian regime, such a step backward can always occur. However, the regime could more easily use other legal weapons, such as the constitutional provisions for declaring a state of siege or a state of emergency in situations of disorder or internal subversion without immediate approval by Congress. Under the state of siege, for example, the government can impose censorship, search private homes, and suspend the freedom of assembly. In addition, the National Security Law forbids a number of actions that are considered threatening and prescribes specific penalties for these. Most of these actions would be considered illegal even in democratic systems. The chief difficulty in the law lies in potentially arbitrary interpretations of its provisions, and the fact that violators are tried before military rather than civilian tribunals. It is encouraging, however, that since the demise of AI-5 the new Figueiredo administration has used the National Security Law only occasionally.

Freedom of Political Expression

An indispensable prerequisite for greater political participation is the opportunity for all authentic political currents in a country to act and to express themselves. Authoritarian systems, such as Brazil since 1964, by definition forbid activities by certain political leaders and organizations. The transition from authoritarianism to democracy implies that publications and the media will be free from censorship, and that all political persuasions can act without restraint.

After 1964, Brazil suffered from both formal and informal censorship, directed against Marxism, Populism, and criticisms that were considered hostile to the regime. Though censorship was sporadic before 1968, after the crackdown of that year tight restrictions were imposed on the press and other media as a measure against terrorism and instability. Editors of newspapers, for example, were emphatically forbidden to discuss certain topics which were considered relevant to national security.

With the beginning of decompression in 1974, most of the restrictions were lifted, although a few journals continued to be censored. Other newspapers and magazines were occasionally told not to discuss certain matters. The most notable feature of the censorship policy during these years was caprice, for while some issues clearly seemed threatening to public order and security, others were arbitrarily censored and in certain cases reflected confusion and ignorance in the censor's office. The same censorship policies applied to radio and television.

The government established another form of censorship in the municipal elections of 1976 and the congressional elections of 1974 and 1978 by forbidding unrestricted campaign advertising. Each party received a block of television and radio time, during which candidates were limited to brief appearances where they presented minimal information about their background and opinions.

Since President João Figueiredo took office in March 1979, censorship has not been an important political issue although public media are expected to behave with good taste. The National Security Law also prohibits actions such as insulting a foreign head of state who is visiting the country. These minor conditions, however, have not prevented the media from playing a decisive role in analyzing national issues and criticizing government actions and policies.

The second key change in encouraging political diversity has been the declaration of amnesty which led to freedom for persons charged with political crimes and the return of hundreds of exiles from abroad. The opposition always emphasized amnesty as a basic step toward normalization. In 1975, a proamnesty organization composed of female relatives of political prisoners was formed, but the movement did not really begin to develop momentum until 1978 when Brazilian Committees for Amnesty were formed, first in Rio de Janeiro and subsequently in other cities. They rapidly attracted the collaboration of organizations which favored more rapid democratization outside the format of the regime and who made amnesty a major focus of their efforts. The Committees adopted as their aim "broad, general, and unrestricted amnesty," covering all actions of opposition to the regime and all persons involved in them.

In September 1978, the Amnesty Committees formed a national organization, followed in November by the First

National Congress for Amnesty in São Paulo. Among the participating organizations were the Brazilian Order of Lawyers, Brazilian Press Association, National Conference of Brazilian Bishops, the MDB, National Student Union, United Black Movement Against Racial Discrimination, Brazilian Society for the Progress of Science, and the National Association of Sociologists. During 1978 and 1979, political prisoners themselves joined these groups in pressing for amnesty by engaging in protests and hunger strikes.

The response of the regime to the amnesty issue demonstrates how successful it has been in its policy of coopting the proposals of the opposition. As early as 1977, Petronio Portella, at that time Arena leader in the Senate and the chief congressional spokesman for the government political program, brought up the matter of a government-sponsored amnesty. In June of that year, the regime continued its gradual approach by eliminating Article 185 of the Constitution, which forbade those who had been removed from public office from reassuming their earlier posts. In 1978, on its own initiative, it revised the National Security Law, abolishing the death penalty.

From April to September 1979, the chief item of debate in the Congress was amnesty. At stake were two different approaches. One was the opposition demand for a broad, general, and unrestricted amnesty. The other was a government proposal for an amnesty with restrictions. Government leaders did not want to completely exonerate those in three categories: (1) those sentenced for crimes of violence such as bank robbing, bomb throwing, and murder, carried out for political reasons, (2) military personnel who had been sentenced on security and corruption charges since complete amnesty would enable them to rejoin the Armed Forces, and the military institutions did not look favorably on this, and (3) members of the Communist Party as the regime regards Communists as permanently engaged in a plot to overthrow the system, by violence if necessary.

By October 1979, when Congress (where Arena had a majority) approved the government's proposal, only fifty-one persons were still imprisoned for political crimes, down from ninety-two in 1978. (The others had been freed by reduction of their sentences for good behavior). Late in November, when only sixteen prisoners were left, Figueiredo announced a Christmas amnesty for most of the common prisoners in the country, including those sentenced for political reasons. By mid-1980, only one political prisoner remained, and his release is imminent.

The government succeeded in controlling the process of amnesty, imposing its own legislation, and eventually undercutting amnesty as an opposition issue. It did not accept the principle of amnesty for acts of violence, but it allowed persons who had committed them to benefit from the standard reductions of civil penalties for good behavior. With the military problem, the government solution allowed for reincorporation into the Armed Forces only by decision of a select commission and ultimately by the ministers of the Armed Forces. The Communists were included under amnesty as individuals, but the National Security Law continues to prohibit them from organizing officially as a political party.

The most prominent effect of amnesty has been the return of numerous Brazilians from compulsory or voluntary exile, including a number of leading politicians who had been active in the period before 1964. The most important returnees are Leonel Brizola, Miguel Arraes, and Luis Carlos Prestes.

Brizola, former governor of Rio Grande do Sul and brother-in-law of ex-President João Goulart (who was overthrown by the military in 1964) represented, more than anyone else in that period, the radical nationalist and leftist position. He is now projecting himself as a moderate, dedicated to building his political base in the former Brazilian Labor Party (PTB). Miguel Arraes, the reformist governor of Pernambuco, was one of the more moderate political leaders punished by the military in 1964. After spending most of his exile in Algeria, he returned as a professed Marxist and an active participant in the successor party to the MDB. Luis Carlos Prestes is the often imprisoned, often clandestine, and often exiled former chairman of the Brazilian Communist Party (PCB) which is aligned with the Soviet Union. Although Prestes continues to express his views in Brazil, he was rudely received by his comrades in the Party. A younger group expelled him as chairman, charging that his Stalinist views inhibited the Party from functioning effectively in the new Brazilian political environment.

Amnesty has opened Brazilian politics to a degree that compares with the period before 1964. When it assumed power, the regime declared its intention to contain both Marxism and Populism; the repression of 1968 occurred partly because both continued to be active. The official plans for a democratic restoration assume that the country has the political capacity to establish institutions and elect leaders who will avoid both of these tendencies. Nevertheless, Marxist and Populist leaders have returned to Brazil, and are presenting themselves to the public as serious political alternatives.

Although the organized effort for amnesty has declined with the passage of the law, the return of exiles, and the release of prisoners, the coalition of organizations in the amnesty movement continues to be an important potential pressure group in favor of further redemocratization. Their future will depend on their capacity to define new objectives and to achieve a consensus on appropriate strategies for achieving them among the constituent organizations.

Revision of the Party System

The two-party system, based on Arena and the MDB, grew out of Institutional Act No. 2 of 1965 which abolished the previously existing parties. Subsequently, the leading politicians of the country regrouped themselves into a majority party, Arena, which supported the regime, and a minority party, MDB, which opposed it. The resulting arrangement has long been criticized for not reflecting Brazilian political sentiment, even though after 1974 the MDB increased its strength and became the dominant urban party on a platform of opposition to authoritarianism and to the economic performance of the regime. Even the MDB, however, had always been a coalition of differing political currents which were not even united in opposing the government. Embracing a spectrum that ranged from Marxists to conservatives, the MDB included factions such as the machine of Governor Antônio Chagas Freitas in the state of Rio de Janeiro which collaborated closely with the government.

After amnesty was settled, revision of the party structure moved to the top of the political agenda. The government favored a change in part because it wanted to divide the opposition and in part because it hoped to establish a more authentic system of representation. Conscious of the increasing strength of the MDB, the political leaders of the regime feared that the increased political freedom would result in a victory of the MDB which would imply a popular repudiation of them. Although the government had resorted to AI-5 and the April political package of 1977 to avoid such an outcome, the long range solution, from the government's perspective, was to exploit the divisions in the opposition by giving them leeway to form new parties.

The MDB was ambivalent about party restructuring. Some leaders hoped to preserve the MDB because of its future potential as the dominant party in Brazil, based on the momentum of recent electoral results among an urban population that is constantly increasing proportionally. Other leaders, to the contrary, objected to the coexistence of radically different political outlooks in the same organization. Many moderates, for example, were anti-Marxists who criticized the presence of Communists and other leftists in the MDB. Correspondingly, the left wing of the Party objected to "collaborationists" or "opportunists" (adesistas) who maintained close relations with the regime, particularly the followers of Chagas Freitas in Rio de Janeiro and a group of MDB federal and state legislators who have chosen to support the Arena governor of Sao Paulo, Paulo Maluf.

Arena was also divided, the most serious cleavage being between adherants of the pre-1965 Social Democratic Party (PSD) and the National Democratic Union (UDN). Especially in townships (municipios), but often extending to the level of governor and senator, Arena was divided between PSD and UDN factions, or simply between supporters of different individual machines. Recognizing the internal conflicts in the official party, the regime maintained in elections a device called the "sublegenda" which allowed separate tickets to compete under the same party label.

The architects of the Law of Party Reform, which was passed in November 1979, were President Figueiredo, General Golbery do Couto e Silva (Head of Civilian Liaison for the Presidency), and the Minister of Justice, Petrônio Portella. They produced a bill that they hoped would retain as many of the "arenistas" as possible as some had made it clear they did not want to remain within a new government party. The principal reason why some "arenistas" decided to join the opposition was their inability to pursue their political interests in states where a rival faction of Arena dominated. Others wanted to abandon the Party because they believed that the regime was losing support under the momentum of increasing political freedom.

The government's political planners hoped that the bill would have two basic effects on the MDB. First, they wanted to make the formation of new parties sufficiently easy that the MDB would break into at least two parts. Second, they did not want to make the requirements for reorganization so easy that many small parties would result. They had observed that the most successful multiparty systems in the world today have only a limited number of political groupings. They were also influenced by the West German model which had prevented parliamentary representation for the Communists and neo-Nazis by requiring a 5 percent minimum vote.

The MDB had long been divided into two principal wings, the "moderates" and, to the left, the "authentics." With the passage of time and new political developments, each of these had tended to fragment still more. One group among the moderates, led by Senator Tancredo Neves of Minas Gerais, refused to remain in a party with Marxists. Neves, one of the country's leading politicians and an outstanding tactician, had served as Prime Minister of Brazil during the brief "parliamentary" interlude at the beginning of Goulart's administration. With great finesse, he attracted many of his congressional colleagues to a new party which was independent of the government, drawing support from anti-Communists in the MDB (including "collaborationists" and "opportunists") and from dissidents who decided to leave Arena.

Another group of moderates, led by the longtime MDB Chairman, Deputy Ulysses Guimarães, and by Senator André Franco Montoro, both of Sao Paulo, led the fight to preserve the MDB. They considered the left essential to the identity of the Party. The MDB left had become so fragmented that the label "authentic" no longer encompassed the differences. The original "authentics" had divided into "historical" and "new" authentics, the former including electoral winners from several years before, the latter composed of the victors from the elections of 1978, who in many instances were more radical. The MDB also included the "popular tendency," a coalition of independent Marxists and non-Marxists, including the prominent young labor leader, Luis Ignácio da Silva (Lula). The "popular tendency" wanted to break with the traditional Brazilian patron-client system and form a new party on a "popular" base. The unity of the MDB was further undermined by ex-Governor Leonel Brizola, who had been seeking support for his revived PTB from the ranks of the MDB.

The Law of Party Reform was the principal item of congressional debate during the latter months of 1979. The MDB decided to concentrate its opposition on only one of the government's proposals: the extinction of the existent parties preliminary to forming new ones. Though the MDB was already falling apart from internal dissensions and its members were negotiating over the new party system, it hoped to blame the government for arbitrarily abolishing the opposition party.

Although Congress added some minor changes to the original proposals, the government's bill passed. The new law allows parties to be formed immediately if they have among their founders at least 10 percent of the membership of Congress, including one senator. Political groups that cannot meet this requirement must receive at least 5 percent of the total vote in the next election for the Chamber of Deputies, including 3 percent in nine states, to be recognized as a party. In the interim, the federal, state, and municipal representatives of aspiring parties can function in their respective legislatures as "parliamentary blocs."

With the passage of the law in November 1979, the divisive tendencies within Arena and the MDB took their course. The first party to organize was the Democratic Social Party (PDS), the successor to Arena. Though its greatest electoral strength lies in the former Arena strongholds of the North, Northeast, and rural areas in general, it also has large delegations from such major states as São Paulo, Minas Gerais, and Bahia. By astute manipulation of patronage and political favors, the PDS managed to retain a slight majority, not only in the Senate but also in the Chamber of Deputies. The Tancredo Neves movement also established itself as the Popular

Party (PP). Neves managed to attract over 30 Arena dissidents in Congress, including his longtime rival from Minas Gerais, Senator José Magalhães Pinto. In addition, about forty senators and deputies from the MDB joined the PP. The PP has exceptional strength and seems likely to control the populous states of Rio de Janeiro and Minas Gerais.

The direct successor of the MDB, the PMDB, has managed to retain about 120 members of Congress, drawn from moderates in major states such as Senator Franco Montoro in São Paulo, Roberto Saturnino Braga in Rio de Janeiro, José Richa of Parana, and Pedro Simón of Rio Grande do Sul, plus the "authentics" and other groups on the left.

The final outcome of the MDB division is still unclear at the time this chapter is being written (August 1980), because a few of its leading figures have not committed themselves completely to any of the new groupings. Though the PP and PMDB can begin to function immediately as parties, Leonel Brizola and his PTB have not been as fortunate. For months Brizola negotiated with various politicians, appearing at times to be on the verge of persuading such MDB notables as Montoro and Simón to join him in the PTB. The harshest blow to his hopes, however, was a court decision awarding the PTB label to Ivete Vargas, niece of former president Getulio Vargas. The Brizola movement recaptured its stride under the name of the Brazilian Democratic Labor Party (PDTB), but it does not have the participation its leader had hoped for.

One other group may also succeed in 1982. Commonly called the Labor Party (PT), its chief leader is Lula, and it includes many of the individuals and organizations which are trying to build a "popular" political movement. Though the components of this group are very vocal, they do not include very many people with vote-gathering credentials. However, by 1982 the PT could well receive 5 percent of the ballots for the Chamber of Deputies. The Brazilian Communist Party could probably attract at least 5 percent of the vote, but it is choosing not to test provisions of the National Security Law which forbid the creation of parties which are aligned with foreign countries or are committed to violence as a tactic. The Party is supporting the PMDB and some of its members hold political offices under that label.

The emphasis in recent months on party realignment has provoked cynical comments about the "artificiality" of the process. The principal individuals involved in the determination of parties, namely federal congressmen, are the same political class Brazil has had for decades. Although Brazil's civilian politicians leave much to be desired, they were, nevertheless, chosen in the elections of 1974 and 1978 and are products of the patron-client system that underlies the political system. The individuals serving in Congress do so fundamentally because of their skill in controlling votes. Brazilians normally do not vote on great issues or for ideologies, but for personalities and factional loyalties. Despite this reality, the party realignment is an indispensable step in the new political model, for at least the following reasons:

1. In any transition from military to civilian control of the top positions, the civilian leaders will come predominantly from those with experience in Congress and in other key posts such as state governors.
2. With the majority government reduced to a bare minimum, President Figueiredo will have to bargain in Congress to pass his program. He must seek support not only from the PDS, but also from the PP, which is not a government party but may collaborate with it. Parliamentary bargaining of this sort contrasts positively with the previous system in which the Arena-dominated Congress basically rubber-stamped executive proposals.
3. The need for congressional support may require the President to base his Cabinet on party representation in Congress, especially if the PDS strength is reduced in the elections of 1982. This could mean more than one party in the cabinet. At present, the Figueiredo Cabinet has no relationship to Congress but is composed of his personal choices. A Cabinet reflecting and responsible to Congress would move Brazil decisively in a democratic direction.

What stands out most clearly from the process of party realignment is the overall moderation and lack of ideology in the spectrum. All of the new parties can be placed on a range from center-left to center-right. The lack of extremism may strengthen the democratic trend by giving the Armed Forces leadership confidence that the political process is not hostile to the regime and that Brazil is not returning to the polarization of 1963-1964. Even though the PMDB includes many individuals who consider themselves leftist, and the Communist Party has endorsed it, its principal leaders are modest reformers. The chief difficulty will be for the parties to distinguish themselves from each other. Though the PDS might be considered center-right, the PP centrist, and the PMDB center-left, individuals of varying political hues support each party. In the proximate future, Brazilian political parties seem likely to continue to depend in large part on the personal attractions of candidates and the capacity of machines to deliver votes.

Elections

One of the unique characteristics of the Brazilian model of authoritarianism since 1965 has been its maintenance of the normal schedule of elections, even though the regime has manipulated them. An important prerequisite for a new democratic model will be elections which nongovernment parties can enter without handicap and with the possibility of capturing the highest offices.

The principal mechanisms the regime has used to control elections have been the abolishment of the pre-1965 political parties, removal of the political rights of critics, and the establishment of indirect elections for governors and the presidency. Governors are selected by state assemblies (with some municipal representation as well), and the President is elected by the Congress. In both settings, Arena has majorities.

Since the congressional elections of 1970 and 1974 and the municipal elections of 1976 maintained Arena majorities, it seemed that the government would have the confidence to allow relatively free congressional elections in 1978. However the impressive showing of the MDB in the cities, and the possibility that it might capture control of the Federal Senate, led Geisel to take the backward step known as the "April package."(6) When the opposition refused to negotiate on a government proposal for judicial reform, President Geisel's distrust of the MDB was increased. Furthermore, he had already decided that the transition would require yet another military president, that the logical person was Joao Figueiredo, and that Figueiredo would need a majority in Congress to guarantee a continued "slow, gradual, and sure" process toward redemocratization.

The April package was designed to guarantee that the regime would win in the senatorial elections of 1979 (it was already certain of winning in the Chamber of Deputies). The package scheduled indirect rather than direct selection of a third of the senators by the state assemblies, in nearly all of which Arena had a majority. In addition, the Falcão Law, which restricted television and radio campaigning, was applied to the upcoming elections, and the presidential term of office was increased from five to six years. Geisel decreed the April package by using AI-5 to close Congress. While it was in recess, he promulgated the electoral changes. Although one should not discount the possibility of extra-legal manipulation of future elections, President Figueiredo no longer has AI-5 as an instrument for doing so.

Two issues involving future elections were settled in mid-1980. First, the municipal elections scheduled for 1980 were postponed until 1982 to coincide with congressional and state elections. Although this decision, which was ratified by the PDS majority in Congress, can be interpreted as a setback on the path toward democracy, it had long been rumored and was not unexpected. The government party, because of its strength on the local level, would undoubtedly have won in most of the municipal contests, but to justify this measure it alleged lack of time for the new parties to organize sufficiently to contest them. The opposition charged, to the contrary, that the government was trying to avoid a test under the new party system. Second, direct elections were reestablished for all members of the Senate and for state governors, in contrast with the previous indirect system. The regime has made clear its intention, however, to conduct the presidential election of 1985 as an indirect procedure by the members of Congress.

The elections of 1982 will consequently be the key indicator as to where Brazil stands in its transition from authoritarianism to democracy. If they are carried out as scheduled, the opposition will have the opportunity, at least in theory, to strengthen itself on the state level by electing governors and gaining control of more state assemblies. More significantly, if it can achieve a majority in the congressional vote, the opposition, or sectors of it, will be in a position to determine who Brazil's next president will be. The government, in turn, is counting on its continued strength in the Congress and the incapacity of the opposition to unite around a single candidate.

The Formation and Activities of Interest and Pressure Groups.

Perhaps the most interesting political development in Brazil since 1974 has been the political activity of a number of groups which represent different segments of the population. The issues on which they have been particularly active are human rights, distribution of economic benefits, further redemocratization, and the defense of Brazilians who suffer from discrimination and neglect.

The most successful democracies in the contemporary world are those which not only have freedom of political expression, representative parties, and free elections, but also intermediate groups which criticize, organize to present their concerns to the public, and pressure for changes of policy. Any analysis of the Brazilian political process must take into account not only what is happening at the top - the President, Congress, and the national political class - but the capacity of society to generate grass root groups that represent autonomous expresssions of individual and group concern to improve society by acting politically.

The pivotal organization behind many of these groups is the Catholic Church.(7) During the decade of the

1970s, the leaders of the Brazilian Church made an important shift in their approach to social problems. They decided to use the influence of the Church to defend the poor, in contrast with their longtime tendency toward association with the upper and middle classes. The Church began giving special emphasis to the formation òf "base" organizations: communities of committed Christians who gather for mutual worship and discussion, but who also analyze common problems and develop means of confronting them. The Brazilian Church hierarchy played an important role in influencing the Puebla (Mexico) meeting of the Latin American bishops in February 1979 to take a similar stance, and in turn the Puebla Document is providing legitimation for what the Brazilians are trying to do. The visit of Pope John Paul II in July 1980 also provided support for the overall strategy of the Church in Brazil.

Although the influence of the Catholic Church on most Brazilians in the twentieth century has been limited, it still maintains the loyalty of many individuals including such population segments as urban slum (favela) dwellers, peasants and rural workers, and indigenous ethnic groups. These are among the Brazilians who most clearly suffer from unemployment and underemployment, poverty, inadequate public services, and discrimination by officials. Traditionally these groups have had little or no political impact because of illiteracy, their relative weakness when compared with more powerful segments of society, and manipulation by politicians. It is on behalf of these people that the Church leadership has chosen to dedicate its principal resources to a pastoral strategy that aims not only at a deepening awareness of Christian faith and values, but also at the formation of organizations for improving life.

In the past decade the growth of such base communities has been phenomenal, and it is currently estimated that over 50,000 of them exist in Brazil.(8) A great many of these already existed for other reasons, such as devotional activities or functions necessary to maintain the parish. Others, however, have sprung up as a conscious result of the expanded pastoral focus on forming Christian communities among the poor. The Church, in fact, currently sponsors what is probably the most extensive network of grass-root organizations in Brazil. While many of these prefer to limit themselves strictly to religious functions, others are already assuming an active role in articulating group interests, making changes in the community, and putting pressure on politicians and public officials to promote policies benefiting their interests.

In each diocese the system of base communities is organized within the framework of pastoral programs. For

example, there may be a pastoral of the land, which operates in rural areas, an urban pastoral, which functions
chiefly in lower class areas, and an indigenous pastoral,
which is a manifestation of the Church's missionary work
among the various native ethnic groups. In addition, the
Church has developed pastorals among migrants, workers,
students, and prisoners. Each of these groups suffers
from various problems. The poor in rural areas are usually either small farmers or salaried workers. The small
farmers frequently have plots that are too limited for
an adequate living, they do not benefit significantly
from government programs of credit and technical assistance, and they receive low prices for their products
because intermediaries control the market. The landless
workers frequently receive less than the minimum wage and
do not enjoy as generous social security benefits as urban workers. Though most of them would like to own their
own land, this hope is frustrated by the absence of an
effective agrarian reform in Brazil, and by the government's encouragment of holdings based on large commer-
cially-oriented production.

The pastoral strategy of the Church assumes that base
ecclesial communities (CEBs) can become the wedge for
achieving a greater degree of justice for these groups.
In many instances the rural poor do not even know what
their legal rights are, much less how to guarantee them.
Though peasant unions are already widespread as a network
for the social security system, many rural dwellers do
not belong to them, and they usually do not serve as effective representatives of peasant interests. The CEBs
are not intended to replace the existent rural labor unions, but to form them where they do not exist, and to
make all of them more effective as ongoing instruments
to guarantee individual rights and pressure government
for benefits and land.

Already, in a number of urban areas, the CEBs have
stimulated significant improvements in the living conditions of the lower class. Individuals in the CEBs began
by discussing common problems and the need for a collective solution to them. Frequently the next step was to
get the support of Protestants and other groups in the
community which shared the same concerns. In a number
of cases, government organizations which supposedly represented the community did not function well and the
Church groups provided the momentum for making them more
effective. By working together, members of the community
solved certain problems through mutual activity or by
calling the attention of public authorities to their
needs. In many cases local politicians and officals are
recognizing that they cannot simply assume the acquiescence of this segment of the electorate, but must respond
to their demands.

There is no question that the CEBs constitute an extremely important political phenomenon in Brazil, although one that cannot yet be fully evaluated. A number
of political figures, impressed with their potential,
have been discretely trying to get their support and some
enthusiasts anticipate that the CEBs will result in a
radically new form of popular participation in national
politics. For the moment, it is useful to stress their
influence on local problems and policies, which is the
level on which many of the needs and solutions of the
relevant groups are found. The elections of 1982, which
will cover all elective offices except the presidency,
will provide a test of their broader impact. One can,
for example, envision the following development: candidates from the local to the national level, seeking to
attract the newly politically conscious Christians as an
important constituency, would try to implement policies
that responded to the general line of their criticisms
and suggestions. The base communities would then constitute a nonpartisan, but politically active, voting bloc
to which politicians and parties have to be responsive,
and the policies implemented would entail social changes
as well as patronage.

Although the CEBs are the prototype of the intermediate organizations that may provide a new, more participatory political content to Brazilian redemocratization,
the leadership of the Church has also acted as an initia-
tor and supporter of other activities. These have included campaigns for human rights (in which the archdio-
cese of São Paulo and its Cardinal, Paulo Evaristo Arns,
have been outstanding) and amnesty (supported by the Brazilian National Bishops Conference). Important individuals and organizations in the Church have also encouraged
more autonomous labor unions and have acted through comprehensive movements in defense of groups which are discriminated against, such as the indigenous population and
blacks.

A second type of intermediate group is the labor union.(9) As a result of the political openness of 1974,
Brazilian labor has been more active than at any time
since 1963 and 1964. The official Brazilian labor union
system has never enjoyed the autonomy that is normally
associated with its counterparts in democratic countries
since the present structure was created during President
Getulio Vargas' "Estado Nôvo" and patterned on corporatist, authoritarian models prevalent in Europe in the
1930s. The government formed the system to prevent the
left, especially the Communists, from establishing a political base among workers. In return for participating
in a controlled labor movement that would not challenge
government interests, the organized workers received a
variety of benefits such as minimum wages, paid vaca-
tions, accident insurance, health care, and pensions.

In the early 1960s, widespread strikes, open Communist leadership in labor organizations, the formation of unions outside the offical structure, and political activities by the unions caused alarm among the Armed Forces leaders and contributed to the coup of 1964. Afterwards many politicians from the Brazilian Labor Party (PTB) had their rights removed, and in a number of cases labor unions were taken over by the government and their leaders thrown out of office. The military regime thus reaffirmed its longtime government domination over the labor movement, a domination which had been challenged only in the years immediately before 1964.

The government also exercised tight control over unions because its antiinflation policy depended on control of wage increases. In the first years after 1964, this policy resulted in a decline of real income among salary earners although, after 1970, the government tried to apply compensatory policies to help the lower income groups regain some of their relative share of national income.

The new political situation after 1974 stimulated labor organizations to press for further advantages. In 1977, they found a means to challenge the government's wage control system when a team from the International Monetary Fund revealed that inflation in 1973 had actually been about 20 percent higher than the official figure. In May and June 1978, a number of major unions in the state of São Paulo went out on strike, insisting that the lost difference be restored to their salaries.

Strikes have been common features of the Brazilian political landscape for the past two years, reaching a special intensity in March 1979 at the time of Figueiredo's inauguration and in a massive metallurgical strike in April and May 1980. The most active unions have been among metal workers of greater São Paulo, but strikes have also spread to groups such as teachers, construction workers, and sugar plantation laborers. In some instances the unions accomplished their objectives, but in others they backed down because of their own internal divisions or because of pressure and cooptation by the companies and the government.

During this period, a number of union leaders, now organized as the Unidad Sindical, tried to develop more independent positions on economic and political questions than the conformist positions of the official labor leadership. The unquestioned leader of this group is Luis Ignácio da Silva (Lula), even though in May 1980 he was removed from his union post on a charge of violating the labor legislation. Lula and his associates represent a younger generation of union leaders who are challenging the "pelegos," the officials who currently direct the official union system.

The appearance of more independent union activity is a decisive expression of increased intermediate group relevance in Brazil. Although the official structure continues to be strong because of the benefits it administers, the new union leadership has received wide national attention because of its initiatives in defense of workers' rights. It is thus in a position to press for expanded unionization and for more rapid redistribution of income in favor of the working class. Although Brazil is now passing through a difficult economic situation, with an inflation rate of nearly 80 percent in 1979 which has led the government to institute new norms on wages, Lula and the unions that work with him have already established themselves as the leading spokesmen in Brazil for labor interests.

In addition to the activities of the Catholic Church and labor unions, the new political situation has led a number of other interest groups to enter the public scene. Two groups which particularly deserve mention are those representing the two Brazilian ethnic groups which have historically been the most obvious victims of exploitation and continue today to suffer various forms of discrimination: the indigenous population and blacks.

Brazil has a large number of indigenous peoples who traditionally lacked mechanisms to defend the preservation of their land against interlopers, the maintenance of their culture, and their very existence against disease, enslavement, and murder. Since the early part of this century, individuals such as the explorer, Cândido Rondon, and professional anthropologists have been exceptional in raising their voices in favor of these groups. However Brazil lacked organizations representing the indigenous population which could also gain the support of diversified sympathizers from other segments of society. The National Indian Foundation (FUNAI), which is supposed to help the natives, was often led by individuals who lacked sensitivity to indigenous problems and FUNAI itself often contributed to exploiting those it was supposed to serve.

Since 1974, this lack is being remedied. Perhaps the most important institution seeking to defend the native population is the Indigenous Missionary Council of the Catholic Church (CIMI).(10) In addition to publicizing violations of indigenous rights, it has promoted meetings, organizations, and protests by the indigenous leadership. CIMI now has regular regional and national meetings which bring the heads of various indigenous groups together to act on their common problems.

In 1978 a government proposal to speed up "integration" of the indigenous population into the national culture through "emancipation" added important new dimensions to the movement. The widely publicized opposition of the indigenous leaders to "emancipation," which they

perceived as a destruction of their culture and their incorporation into the poorest and most marginalized segments of the national population, led to the formation
of Pro-Indian Committees in a number of Brazilian cities.
Various other concerned groups joined the protest and in
1979 compelled the government to withdraw its proposals
for "emancipation." As a result, a widespread movement
is now active throughout Brazil which is aimed at recognizing indigenous culture, protecting the rights of the
native population, and pressuring for greater justice for
them.

Brazil's blacks also experience various kinds of
discrimination, especially in employment and wages.(11)
However most blacks have been disinclined to join movements in defense of their rights because the national
racial perception distinguishes between mulattos and
blacks in the population of African background, and the
culture encourages people to aspire to whiter identity
and racial characteristics than they actually have. In
spite of this, black cultural, and even political, movements existed for limited periods of time between 1920
and 1950.

With the recent political openness, a number of Brazilians of African background have responded to the emphasis on black identity, cultural values, and political
participation which have appeared in such places as Africa, the West Indies, and the United States. One expression has been black cultural associations, which now
exist in a number of Brazilian cities. The only clearly
political organization is the United Black Movement
Against Racial Discrimination (MNUCDR).

At present MNUCDR is a relatively small organization
led by middle class black intellectuals. Although they
recognize that their movement has a long way to go, they
are currently focusing on two types of strategy. One is
joining with other organizations in pushing for redemocratization, on the assumption that they can best achieve
their aims in a more open society. The other strategy
is carrying on activities in favor of black rights and
opportunities. In preparation for the elections of 1982,
the MNUCDR is trying to increase political awareness,
especially among lower class blacks, with special emphasis on the problems affecting blacks as a race. Its leaders hope that, in major states like Sao Paulo and Rio
de Janeiro, candidates representing MNUCDR will run under opposition party labels. In other cases they will
support candidates who sympathize with the objectives of
the organization.

Although the MNUCDR and other organizations of black
consciousness are relatively new and still small, they
represent an important symbol of political action by the
largest racially discriminated minority in Brazil. Their
objectives are difficult ones because Brazilian political

leadership, including the present regime, denies that Brazil has any kind of racial problem at all. Questioning this assumption is delicate, even for the scholar, and certainly far more so for victims of racial discrimination who want to bring about changes.

Another type of intermediate organization is the National Student Union (UNE), which was an important political actor on the left in the early 1960s. Although "abolished" by the military regime, UNE continued to play an effective role until the crackdown of 1968, when it became clandestine. The political openness enabled it to reemerge and reconstruct its organization. Since 1976, UNE has been a public participant in practically all antiregime causes. In 1979 it held nation wide elections (though only a minority of the students voted), in which the most radical slate won. At present, it probably represents, at least in rhetoric, the farthest left position among the political actors in Brazil.

The leading instance of a developing national concern during 1979 and 1980 has been the question of legal justice, which includes treatment of persons detained for crimes, the effectiveness of the judicial system, and conditions in the country's prisons. The murders of petty criminals by "Death Squadrons" composed of off-duty policemen have long been a national scandal, with the government having charged and sentenced only a few of those involved. More recently, wide publicity has focused on cases of individuals who were arrested and then mistreated by the police. In several prominent trials, persons with influence were freed although they were obviously guilty. This has drawn attention to the heavy sentences that people who lack influence regularly receive. The slow pace of judicial procedures often results in release for serious criminals, while innocent people often spend more than a year in prison before they have a chance to prove their innocence. In the prisons themselves, the privileges of those with resources contrast to the shabby treatment of persons who are poor.

The abuses of criminal justice have thus far not produced a concerted movement for change, but this is clearly an important issue of human rights. The Brazilian Order of Lawyers (OAB) has been active in highlighting problems of this sort and in making suggestions for improvement. The Catholic Church is also developing a prison pastorate in certain parts of the country. The fact that prisoners are now commonly believed to be the principal victims of human rights violations suggests that further organizational efforts and political activities in their defense may emerge in the proximate future.

Another issue destined for greater group activity is women's rights. For several years, social scientists have been making studies of the condition of Brazilian women and the discrimination which certain segments, like maids, undergo.

Finally, mention should be made of ad hoc movements responding to temporary crises. Brazil has a certain tradition of mass demonstrations, often by women, in response to government policies or economic conditions. The most recent example emerged early in 1980 when women's groups in a number of Brazilian cities protested the high price of meat. Though this movement clearly represents a privileged group, namely those who eat meat regularly, it is nevertheless a legitimate expression of the group awareness, organization, and pressure by which ordinary Brazilians are expanding their participatory experience and contributing to democratic processes.

CONCLUSION

The Brazilian process of redemocratization will be decisively tested between 1980 and 1985. The next major item on the agenda may be constitutional changes, carried out either by Congress or by a specially elected commission. These changes could involve matters like the allocation of relative power to Congress, the President, and the Ministers, the replacement of proportional congressional representation by districts, changes in the National Security Law, and a definition of the specific role of the National Security Council. The elections of 1982 and 1985 should further clarify the political opinions of the electorate, strengthen the new parties, and increase the role of Congress. During these years interest group activity should grow and involve a larger public in a still wider range of local and national problems. If all goes well, Brazil might make the transition from an authoritarian to a democratic regime during this period.

This optimistic forecast may be sidetracked by several problems. As political activity increases and the time for a transition draws near, certain groups within the regime may become frightened and return to a policy of political manipulation or even try to halt the process. It is well-known that many medium-ranked officers are concerned about forms of political activity and the relative freedom Communists now enjoy. This view is shared by some business and political leaders.

Brazil's economic crisis may also provide an excuse for stopping the political process. Brazil is currently undergoing extremely high inflation, serious balance of payments deficits, and the prospect of a mushrooming external debt. In 1979, President Figueiredo, by appointing Antônio Delfim Netto as Minister of Planning, reestablished the system that had prevailed from 1964 to 1974 of vesting control of the economy in a single czar. This shift reflected a perceived need that the government could not confront the economic problems of the country without more effective control. In the worst of projections, Brazil might enter a massive economic crisis that would lead the regime to conclude that it could not tolerate the luxury of further democratization and might even result in a reversal of this process.

Brazil can also move toward a situation in which certain formal democratic processes coexist with authoritarian features which undermine their effectiveness (as in Mexico). Even in its most democratic periods in the past, Brazil experienced military meddling in politics, government control of labor unions, and a concentration of power in the presidency and the bureaucracy. All of these characteristics have been strengthened as a result of military rule and are now very difficult to eliminate. The Armed Forces, through their high administrative posts in the National Information Service (SNI), and state-owned enterprises in petroleum, steel, transport, and communications, seem likely to continue their prominent role in governing Brazil. Labor unions are weak, and the corporatist union structure cannot be easily changed to a more autonomous one, despite the increasing influence of more independent labor activities. The federal bureaucracy has grown so much since 1964 and assumed such powers, especially in the economic area, that it constitutes a powerful political group eager to defend its prerogatives against attempts to transfer them to, for example, Congress.

Other democracies today face similar problems. Redemocratization in Brazil is a process, an adventure and struggle by the Brazilian people, though a true transition will have occurred when the opposition has an authentic possibility of contesting power on all levels.

NOTES

1. For a detailed discussion of the use of the moderating power in Brazil, cf. Alfred Stepan, The Military in Politics: Changing Patterns in Brazil (Princeton: Princeton University Press, 1971), pp. 62-187.

2. On the early stages of the Brazilian transition, which at the time was called "decompression," cf. Fernando Pedreira, "Decompression in Brazil?," Foreign Affairs, April 1975, pp. 498-512; and Thomas G. Sanders, "Decompression in Brazil," American Universities Field Staff Reports, East Coast South America Series, Vol. XIX, no. 1 (December 1975).

3. The Background of the 1968 events is discussed in Ronald M. Schneider, The Political System of Brazil: Emergence of a "Modernizing" Authoritarian Regime, 1964-1970 (New York: Columbia University Press 1971), pp. 241-78.

4. Ibid., pp. 279-329.

5.   _Veja_, 1 November 1978.
6.   On the intentions of the Geisel government in decreeing the "April package," cf. André Gustavo Stumpf and Merval Pereira Filho, _A Segunda Guerra: Sucessão de Geisel_ (São Paulo: Brasiliense, 1979), pp. 111-124.   An especially helpful book for understanding the Geisel administration is Walder de Góes, _O Brasil do General Geisel_ (Rio de Janeiro: Nova Fronteira, 1978).
7.   Our understanding of Brazilian Catholicism is greatly assisted by the works of Thomas C. Bruneau, cf. _The Political Transformation of the Brazilian Catholic Church_ (London: Cambridge University Press, 1974).   For the shift of Catholic attitutes and strategy during the 1970's, cf. his _Religiosity and Politicization in Brazil: The Church in an Authoritarian Regime_ (Austin: University of Texas Press, 1981).
8.   The literature on base communities is extensive. Cf. Bruneau, _Religiosity And Politicization in Brazil_ and "Basic Christian Communities in Latin America: Their Nature and Significance (especially in Brazil)," in Daniel H. Levine, ed., _Churches and Politics in Latin America_ (Beverley Hills: Sage, 1979), pp. 225-237.   Among the numerous works published in Brazil, the most important is _Comunidades Eclesiais de Base: Uma Igreja que Nasce do Povo, Encontro de Vitoria, ES_ (Petropolis: Vozes, 1975).
9.   On Brazilian labor unions, see Kenneth Paul Erickson, _The Brazilian Corporatist State and Working-Class Politics_ (Berkeley: University of California Press, 1977).
10.   The principal source of information on indigenous problems and organizations in Brazil is the _Boletim do CIMI_, published in Brasilia by the Conselho Indigenista Missionario.
11.   For an insightful analysis of various movements, including the CEBs, Indians, and blacks, see Charles A. Reilly, "Cultural Movements as Surrogates for Political Participation in Contemporary Latin America" a paper presented at the 1980 annual meeting of the American Political Science Association, Washington, D.C.

10
The Labor Movement and the Crisis of the Dictatorship in Brazil

Ronaldo Munck

In the last few years the Brazilian labor movement has shown a vitality which took most observers by surprise. What appeared to be a long-term acquiescence to the rule of the military dictatorship imposed by force of arms in 1964 was dramatically broken. Today the Brazilian labor movement is facing vital programmatic and organizational questions, the answer to which will play an immense role in Brazil's future political development. To even begin to understand these political debates, one must delve into the history of Brazilian labor. This chapter therefore begins with an examination of the corporatist controls imposed on labor by the state in the 1930s and 1940s. This is followed by a synthetic appraisal of the populist period of the 1950s and early 1960s, which was important in shaping labor's political consciousness. The major characteristics of labor under the dictatorship which came to power in 1964 are outlined, and a discussion of the brief resurgence of labor in 1968, the few sparks of labor revolt in 1973, and the sustained and massive upsurge of labor militancy since late 1977 sets the scene for a discussion of some of the major questions, both theoretical and political, posed by the challenge to the dictatorship from the Brazilian labor movement.

This is not the place for a full historical account of the development of the Brazilian working class. Our purpose is simply to outline the structural characteristics of the Brazilian labor movement (understood as the class, union, party triad). As Tim Harding notes in his definitive political history of Brazilian labor, it was "with the coming of the Estado Nôvo in 1937, /that/ all radical and independent labor leadership was suppressed, and unions were carefully regimented into a corporatist system. An elaborate structure of labor legislation enveloped union activities, denying the right to strike and converting the unions into government agencies."(1)

The main characteristics of this corporatist structure
can be summarized as follows:

1. The state, with the explicit aim of concili-
    ation, retained for itself the right to
    guarantee certain minimal rights to labor,
    (related to the work situation, etc.) rather
    than allowing an unmediated conflict between
    capital and labor.
2. A system of labor tribunals was set up and
    became a key element in cushioning the class
    struggle, taking the employer/employee con-
    flict out of the work place and channeling
    the struggle into the state apparatus it-
    self.
3. A type of union structure was established
    with horizontal bodies which could coordi-
    nate unions and federations through a cen-
    tralized trade union structure and the ex-
    plicit prohibition of trade union organiza-
    tion in the work place.
4. A social security system was set up which
    corresponded to the tendency of the state
    towards social intervention and, at the same
    time, reinforced the mass base of the popu-
    list governments.(2)

Prior to 1945 the main aim of Vargas's labor policy
was to suppress labor, not to mobilize it in support of
populist policies. As the corporatist Estado Novo gave
way to parliamentary democracy, this was to change. The
unions launched a series of strikes in 1945-1946, but
Vargas was overthrown before he could forge a populist
"pact" similar to that created by Peron in Argentina
during the same period.
    In retrospect, we can see that the incorporation of
the trade unions into the state apparatus was most
clearly defined and systematized in the period of 1945-
1946.(3) This was the first attempt to create a "populist" syndicalism through the political alliance of Vargas and the Brazilian Communist Party (PCB), and it was
this same model which shaped the union structure when it
achieved maturity in the mid-1950s. Its main characteristics were a subordination to nationalist ideology and
a policy of reform within a class-collaborationist structure, a framework maintained by João Goulart and the
other populist politicians from Vargas onwards.
    It was the so called "populist period" in Brazilian
political history which largely shaped the consciousness
of the Brazilian working class. It was during this period that the labor movement expanded, acquired its predominantly nationalist political consciousness, and, after seriously challenging the rule of the bourgeoisie in

the early 1960s, collapsed in disarray in 1964. This was a period when the working class burst onto the political scene in a process of simultaneous social mobilization and political containment promoted by the Bonapartist figures of Peron in Argentina and Vargas in Brazil. Populism, in Ianni's words, "is a form of political organization of the relations of production, in a period of expansion of the forces of production and of the internal market."(4) It is a period of intense politicization of the working masses, a politicization which was to become the main contradiction of Latin American populism. Again following Ianni, populism "depoliticizes social classes, through politicizing the alliance and harmony between classes."(5) The Bonapartist role of the populist leaders, in standing "above" the class struggle (at least in appearance), led to the development of the trade unions as a means of controlling the expanding working class.(6)

Vargas was elected to the presidency in 1950 on the basis of a nationalist economic programme and a "populist" social programme. He committed suicide in 1954, under pressure from both within and without Brazil. During his period in office, the working class began to assert its growing social weight. A watershed in the struggle of labor was undoubtedly the São Paulo general strike of 1953 which mobilized engineers, glass workers and typographers in a fierce struggle lasting twenty-nine days and marked by big demonstrations and police repression. It was at this time that labor effectively regained the right to strike.(7) This strike was particularly significant insofar as it saw the widespread development of factory committees which were later revived in isolated cases such as the Rio shipyards, taking the place of the more generalized unions which were not developed until the late 1970s.

The state-wide strike in São Paulo in 1954, one of the greatly increased number of strikes in 1954-1955 as compared to the preceeding period, gave rise to the "Pacto de Unidade Intersindical" (PUI), an organization which was to effectively coordinate labor struggles in Sao Paulo until 1960. Another state-wide strike in 1957 drew half a million workers and made the PUI a mass organization built on rank and file initiative sufficient to make up for the lack of central labor organization.

After 1959, a new wave of strikes resulted from the growing rate of inflation. "Sindicalismo de base" currents developed and broke off from the PCB. There were strikes in the rail, road transport, and port sectors among others, as well as important strikes by government employees who had just gained the de facto right to strike. There were further increases in labor struggles during 1960, including general strikes against the effects of inflation. During this wave of strikes, which often escaped the control of the "pelegos" (labor leaders

domesticated by the government), the campaign for a central union body was renewed and came to fruition in 1962
with the formation of the General Confederation of Labor
(CGT).(8)

The period of the Quadros government (1960-1961) was
one of realignment within the labor movement, and his
fall from power raised the problem of Goulart's succession. This campaign was marked by mass public meetings
and culminated in a general strike which took place (at
least partially) in spite of the arrest of hundreds of
union leaders and a severe repression of the labor movement. An indication of the climate during this episode
of the class struggle was Porto Alegre, where Brizola
(the "radical" populist governor) was actually distribut-
ing arms to the workers. Without doubt, the period 1961-
1964 is critical for the labor movement, highlighting
both its strength and its grave political weakness. According to Harding, a general radicalization of the mass
movement developed in this period and the populist manipulation of labor was seriously hampered by mass pressure
and radical demands. After a series of strikes in late
1961, union leadership focused on the struggle for the
return of full presidential powers to Goulart. Goulart
had to use his full authority to call off these strikes
before specifically working class demands were won. By
1963, however, "political" strikes were increasingly directed against Goulart, one example being the massive
mobilization of the state railway workers, CGT opposition
forces, the National Students Union (UNE), and others
which prevented Goulart from establishing a state of
siege during the crisis provoked by the Brasilia Sar-
geants Revolt. General strikes were called to demand
changes in Goulart's cabinet and also to oppose the Plano
Trienal (Three Year plan) of 1963. In effect, the working class was effectively exercising a "right of veto"
on crucial questions in the political arena.(9)

A key element in the actual implementation of the
corporatist union structures was a particular type of
"organizing cadre" promoted by the Ministry of Labor with
the aim of controlling the unions. Known as the "pelegos," these people had functions akin to a trade union
officials and became the lynch-pin of the collaboration-
ist union structure. The "pelegos" helped achieve the
dual purpose of the union structure, that is, to maintain
the proletariat in submissive passivity (accentuated by
the paternalist relations in the work place itself) while
developing a mass base for the populist governments which
depended on popular support for political survival. From
the mid-1950s onward, the "pelegos" were consistently
removed from the leadership of the larger, more militant
unions, and were replaced by a new organizing cadre which
was just beginning to consolidate itself in 1964. This
new group, composed primarily of factory delegates and

organized in factory committees, was potentially the backbone of a new workers movement. It played a crucial role in the development of working class struggles, organizing pickets, etc., and taking an important part in political education. This made it a key element in the development of class consciousness and the recovery of the labor movement from the "pelegos." Some idea of the extent to which the phenomenon was occurring can be seen in a 1960 survey of São Paulo textile workers which found that of thirty firms, eleven had factory delegates and seven had factory committees.(10) Considering the degree of persecution to which these delegates were subjected, this survey is certainly an underestimate. One can assume that the massive wave of strikes in the period 1960-1964 also led to increased importance for this new organizing cadre.

Perhaps the most fundamental characteristic of the Brazilian labor movement is the particular history and structure of the trade unions which left them without any real roots in the factories. In the beginning this was due to rulings in the labor laws, but the evolution of the trade union movement after that time did nothing to alter the situation. This lack of organic structures in the work place, and the predominance of populist relationships between the leaders and the masses in demonstrations and assemblies, etc., can be seen as a major cause of the near total collapse of the workers' movement in the face of the military coup in 1964. According to Almeida and Lowy,

> ... for these reasons, the military dictatorship was easily able to decapitate the labor movement by persecution of the top labor leadership. The base was totally formless, without any organic structure at the factory level to react to a rapid deterioration of purchasing power and the loss of all means of expression. Even had the former labor leadership wished to do so, it would have been very difficult, lacking a rank and file structure, to mobilize the workers under the clandestine situation to which they were reduced. The labor movement, losing its top leadership, found itself completely atomized and unstructured.(11)

However we wish to avoid an interpretation, common amongst PCB writers, which proceeds from the rural origins of the class, or the corporatist nature of its trade unions, to draw conclusions on the political level regarding the working class. This procedure, which ignores the mediations between the economic and the politico-ideological, has been used to explain the "backwardness" of the class. But, as Poulantzas correctly notes in a different context, to understand the trade unionist or corporative mentality of a given working class, it is not sufficient to refer to its lack of a hegemonic class consciousness (or conception of the world) but one must refer for explanation to an analysis of its political organization, to the structure of the working class party, and to the global political strategy of this party.(12) In the Brazilian case this means subjecting the Communist Party to critical investigation. In the evaluation of any working class political party, a key question is its trade union policy. On this score the PCBs failure is clearly revealed. According to Almeida and Lowy, between 1945 and 1964 the PCB made no attempt to win autonomy for the labor movement, to transform the union structure into an independent instrument of the working class, or even to create a grass roots labor organization in the work place capable of escaping state control. The PCB's failure to take up the task of breaking the crippling ties between the trade unions and the bourgeois state is manifested in its ambiguous policy towards the "imposto sindical," the trade union tax which was administered by the state. Although on occasion voicing its opposition to the paralyzing effects this tax, the PCB eventually capitulated. On the various occasions when the PCB strove to organize parallel trade union structures, it in fact only helped to revitalize the rigid corporatist structure; although outside the rules, these projects were actually broadly compatible with the official framework. Fundamentally, the PCB never attempted to organize a coherent class-struggle tendency in the unions which could fight the collaboration of the labor bureaucracy. (13)

The year 1964 periods was one of those historical in which a dramatic condensation of contradictions occurred. The aim of the military coup was to ratify, at the level of political hegemony, the economic dominance already achieved by monopoly capital. The coup put an end to the ambiguity of late populism and ensured the social and economic conditions necessary for the continued expanded reproduction of capital. In the wake of the coup, a large number of trade union militants and leaders were arrested and the corporatist legislation was applied with a vengeance. The right to strike was effectively removed and the living standards of the masses were driven down: real minimum wages fell by 55 percent between 1961 and 1973. However the labor movement was not totally disorganized, and in 1968 it was able to wage a number of important battles. In April, a largely spontaneous strike was launched in Contagem (an industrial suburb of Belo Horizonte). This radical revolt, involving twenty firms and roughly 20,000 workers, culminated in the occupation of the Belgo-Mineira company. The "Oposição Sindical" (union opposition), which had played a prominent role in this action, then organized an effective protest during the official May Day demonstration. This was followed by the Osasco strike movement in São Paulo's industrial belt, in which an occupation of the Cograsma factory soon spread to five other plants, involving approximately 6,000 workers. Sharp repression broke this strike and the workers returned to work in disarray. In retrospect, however, these strikes prefigured the post-1977 wave of strikes. In his assessment of both strikes, Weffort shows how they pointed to future trends: "Contagem and Osasco represent, in different degrees, the same process of internal rupture in populist trade-unionism ... a partial rupture ... though sufficient to show evidence of some characteristics of working class independence which contrasts clearly with the dominant tendencies in the country's trade union movement since the 1950s."(14)

From 1968 to 1978, while no major strike occurred in Brazil, this clearly did not mean that all working class activity ceased. Instead, labor protest was directed towards restructuring the movement to meet the increased exploitation unleashed after 1968. There is no doubt, however, that defeatism was the dominant mood, and activity was channelled in a legalist direction, such as through the Church.(15) However, by mid-1973 there were signs that a struggle was beginning, with a series of strikes in São Paulo, at the Villares Steel plant, and at the Volkswagen and Mercedes-Benz car factories. Most significantly, this renewed phase of labor activity marked the emergence of the "Comissões de Fábrica," factory commissions which historically, whether in 1919-1920 and post-1969 Italy, in Spain during the Franco regime, or in Argentina since the 1940s, have structured the working class at its base. The importance of these rank and file bodies was particularly stressed by the "Oposição Sindical" organized in a number of unions. As Almeida and Lowy noted at the time,"departing from previous experience, in this phase the labor movement based itself on the factory commissions. It had not yet reached the point of commissions representative of the workers in the whole plant, since to look for across-the-board representation would be suicidal in the current state of repression. Commissions are made up of the more conscious activists who assume the propaganda and organizational work at the factory level."(16) Compared to the Argentinian "comisiones internas," these bodies were as yet unrepresentative of the workers, having developed more among the political vanguard. In the years since 1973 they have become somewhat more representative, although it appears that they may have been partly outflanked by the new "militant" union leadership.

The period from 1974 to 1977 was one of organic changes within the labor movement, with a noticeable increase in the level of internal union life. These changes culminated in a number of strikes in late 1977 which marked the beginning of a qualitative transformation in the relation between labor and the military state. The metal workers began to campaign for "reposição salarial" (or wage recovery) which involved combating the government's falsification of cost of living indexes in the previous year. The union demanded a 34 percent wage increase to compensate for the losses caused. In 1977, during the wage negotiations, strike action was increasingly discussed in the union assemblies. In November of that year the Fiat-Diesel plant near Rio went out on strike for three days.

However it was the largely unexpected May 1978 strike at the Saab-Scania factory (São Bernardo) which marked the beginning of an unprecedented upsurge of labor activity in Brazil. This strike spread throughout most of the motor industry, largely organized by an in-plant leadership seeking wage increases. This unprecedented wave of labor activity did not stop with the motor industry, and it is estimated that in the four months following the Saab-Scania strike, 280,000 workers in over 250 firms went on strike. Furthermore, at least 1 million workers were directly or indirectly affected by wage settlements negotiated as a result of such stoppages.(17) Following this, there was another round of strikes by metal workers in November 1978 and again in March 1979, involving roughly 250,000 workers each time. Overall, from the time President Figueiredo came to power in March 1979 until the beginning of August 1979, there were 1.2 million workers on strike and 14.3 million work days lost. New forms of action were tried, such as picketing which had virtually disappeared after 1964, and the "pelego" leadership came under growing pressure from a new, more responsive, type of union leader. Also, as one report notes, recognition of shop-floor delegates became a major issue.(18) The major characteristics of these strikes have been the advanced forms of organization practiced, such as the "General Strike Committee," frequent struggles across occupational lines, and massive militant street demonstrations.

Some idea of the extent of this strike explosion can be seen from Table 10.1. By mid-August 1979, the number of strikes for the year had reached 83 and the press was anxiously comparing this with the 131 strikes in 1963, that year of "Anarchy and Subversion." By November the number of strikes had passed 200, and the magazine Veja was speaking of an "extravagant" wave of strikes, "taking in practically everyone, from the building workers of Goiania to the commercial employees of Belo Horizonte. Even reaching the Rio Police ...."(19)

Table 10.1
Strikes 15 March 1979 to 30 June 1979

Industry	No. of Strikes	Man Days lost	No of Strikers
Metallurgical	6	2,780,000	200,000
Others	3	10,000	10,000
Total	9	2,790,000	210,000
Service Sector			
Bus drivers	8	223,000	120,000
Teachers	13	9,035,000	400,000
Doctors	9	370,000	15,000
Refuse Collectors	4	5,400	2,200
Journalists	1	12,000	2,000
Others	2	34,000	15,000
Total	37	9,679,000	544,000
Overall Total	46	12,469,400	754,200

Source: "Greves do Governo Figueiredo," Veja, 11 July 1979.

The November 1979 metal workers' strike in Sao Paulo was, by all accounts, rather confusing. It was launched by the "Oposição Sindical," and though at first it was widely supported, it collapsed after eleven days by which time only 20 percent of the workforce was still out. The powerful president of the Union, Joaquim dos Santos Andrade, regarded by many as the archetypal "pelego," weathered the storm with the support of the PCB. The sharp repression of this strike seemed to indicate a successful clampdown by the state on labor agitation. Allied to this was the new wage legislation which placed a premium on productivity bargaining, clearly designed to defuse working class militancy. However this mixture of repression and cooption was not successful for long, and the strikes continued.

In March 1980, more than 12,000 dockers in Santos came out on strike against the recommendations of the "pelego" leadership, in spite of the strike being illegal as Santos is a "national security" area. On 1 April 1980, some 300,000 metal workers in São Paulo's ABC industrial suburbs struck over wages, but also, significantly, for the forty hour week and the right to elect

shop stewards. The strike was ruled illegal and the union leadership, including Lula (Luis Inácio Da Silva),
were arrested. The Church and most of the political
parties supported the strike and while some of the workers voted to accept the wages offered by the courts, the
rest stayed out for the broader demands. This seemed to
constitute a definitive blow against the "pelego" system.
After forty days the strike appeared to be deadlocked as
the government had banned any further negotiations. At
the beginning of May the drift back to work began, but
not before a militant 100,000 strong May Day march in Sao
Bernardo. A humorist in the magazine Isto É mocked the
government's arbitrary powers with the suggestion to "Let
Saints André, Bernardo and Caetano (after which the ABC
suburbs are named) be expelled from heaven, and in their
places let Ford, Volkswagen, and General Motors be canon-
ized."

How can we explain and analyze these tumultuous
events? First, they must be set in the context of the
new model of capital accumulation generated since 1964.
This is not the place to fully analyze Brazil's accelerated economic growth, particularly during 1961-1973 when,
on the basis of a sharply increased exploitation of labor, increased integration into the international circuit
of capital reproduction, and a strongly interventionist
state, the so-called "economic miracle," with all its
contradictions, emerged. What interests us here is only
the effect this had on the composition of the working
class. Between 1960 and 1970 the number employed in industry grew by 52 percent and between 1970 and 1974 it
increased again by 38 percent. Perhaps an even clearer
illustration of the great expansion of the Brazilian
working class is the fact that between 1970 and 1977 industrial workers rose from 15 percent to 20 percent of
the total workforce. Within the working class, there
was a greater relative expansion of those sectors involving the most skilled and potentially most advanced
contingents of the class. Metal workers represented 30
percent of total employees in the transformation industry
in 1960, 38.9 percent in 1970, and 41.3 percent in 1974.
(20) The objective conditions are present for a powerful
labor movement; the question is whether the subjective
conditions have been attained. One obstacle may be that
this "new" working class has become a relatively privileged sector compared to the mass of impoverished workers
and peasants.

One must consider more precisely the character of
this "new" working class, which was the main actor in the
recent strike wave, although largely absent from the big
1962-1964 strikes. A term which immediately springs to
mind is that of "labor aristocracy." Lenin, in particular, popularized this term and used it loosely to cover
the trade union leadership, an upper stratum of the

working class, and even the whole working class in imperialist nations. As Stedman Jones accurately points out,
"the term has often been used as if it provided an explanation. But it would be more accurate to say it pointed
towards a vacant area where an explanation should be."
(21) I suggest that we have to confront two distinct issues: (1) whether certain elements of the working class
have attained a relatively privileged economic position,
and (2) whether these elements have become a politically
reformist layer, allied with the owners of capital.

The structural heterogeneity of the working class is
perhaps the main issue in question. The development of
monopoly capitalism tends to produce a degree of differ-
entiation within the working class. A "modern" layer of
the working class will tend to emerge with considerably
higher wages than average. What does not follow is that
these workers will become conservative. In fact, they
have often been in the vanguard of the class struggle,
articulating the most advanced antibureaucratic demands
and raising issues of workers control. This does not
mean they cannot become a conservative influence in the
labor movement, but this depends on the whole political
context in which they operate, and on the type of orientation which predominates within each union. In fact the
basic problem with most "dual labor market" theories is
that they attribute undue primacy to technological change
and neglect the role of workers' organizations. Trade
unions are quite capable of gaining better wages and conditions across the category, including the big multinational and the small workshop. Bearing in mind the real
conflicts, the structural heterogeneity of the working
class need not result in a political split within the
labor movement.

The debate on this question in Brazil has polarized
around two main positions. Tavares de Almeida, in particular, has stressed the structural contradictions between the "new" proletariat of the dynamic industrial
sectors and the old trade union structures.(22) He
points to the development of a current within the labor
movement, organized around demands - wage adjustments in
accordance with increases in productivity, collective
bargaining at plant level, and recognition of union organization within the factory - which could not be dealt
with through the corporatist structures. The logical
outcome of this would be a tendency towards "business unionism" along North American lines, a technically profi-
cient union organization noted for wage militancy, yet
conservative. Another view is to argue that these modern
sectors of the working class, far from being incorporated
or "bought off," are in fact at the forefront of the economic and political advance of the working class as a
whole. John Humphrey has argued coherently for this position, and his careful analysis of the Brazilian motor

industry workers concludes that "far from being an aristocracy of privileged, self-interested workers, they have
acted as a class vanguard because they have taken up positions on the right to strike, forms of negotiations and
opposition to the employer and the state which have been
followed by other groups of workers."(23)

In reality things have not polarized quite so clearly
in either direction, and both positions ("optimistic" and
"pessimistic" for short) reached conclusions which were
far more definitive and specific than warranted by the
limited empirical studies on which they were based. This
has now been recognized by Tavares, who notes that there
is no inherent contradiction between "business unionism"
and "class struggle unionism," which can in fact coexist
quite easily.(24) Further, whether militancy is absorbed
and institutionalized or instead exacerbates the class
struggle depends not only on the "condition ouvrière" but
on the overall environment which determines the content
and sense of each demand.

Alongside the term "labor aristocracy", and often
confused with it, is the category of "labor bureaucracy."
One of the major issues posed by recent strikes is the
crisis of the "pelego" system. At first implicitly, and
increasingly explicitly, they have been attacked by opposition in the unions, and a more representative leadership, the "auténticos," has tended to emerge. During the
strikes of 1979, the "new unionism" of Lula promoted a
genuinely open and more democratic form of leadership,
although quite capable of secret negotiations and the
quelling of revolt within the rank and file when necessary. This militant/conservative quality was best seen
during the Belo Horizonte construction workers strike in
mid-1979 where Lula played a major "advisory" role to the
local unions.

This wildcat strike by 15,000 workers was effectively
settled through Lula's intervention which was designed
to channel spontaneous action into "effective" union activity.(25) This intervention by the de-facto leadership
of the Brazilian trade union movement may have suggested
to the government that a central labor organization would
not only strengthen labor, but could also "institution-
alize" it. It appears that the Communist Party is
throwing its weight behind the Central Unica dos Trabalhadores (CUT) in a bid to recreate the CGT of the early
1960s. But, as one commentator notes, "if it gets off
the ground, the CUT is likely to be an unholy alliance
of PCB unionists and pelegos, who still hold power in the
majority of unions."(26) How questions about the "pelegos" and the development of a central labor organization
will be settled in practice depends on the degree of activity of the working class, and on its political leadership.

The trade union bureaucracy has been referred to as the "labor lieutenants" of capital, or as Hyman more elegantly puts it, "those continuously engaged in a representation capacity perform a crucial mediating role in sustaining tendencies towards an accomodative and subaltern relationship with external agencies (employers and state) in opposition to which trade unions were originally formed."(27) The "political space" occupied by a labor bureaucracy is mainly space ceded by a demobilized working class. The Brazilian working class has now broken out of this passivity and is beginning to threaten the hegemony of the old labor bureaucrats, the "pelegos."

The state certainly needs, and will do everything in its power to obtain, a stable and reliable mediator between itself and the working masses. This is needed to absorb and defuse the struggles of labor. If the "pelegos" can no longer serve this function, then clearly capital will begin to groom the "autenticos" to fill their place. In that case, this current, which has until now reflected the antibureaucratic nature of the mass struggle, will have to confront the workers. The workers as a whole have placed critical importance on their autonomy, i.e., the independence of their unions from the state, a break with the corporatist labor legislation (especially the "imposto sindical"), and a recognition that the bosses are to be confronted (as against those seeking a recreation of the "National Democratic" alliance). The political project of the "autenticos" is still unclear, but the critical break with corporatist/bureaucratic practices has been made and will only be reversed through a dramatic defeat of the working class.

At this stage we must discuss the major organizational questions currently confronting the Brazilian labor movement, primarily the role of the democratic organs for workers power. A labor movement is more than just an organ for self-defence achieved through combination by the trade unions. It is a whole series of intermeshing networks - economic, political, and social - which change the natural atomization of labor under capitalism and turn it into a movement. A social phenomena like this can become thoroughly routine and even conservative, as the British labor movement shows. However, when workers are part of a social movement, they are in a different position from those workers who are just election fodder for bourgeois parties. British laborism and Peronism in Argentina may be politically bourgeois-reformist, but they represent proletarian organizations. When workers organize in the work place, they begin to think and act collectively and can become a social movement. When this movement endures long years of clandestine activity, confronts repressive military regimes, and structures a broad nationalist movement, as in Argentina, it accumulates an immense wealth of experience. It is only within its own movement that the class builds up its confidence, exchanges experiences, and elaborates its class perspectives. In Brazil, it is difficult to actually speak of a labor movement as such. That is, there has not been the degree of unity, cohesion, and organization necessary for the crystallization of a basic class consciousness. Whether or not this will emerge from the recent upsurge of labor activity is still an open question.(28)

What is certain, however, is that the factory commissions have an absolutely crucial role to play in this process. Throughout the history of the international workers' movement, periods of upsurge have led to the creation of new organs for the self-expression of the class, based on active and direct democracy. To the extent that this process takes place, workers cease being just a class defined through its opposition to capital and become organized as a class "for itself." In periods of downturn these bodies can become bureaucratized, but in an upsurge of rank and file activity they can take on the role of the classic workers soviets.

The factory commissions were built on what is only a very weak tradition in Brazil's labor history, but today they are rapidly becoming an important component of the struggle. During the November 1979 metal workers strikes, some 200 factory committees were formed in Sao Paulo alone, although these have not yet become fully stabilized. A partial demobilization after the strike, which was not really successful in its aims, saw the number of commissions fall to fifty, of which ten are recognized officially by management. By 1979 it was calculated that some 60,000 workers were employed in workplaces with functioning factory committees. When one considers that there are 300,000 metal workers in São Paulo alone, we see what a limited extension these commissions have, even in the industrial heartland of the South-East.

The "Oposição Sindical" movement recognizes the centrality of factory commissions.(29) This emerges in the following quote from their 1976 programme:

The total independence of the Opposition in relation to the trade unions is only possible if it turns to the broad working masses who find themselves disorganized in the factories and organizes them in workers'commissions. Only with organizational autonomy can the union opposition adopt an independent political line in relation to the unions. Only in that way will the union opposition, based on the workers' commissions, appear in the eyes of thousands of workers as an alternative to the official unions. The workers' commissions are the place of unity of all the workers who are prepared to organize and fight for their interests, even the most immediate ones. In each factory, in each work-place, in the communities, wherever there is the need and disposition to struggle, it is possible and necessary to organize workers' commissions.(30)

The main problem with regard to the "Oposição Sindical" is of course their very restricted social base. Their approximately 200 activists grew to 500 in the 1978 strikes. These are in the vanguard sectors of the class, and only some of these, during limited periods of time, have moved along these advanced organizational lines. The more traditional sectors of the class, such as the rail and port workers who are organized along more orthodox trade union lines, will take longer to mobilize. The danger is, of course, that the vanguard elements will move too far ahead of the majority of the class.(31) There is a clear need for a dialectic of intervention in the commissions and through the official union structures.

Last, but not least, we turn to the programatic questions facing Brazilian labor, among other things the issue of labor's political representation. When the corporatist bonds began to break, labor naturally turned toward the formation of its own political organ. Early in 1979, the Sao Paulo metal workers union voted to struggle for a workers' party on the grounds that, "history has shown us that the best instruments the workers can use to carry out the struggle is their own party." (32) This call came to fruition with the formation of the "Partido dos Trabalhadores" (P.T.) which brings together many of the activists of the "Oposições Sindicais," as well as more established union leaders such as Lula. The demands for organizational autonomy in the labor movement are now being matched by a clear call for the class independence of the proletariat in politics.

The multi-class opposition front, the Brazilian Democratic Movement (MDB), was questioned by leaders of the labor movement. They wanted, in Lula's words, a party "without bosses, without foremen and without sell-outs, a party that would fight to defend the economic and democratic rights of the workers and for socialism."(33) Throughout the country, union meetings and political discussions are considering the issue of a Workers Party. Against President Figueiredo's panicky proposals of a "democratic opening" (the "abertura"), these trade union and political forces are putting forward the slogan of "a free and sovereign constituent assembly." Along with the demand for the dismantling of the repressive apparatus, another major plank is the issue of trade union unity and the building of a United Workers Federation. Those interested in a Workers Party declared themselves to be against vertical union structures, a relic of the

"Estado Nôvo," and have drawn up proposals to overcome the division and atomization of the workers movement. The primary weakness in this political project remains the low level of political consciousness, even among the leaders in this new class struggle. However, as the leader of the São Paulo leatherworkers union declared recently, "the Workers Party is the reflection of all the struggles for the demands of the working class.... The presence of the Workers Party provide(s) a certain form of continuity to the struggle, restoring the workers' full confidence in their ability to lead the struggle, side by side with the Workers Party, towards a workers' government."(34)

It would be unrealistic to assume that the PT is at present a viable organ for Brazilian working class demands. Certainly the PCB would contest its right to call itself the workers party, which by definition is the label for the "Leninist" party alone. But the PCB is going through an unprecedented crisis and out of it, as before, a renewed turn to the right is emerging. Its legendary leader, Luis Carlos Prestes, is totally marginalized and has called on rank and file members to take control of the party, blaming the leadership for its "opportunism, total absence of internal democracy and personality struggles."(35) Underlying this spectacle is the rightist "Eurocommunist" policy being pursued by the party, against the "Oposição Sindical" and for the "pelegos" in the unions and, in the broader political scene, in support of the MDB's successor, the PMDB. When calling for an alliance of the PMDB, the PTB, and the PP (Partido Popular, a dissident business party) in the 1982 elections, Prestes could declare "they defend even the banker's party."(36) This party is certainly not growing amongst the militant metal workers of São Paulo.

Finally, in the very fluid panorama of Brazilian party politics, the Brazilian Labor Party (PTB) appears to be the one possible social-democratic option. Currently being revived by Brizola, this party has dusted off its old populist/nationalist mantle and has added a few "socialist" overtones. From the perspective of stability this option is a rational one, and one which is probably influenced by European, especially German, Social Democracy. Without entering into this whole debate, with its many pitfalls, I think that it would be premature to write off the possibility of a "populist" reappearance in the 1982 elections (much like Peron's return in 1973). Nationalist and democratic ideology has an immense capacity for recovery among the masses, and even the Goulart years look rosy after sixteen years of military dictatorship.

The recent upsurge of the labor movement in Brazil has thrown into question many assumptions as to the nature of this movement. The idea of an inherent "backwardness" in the Brazilian working class makes little sense today, if it ever did. The explosiveness of the situation makes it impossible to predict future developments with any degree of precision. Certain things, however are clear. The industrial proletariat as a whole is in the forefront of a great upsurge in the mass movement. Economic conditions, though not as buoyant as in the years of the "Brazilian miracle," will allow capital more flexibility than in, for example, Argentina. This situation makes it likely that an attempt will be made to create a labor aristocracy. The question of working class unity would then become a burning issue. If a Labor Party based on the trade unions were created, it would seem to indicate that Brazil will follow a pattern analogous to that of the rise of Peronism in Argentina in the 1940s. Whether this broad political unity, albeit reformist, would be coopted by the likes of a Peron (perhaps Brizola?) remains to be seen. The other issue posed by these developments is that of the labor bureaucracy. The "pelego" type figure is probably on the way out, but it is possible that the new militant trade union leadership may become something akin to the Peronist union oligarchy.

If one thing is certain today, it is that the battle for political leadership in the Brazilian labor movement is now on in earnest. At one stage is could have been said that while the struggle in Argentina was over control of the labor movement, in Brazil it was over the question of forming such a movement. This process is now well under way, but the fight between class-struggle tendencies and reformists of all types is just reaching the critical stage. The question of leadership is always critical in the workers' movement, but in certain historical periods it becomes an overwhelmingly decisive issue. This would seem to be the case in Brazil today as poor leadership could direct the movement down a "populist" blind alley, while a correct approach could put the movement in a position in which it could deal the final blow to the "economic miracle" which has been in crisis since 1974.

It would be tedious to repeat our partial conclusions from each preceeding section. It would also be futile to engage in any further speculation on the future on the basis of scarce and very patchy information. However, it is absolutely essential to pose the question of labor and dictatorship today in the correct context. We have worked on the assumption that the capital/wage labor relation is the very kernel of bourgeois society. Certainly the labor movement in Brazil has conquered a significant political space through its own struggles. But, to understand the future role of labor in Brazil, one must see it in the context of the overall unfolding class struggle.

This leads us to a bit of "self-criticism," a good note to end on. This discussion has completely neglected the rural dimension; in April 1980 over 500,000 farmers and rural workers took to the streets protesting against the soya export taxes, which were subsequently dropped. This unprecedented action should sensitize us to the critical role of Brazil's rural working population. We have also neglected the global political struggle - how can you discuss the 1978 strikes without discussing the victory of the opposition in the November 1978 elections? To say that labor "created" its own political space is only half true - the "abertura" also opened up the political scene, perhaps a necessary precondition for labor's reemergence. Finally, we have neglected the debates and strategies of the Brazilian bourgeoisie. An intelligent policy of labor cooptation is emerging, with a restricted role allocated to the shop stewards, and management is putting more emphasis on its industrial relations departments (sorely neglected since 1964). Herbert Brenner, personnel manager of General Motors do Brasil, puts it like this, "Undoubtedly, we're getting into a new era. About the best we can hope for is that labor-management relations will be conducted here on the same basis as in any democratic country."(37)

NOTES

1.   Timothy Harding, "The Political History of Organized Labor in Brazil" (Doctoral thesis, Stanford University, 1973), p. 16.
2.   M. H. Tavares de Almeida, "O Sindicato no Brasil: Nôvos Problemas, Velhas Estruturas," Debate e Critica 6 (1975):   53-56.
3.   Francisco Weffort, "Origens do Sindicalismo Populista no Brasil (A Conjuntura de Apos-Guerra)," Estudos CEBRAP 4 (1973).
4.   Octávio Ianni, "A Formação do Estado Populista na América Látina," Civilização Brasileira, 1975, p. 135.
5.   Ibid, p. 115.
6.   The industrial working class grew from 83,998 in 1920 to 254,771 in 1940, 449,084 in 1950 and 1,509, 713 in 1960.   This growth rate is even more rapid in Sao Paulo, which contains about half the total members of this class.
7.   José Moises, "La Huelga de los 300 mil y las Comisiones de Empresa," Revista Mexicana de Sociologia 40, no. 2 (1978).
8.   Timothy Harding, "The Political History of Organized Labor."

9.   Kenneth Paul Erickson, The Brazilian Corporative State and Working-Class Politics (Berkeley: University of California Press, 1977), Chapter 6.

10.   J. A. Rodrigues, Sindicato e Desenvolvimento (São Paulo: Difusão Europeia do Livro, 1968), p. 148.

11.   A. Mendes de Almeida and M. Lowy, "Union Structure and Labor Organizations in Contemporary Brazil," Latin American Perspectives III, no. 1 (1976): 108.

12.   Nicos Poulantzas, "Marxist Political Theory in Great Britain," New Left Review 43 (1967).

13.   This is not the place to enter into the reasons for the PCB orientation, which center around a blind allegiance to Comintern mandates and the general priority of "democratic" alliances. See however R. Chilcote, The Brazilian Communist Party (New York: Oxford University Press, 1972).

14.   Francisco Weffort, "Participação e Conflito Industrial: Contagem e Osasco, 1968," Cadernos CEBRAP 5 (1972): 87.

15.   I do not mean to imply that the grassroots "comunidades de base" which are organized by the Church are conservative. In fact, they played a crucial role in the reactivation of the labor movement in the 1970s. See, for example, Thomas C. Bruneau, "The Catholic Church and Development in Latin America: The Role of the Basic Christian Communities," World Development 8 (1980): 535-544.

16.   Mendes de Almeida and Lowy, "Union Structure," p. 117.

17.   J. Humphrey, Labor in the Brazilian Motor Vehicle Industry (Liverpool: University of Liverpool, 1979), p. 27.

18.   J. Green, "Liberalization on Trial: The Workers' Movement," NACLA Report, May/June 1979, p. 22.

19.   "Greves do Governo Figueiredo," Veja, 11 July 1979.

20.   T. Vigevani, "Notas sobre la clase orbrera Brasilena," Coyoacan 6 (1979).

21.   G. Stedman Jones, "Class Struggle in the Industrial Revolution," New Left Review 90 (1975): 61.

22.   Tavares de Almeida, "O Sindicato no Brasil," pp. 68-73.

23.   Humphrey, Labor, p. 31.

24.   M. H. Tavares de Almeida, "Desarollo capitalista y accion sindical," Revista Mexicana de Sociologia 40, no. 2 (1978): 488.

25.   Latin America Political Report 13, no. 31 (1979): 242.

26.   Latin American Political Report 13, no. 41 (1979): 322.

27.   R. Hyman, "The Politics of Workplace Trade Unionism: Recent Tendencies and Some Problems for Theory," Capital and Class 8 (1979): 54.

238

28. See, however, the articles by José Moises and
J. Humphrey, "Brazil I: Capitalist Crisis and Workers'
Challenge," Latin American Perspectives 6, no. 4 (1979).
29. The position of Lula is more ambiguous: "In my
view, the factory commissions inside a free labor-union
movement would have to remain subordinate to a broader
coordination by the union .... We cannot propose freedom
for unions and at the same time want commissions parallel
to the unions." (Interview in Latin American Perspectives 6, no. 4 (1979): 96.) It seems that even the most
militant union leaders perceive the threat to their position (and to the very role they perform) implicit in the
self-organization of the working class.
30. "Ante-Projecto de Programa da Oposição Sindical
de São Paulo," 1976.
31. T. Vigevani, "Del Golpe militar (1964) a las
comisiones de fabrica (1979)," Coyoacan 7/8 (1980). The
preceding discussion on factory commissions owes much to
this vital article.
32. Green, "Liberalization," p. 24.
33. Lula, Intercontinental Press, 5 November 1979,
p. 1080.
34. Ibid, p. 1083.
35. Luis Carlos Prestes, Veja, 2 June 1980.
36. Ibid.
37. H. Brenner, Business Week, 17 March 1980.

29. The position of Lula is more ambiguous: "In my view, the factory commissions inside a free labor-union movement would have to remain subordinate to a broader coordination by the union .... We cannot propose freedom for unions and at the same time want commissions parallel to the unions." (Interview in Latin American Perspectives 6, no. 4 (1979): 96.) It seems that even the most militant union leaders perceive the threat to their position (and to the very role they perform) implicit in the self-organization of the working class.

30. "Ante-Projecto de Programa da Oposição Sindical de São Paulo," 1976.

31. T. Vigevani, "Del Golpe militar (1964) a las comisiones de fabrica (1979)," Coyoacan 7/8 (1980). The preceding discussion on factory commissions owes much to this vital article.

32. Green, "Liberalization," p. 24.

33. Lula, Intercontinental Press, 5 November 1979, p. 1080.

34. Ibid, p. 1083.

35. Luis Carlos Prestes, Veja, 2 June 1980.

36. Ibid.

37. H. Brenner, Business Week, 17 March 1980.

11
The Ethic of Umbanda and the Spirit of Messianism: Reflections on the Brazilian Model

Roberto da Matta   •

INTRODUCTION

My title needs to be explained; it indicates neither an intention to refute Max Weber's thesis using Brazilian data, nor to naively demonstrate its validity. Why, then, such a pompous title? I want, first, to indicate my intellectual affiliation with the sociological posture that Weber pioneered. It is important to remember that for Weber - as for Durkheim - the social is a dimension of human existence with its own specific space, rules, and properties. To be understood and interpreted, the social phenomenon - or rather, the social dimension of the human phenomenon - has to be seen as independent from other dimensions of collective life. Durkheim discussed the study of the social as matter precisely in this sense. According to him, the social should be studied on its own, independent of psychological, individual-istic, utilitarian, geographical, or biological connec-tions. Similarly, Weber stressed the value or moti-vational aspects of social phenomena as more important than attempts to reduce the study of the social to other levels of the collective reality which are believed to be more real or concrete. Rather than trying to explain the social universe as if it were composed of individual-ized elements possessing greater or smaller degrees of reality, Weber studied relationships and simultaneities of the social phenomena.

Weber did not deal only with the external aspects of social phenomena, such as numbers and aggregates of in-dividual actions found in statistical charts, nor only with the formal decisions taken by a government at the national level; he studied the inner side of the economic and political phenomena for he was trying to discover how a given group of ideas became the basic element in the orientation and determination of certain social configu-rations. Weber, therefore, rejected the study of the ex-ternal and formal aspects of social and political events, focusing instead on their internal relationships, values, ideologies, and motivations.

One of the most important aspects of this position is the search for a better interpretation of the internal dynamics of social actors. The essential is not to determine the "spirit of capitalism" by means of external signs chosen by researchers from a group of norms and institutions, but to learn how a given set of social actions and subjective motivations became objective and were transformed from individual preferences into collective and dominant values. The question, then, is not to recognize "capitalism" as defined by external factors and according to rules devised by the researcher himself, but to recognize when the combination of hard work, desire for profit, ideas for organization of productive activities, individualism, vocation for productive work, sobriety, and greed sufficient for massive investment becomes a compact value configuration, a dominant and normative ideology - an ethic as Weber himself stressed. This study, then, not unlike the "démarche" characteristic of the French sociological schools, begins by distinguishing between aspects that are empirically inherent in the social system and can be easily perceived by outside observers, and those traits which the system incorporates and utilizes in ways that make it unique and special. To distinguish between these modes of internal perception of each system is a necessary sociological task, for it is only then that we will be able to obtain the key to certain specific configurations which are universal in the course of the human experience. We have to distinguish between the virtual (found in all social systems) and the real (or the historical given), i.e., that which each system establishes as real and sociologically significant.

Weber warns us that various elements of "modern capitalism" were already present in several precapitalist commercial experiences, wherever and whenever the act of trade occurred. The idea of profit and the desire for wealth are universal characteristics of the acts of trade, present even in lootings where an attack against the "others" was legitimated for the looters by the belief that they were dealing with "the unfaithful" or even with "nonhuman beings." Weber is fully aware that the "greed for gold" is as old as mankind since greed is a characteristic of the human experience, traditional or modern. Consequently, by itself, it cannot be used to define "modern capitalism." To do this would be to confuse the virtual and the universal with the real and the historically given. It would be to commit the mistake, so common to contemporary Brazilian sociology, of reducing social phenomena of high complexity and of multiple planes, such as Umbanda, carnival, and soccer games, to mere "opium of the people," for it would be to use a

universal characteristic (the fact that all social structures are illusory and create their own realities) to explain particular, essentially Brazilian, characteristics.
(1)

It is not, then, only in the idea of profit and/or
in the greed for gold that one can find the distinctive
trait (or the "spirit," according to Weber) of modern
capitalism. On the contrary, unlimited greed for gold
and the idea of profit at any price signify an enormous
attachment to tradition and not the opposite. When trade
takes place outside an ethical or ideological framework,
it is close to war as it is an instance in which everything is valid and possible so long as those who are
dealt with are "foreigners" or "strangers." The corol-
lary of this kind of social classification is obvious:
a system in which the trade spheres are separate. One
does not exchange objects or services with brothers and
fellow villagers, but only with outsiders. Because one
can only trade with outsiders, profit and deceit, characteristics typical of warfare, are valid forms of relationship. Among persons of the same group, family trans-
actions are marked by gifts and by long circuits of
trade.(2) With outsiders (who are potential enemies) the
interchange acquires the characteristics of a commercial
exchange. In this case the links of reciprocity are
short - one gives and receives at once - denoting an
absolute lack of confidence.

In other words, according to Weber, social systems
that incorporate the idea of profit practice it only in
their relations with the outside world. They are, then,
societies that possess double ethical patterns. These
are systems in which, as we saw above, the activities are
even more scrupulous given the absence of an ethical code
to regulate commercial activities, turning them into positive endeavours. About this, says Weber,

> "The universal reign of absolute unscrupulous-
> ness in the pursuit of selfish interests by the
> making of money has been a specific characteris-
> tic of precisely those countries whose bour-
> geois-capitalistic development, measured ac-
> cording to Occidental standards has remained
> backward. As every employer knows, the lack of
> the "coscienziosita" of the laborers of such
> countries, for instance Italy, as compared with
> Germany, has been, and to a certain extent still
> is, one of the principal obstacles to their ca-
> pitalistic development. Capitalism cannot make
> use of the labor of those who practice the doc-
> trine of undisciplined "liberum arbitrium," any
> more than it can make use of the business man

who seems absolutely unscrupulous in his dealings with others, as we can learn from Benjamin
Franklin.(3)

It was only much later that social anthropology discovered that many traditional systems possessed "spheres of
exchange"(4) and a double, or even triple, ethic because
articles traded within a domain could not be traded in
all other domains. As Weber stresses, one of the dominant traits of traditional societies is the multiplicity
of spheres and/or domains which do not allow the system
to define itself around one single ethic. In this way
commercial activity was confused with piracy and with war
as being appropriate only to those not belonging to the
group. The double ethic, says Weber, "has permitted here
what was forbidden in dealings among brothers."(5) That
is, what was valid for the outside world could not be
applied within; trade could not be separated, as an activity, from other types of social exchanges essential
to the life of the group.

I believe that the idea of a double ethic is relevant
to the interpretation of the Brazilian case and that Weber was making an important distinction in stating that
there is a double ethic in traditional systems. This
distinction permits us to explain the negative connotations of commercial activities in traditional societies
where the above-mentioned spheres of trade are differentiated and possess equally differentiated ethics. I am
convinced that this occurs in Brazil. However, Weber
stressed that it was possible to eliminate these multiple
spheres and to devise a code common to all society. It
is precisely the acceptance of this single ethic that
allows us to perceive work and business in a positive
way, as acceptable and moral activities. The desire for
profit is as old as the history of man, but this universal trait was not sufficient to give rise to modern capitalism. An ethical code for commercial activities was
necessary to transform the "auri sacra famis" (the mere
greed for gold) - always condemnable in traditional societies - into something positive, making it possible for
Weber to affirm the following: "The 'auri sacra famis'
of a Neapolitan cab driver or of a 'barcaiulo' and certainly of the Arabic representatives of similar trades,
as well as the craftsmen of southern European or Arabic
countries, is, as anyone can find out for himself, very
much more intense and especially much more unscrupulous
than of, say, an Englishman in similar circumstances."(6)

In other words, when we have a society internally
divided into multiple spheres of trade, the commercial
activity is always forbidden to one of its groups - usually to the group where we find "our brothers." Because
it is forbidden to this group, it is always used as a
tool against enemies or persons who are not part of "our

humanity." These activities are only transformed into ends in themselves when framed by an ethical code that transforms mere negative sentiments, appropriate only to enemies or "outsiders," into a positive and all-embracing ideology, valid for all spheres of life.

It is precisely because the traditional systems possess multiple codes and varied spheres of trade that modern capitalism has to be characterized by a series of positive traits. In addition to universal factors such as greed for gold and desire for profit, it includes other essential elements such as vocation and the related idea of work. In this way, then, work stops being something natural and begins to be perceived as a vocation or calling; it becomes an individualized activity that should be of moral benefit to the individual who practices it but no longer needs to benefit his whole family, village or social segment. Work is then no longer a punishment or a means to obtain resources, but becomes instead an end in itself. It can thus become as isolated as the worker himself who, to use Karl Polanyi's terminology, ends by freeing himself from the net of social relations which in the traditional systems rigidly determined with whom one could, should, or would have to work. (7) Thus Protestantism, especially in its most radical variations such as Calvinism, allowed the separation of work from social relations. Thus freed, work became something measured in individual terms, being no longer a means for the social existence. Weber related this change to a basic form of rationality and individual planning: being now on his own, each man could count only upon himself. Work was no longer only a way to acquire wealth, to ritualize the most sacred social relations and so save his soul. Work became a richness in itself and the only guarantee of salvation.

In Weber's theory the notion of work as an end in itself suppresses all other mediating spheres. Thus Protestantism, in its most extreme modalities, by eliminating priests, rituals, and even the Church, and by no longer allowing the alleviation of man's anguish regarding salvation through the doctrine of predestination, ended by affecting a division between work and all social relations and symbols (such as rituals) that could divert one's attention from the final goal: between God and men, there is nothing but work seen as a vocation. Life is no longer lived according to a multiplicity of codes but is now unified by a single ethic: an ethic of sobriety, of hard work, and of individual growth or accumulation of wealth.

I believe that this is the valid interpretation of the basic question of Weberian investigation: the problem of the apparently contradictory association of a religion with a strong and accentuated secular ascetism, provoking what Weber dramatically characterized as an "incredible inner solitude" associated with the accumulation of wealth that characterizes modern capitalism. It was only when Weber recognized this secular and individualistic ascetism, which suppresses all intermediaries by putting everyone directly before God, that he finally realized that it was precisely this apparently negative force that made modern capitalism possible and highly dramatic. Work as an end in itself became not only a possible motivation, but also morally desirable. The problem for Weber, therefore, was not to explain the elements of the capitalist system as individualized elements, as many modern social scientists did with their variables and their positivism, but to look for a specific and singular meaning for the social configuration. His aim was not simply to explain the congruities between certain elements, but to interpret the apparently contradictory relations between a doctrine that required sobriety and the tremendous wealth that its adherents were able to accumulate. By shying away from the world and by avoiding worldly distractions and pleasures associated with celebrations and festivities of social and political events, the Calvinists unwittingly created the basic anxiety which led to the idea that the system needed to free itself from the rules that considered commercial activities and work as means but never as ends in themselves.

My title, then, intends to evoke a certain methodological position and some of its substantive aspects. It attempts to apply an idea developed by Weber to the sociological study of the Brazilian society. I am referring here to the implications of Weber's theory for societies in which capitalism is only partly developed and in which double ethics are prevalent. It is precisely in these systems that the exploitation of manpower assumes unscrupulous and brutal forms, creating a bold kind of capitalism, savage and irresponsible, in which profit is at the service of the maintenance of personal privilege and the state and its bureaucracy are mechanisms which subjugate individuals and block all forms of social justice and political equality. It is my thesis that this occurs in Brazil because Brazilian society has a type of social dynamics very different from those found in systems in which the Protestant creed is dominant. In societies with an explicit Calvinist creed, anxiety about one's salvation is a basic component of social values and moral paradigms and consitutes the basic material for the dominant ethic. In Brazil, the basic religious sense usually involves the alternation between different sorts of tensions and anxieties so that the system operates by means of compensation and a logic of mutuality. Thus in the Brazilian system the sources of anxiety in one sphere are altered by other spheres: what is oppressive on one plane can be compensated for on another. The ethic represented by the types of religion dominant in Brazil, such as Umbanda and the so-called "popular Catholicism," serves this purpose.

To demonstrate this thesis I will present an overview of the most important national rituals in Brazil. Then I will tackle questions connected with the diverse forms of power, authority, and prestige found in Brazil. Finally, I will try to indicate how Umbanda (together with other forms of popular religiosity) is an expression of a subsidiary system that is gradualist, hierarchical, and compensatory: a system possessing an enormous and clear multiplicity of spheres, motivations, and ideologies.

BRAZILIAN RITUAL SYSTEM

The Brazilian ritual system I have studied concerns festivities. I do not see them merely as a kind of bankrupt super-structure, as mere expressions of more real and concrete social strata, but rather as specific manifestations of Brazilian society in the same way that politics and economics are also manifestations of certain social relations and embodiments of the prevalent values. I do not consider these festivities as isolated manifestations, independent of each other, but as a system. I distinguish national rituals or festivities from regional ones, which are celebrated only in specific regions, cities or towns and are irrelevant as sources or reinforcements of more embracing social identities.(8)

It is impossible to study Carnival (probably the best known and most famous Brazilian national ritual) without mentioning at the same time civic-military rituals, such as the "Day of the Nation" (celebrated as part of the Week of the Brazilian Nation in September, when Brazilian independence is commemorated) and the religious rituals, originally sponsored by the Roman Catholic Church, such as the processions of devotion to the protecting saints or the rituals related to Holy Week when the whole country commemorates the death of Christ. Viewed as a system of relations and transformations, Carnival, National Week, and Holy Week form a triangle of rituals. That is, they give us three ways to "read" Brazilian society. One way is through the rigorously hierarchical perspective of the civil-military commemorations, manifested in the military parades, in which the state's most authoritarian facet is represented by the Armed Forces as symbolizing Brazilian reality. There is another reading, more disorganized and complex, suggested by the analysis of religious festivities in which the saint (or saints) of the Church are believed to belong to everyone; all social and political differences are neutralized by the ethic of Holy Communion and of charity which emanates from the

saints and can embrace and encompass all the participants. And, finally, there is a third reading of Brazilian society made possible by observing the model crystallized by Carnival, when the whole society temporarily
changes and adopts a manner of social intercourse characterized by individualization of action and creativity of
gestures and institutional relations. During Carnival
there is a tendency toward greater individualism, equality, and acceptance of more open forms of competition.
In fact the carnival parade, as opposed to the religious
and military parades, is an enormous contest.

The civic rituals represent the state and emphasize
order and duty, gestures typical of what we call patriotism. The Church processions recall the sphere of renun-
ciations, suggesting the realm of an invisible power, a
plane in which mankind can be united under the mantle of
a saint or of someone who knows how to be the vehicle of
divine messages. In contrast, the rituals of Carnival,
as well as some movements of spontaneous or violent character such as the "quebra-quebra" or the vandalism of
buses, boats, or trains of the Brazilian Central Railroad, belong to the sphere of an egalitarian ethic that
sees pleasure and necessity as the prime movers of certain social impulses. The processions are organized by
the Church, the military parades (and the civic rituals
in general) by the state and the Armed Forces, but Carnival belongs to the people and to the free associations
organized and structured by the people.

If we relate this triangle of rituals to other dimensions of Brazilian society, we can create a powerful analytical framework to help us discern the rationale of the
system. On this rationale Brazil is a society in which
there exist a series of spheres in which various elements
can manifest themselves freely, as, for example, the
state during its own week of celebrations or the Church
during her festive days. For each institution or powerful group there is an assigned area or social sphere. If
the military parades and the rituals in general exemplify
the hierarchical separations, and the religious rituals
provide the means for a permanent reconciliation of the
conflicts, the "fits of disorder," such as Carnival,
present the world "upside down," as being egalitarian,
individualized and free. Some Brazilians perceive this
as "folly," hence the name "folião" deriving from folly
or madness ("fou" means crazy), used to describe those
dancing in the carnival.

Table 11.1 presents various dimensions of the contrasting ritual moments, indicating how relationships are
distinguished in these three very different events. In
fact, one could say that each one of these festive occasions celebrates a certain way of behaving and of perceiving the Brazilian world which excludes, and at the
same time suggests, another alternative way. Without an

Table 11.1
A Schematic Representation of Brazilian Rituals

Brazilian Rituals	National Week	Holy Week	Carnival
According to the temporal plane they recreate:	historic	historic and cyclic	cyclic (and repetitive)
According to the types of expression that they use:	marches, uniformity of movement, unity, tradition, speeches, national anthem	prayers and religious psalms, unity, religious tradition, sermons	pageants, creativity, songs and dances, music and movement
According to the cultural symbols that they use:	uniforms, formal attire, solemnity. Emphasis on structural & hierarchical positions, arms, power in its pure form.	formal attire and uniforms. Power of the saint, the Church	Informal clothes, costumes, open sexuality, communication, practical jokes, lifting of social & economic barriers.
According to the social groups that they organize:	impersonal corporations, highly bureaucratic, authoritarian. Emphasis on hierarchy & external symbols, uniforms, positions defined by law.	fraternities, voluntary but some control by church. Mystically involved with saint; groups based on friendship, sympathy, not family. Respect.	schools of Samba, Blocks, etc. Voluntary associations. Performance of a member important, not kinship. Friendship & equality, cooperation.
According to the social group that is mobilized:	armed forces, government officials, state officials	Church, Ecclesiastical authorities, saints.	People in general. Authorities called in to legitimize, but not essential
According to the ethics and ideologies invoked or mobilized:	ethics of duty, nation, obedience, hierarchy	renunciation, power, respect, diffuse obedience, hierarchy	hedonism, pleasure for pleasure's sake, equality
According to the values that they stimulate:	worldly values, nationalism, patriotism	this and the other world. Church as bridge; festivities are the means, discreet renunciation of the world.	Away from the daily routine of work and family life; Hedonism. Sex and sin.
According to the stereotypes that they recall:	"Caxias": square persons, who are authoritarian; who obey the law	saints, priests, ascetics in general in several gradations	"Malandros": persons who fluctuate between spheres of law and crime
The political plane to which they are associated	coups d'état to maintain the status quo, authoritarianism.	doctrines of conciliation or reward.	"Populism"; Ways to invert the existing social and political order.

occasion associated with an ethic of enjoyment of life,
happiness, irresponsibility, and pleasure for pleasure's
sake, as in the case of Carnival, there would be no need
for an institution equally turned towards devotion (as
in the case of the religious festivals) and toward duty
(as happens during civic-military rituals in general)
when the nation is celebrated and the citizens' duty toward its most sacred symbols (the flag and the national
anthem) is stressed. Without one of these, the whole
would be incomplete. The system can only be understood
in its fullness when we have all three spheres interacting. Their relations, therefore, delineate the totality
of the system and it is in these relations that one finds
the key to the originality of Brazilian society.

Even more curious, as I attempted to show elsewhere,
(9) is the study of these three positions in their systematic relations. In a sense, the history of Brazilian
national life can be interpreted as a story or a drama
in which one of the "sides" of the triangle of rituals
was dominant. When the people were theoretically closer
to power, Brazil had periods of politically open and populist leaderships which some conservative observers of
national life described as anarchism, chaos, and the
collapse of social and political life. When the Church
was dominant, Brazil had a semitheocratic state, effectively the visible and global power during the colonial
period. Finally, when the secular state became dominant
and a power in itself, Brazil developed dictatorships or
authoritarian regimes as in the case of the military coup
of 1964. We have, thus, tensions and conflicts between
the various understandings of Brazilian society but, until now, it seems that no group was able to cut its relations with the other sides of the triangle. This is very
important as it indicates that the relations between the
spheres are more important than the vision that each one
suggests in isolation. Hence, no doubt, the preference
in Brazil and in the Brazilian political system for conciliation and negotiations, a fact noted by many observers.(10) The most recent example of this is the political "liberalization" of the Church, in clear contrast
to conservative and reactionary positions (prior to 1964)
when the Church was opposed to the Goulart regime.

This discussion reemphasizes an important fact already mentioned. In this "Brazilian ritual triangle" -
equivalent, as I have shown, to a true popular paradigm
for the Brazil system - we have three different ways of
representing power and social dynamics. One side of the
triangle, the side of Carnival and of the people, of
spontaneity and of creative and egalitarian liberty, indicates a form of familial and personal relationships in
which the ethic of personal relations and of patronage
is dominant. Thus Brazilian populist leaders were always

depicted to the masses as fathers, godfathers, or benev-
olent and understanding masters. Their political rhetoric always suggested the magic possibility that the masses could climb the socio-economic ladder and have better
salaries, housing, working conditions, and transport
without anyone else losing anything. The social world
was presented as a carnival because everyone would, at
long last, have an important role to play. The leader
appeared to be the father of the people (as in Vargas'
case), an older and wiser brother (as in the case of
Jânio Quadros), or the best master (as in the case of
Adhemar de Barros).

But if Carnival and the populist modes of the triangle present facets dominated by the ethic of personal relations, of positive patronage, and of the most sincere
friendship, that is hardly the case with spheres that
find expression in the civil-military or Catholic rituals; in these spheres the social world has to be controlled by laws and impersonal rules, by means of a hierarchy that commands the world. The political conceptions
of leadership emanating from these areas, as well as the
models of society they suggest, are therefore much more
integrated into clearly restricted schemes. This was the
case with the rhetoric of a leader like Carlos Lacerda,
who was committed to fighting for the reestablishment of
social order. It was also noticeable in the rhetoric of
Janio Quadros, whose political emblem was a broom indicating his desire to completely clean the economic and
political world.

Curiously enough, the sphere that does not appear in
the triangle is the economic one. In the Brazilian social unverse there is no place for the auctions and rum-
mage sales so common to the North American social universe where socializing is tied to economic motives – to
the purchase or sale of a product. In the Brazilian
case, however, in all festivities, whether at the regional or the national level, economic factors are controlled
directly by the ideological lines that define the comme-
moration. Thus during a saint's day the aim is to pay
hommage to the saint, even though there are a few suppor-
tive elements of economic character (such as auctions,
raffles, exchanges of goods and services). Even during
Carnival, when economic factors and competition are obvious, these aspects are subordinated to the dominant
guidelines of the festivity, guidelines defined socially
in terms of happiness, freedom to play, dance, and have
fun, sex, enjoyment of life, etc. That is, the market
and the individual as an economic agent are not the basis
of celebration in the Brazilian ritual system in which,
even for birthday parties, the ritualization covers not
only the person celebrating the birthday (in a clearly

individualistic celebration) but also his social relations. The economic factor remains outside the Brazilian
ritual triangle.

THE QUESTION OF POWER AND HIERARCHY

     Investigation of the ritual system, examining the
festivities that characterize Brazilian society and form
the basis of its system of social identification, reveals
the possibility of three codes of diverse and complementary ethics. But it also indicates forms of domination
and of authority that are different or dissociated. Indeed, what can we observe in Brazilian hierarchy and power? Is it a personalized system centered on a single and
exclusive logic, characterized by a single goal? Or
centered on a milieu in which social relations are controlled by well known rules? Or around an axis of money
in which the only scale of success is who has money? Or
around commercial ability and consumption that reveals
those who are closer to salvation and to God? After in-
vestigating rituals and studying other domains of the
Brazilian society, I am convinced that the system values
the economic axis (and turns it into a source of power
and prestige), but also values other social goods because, precisely as in other traditional societies, hierarchy is dissociated from power and the hierarchy is always favored, as I have tried to show elsewhere.(11)
     The festivals express, in their own way, the differ-
ent "lines of power" found in the Brazilian system. Thus
the civil-military commemorations ritualize the relations
and the instruments of temporal power. This power is
legitimized by what it can accomplish for individuals who
are in this world and who are theoretically represented
by this form of power. Here all are equal before the law
and inclusion is defined by impersonal laws voted for by
the people through their representatives. This is a form
of power characterized by a single logic and a single
point of view: the equality of all before the law. It
is very different from the forms of power used by privileged governments such as those in several European countries before the French revolution where each segment (or
stratum) had its own laws. Privilege as a juridical fact
is the institutionalization of inequalities at all levels and results in a multiplicity of legal and economic
systems in the same social body. Thus, in a traditional
society, the same crime when committed by persons of different social orders is judged differently. There were,
as is still the case in Brazil today, as many possibilities of escaping universal legislation as there were different social orders.(12)
     In systems like Brazil there are, side by side with
modern and egalitarian forms of power (in which the individual is the center of the system), other sources of

social and political privilege. One, represented by the Church rituals, is made possible because it exercises power hierarchically and is characterized by closeness with the sacred (God, the saints, etc.). Another is the Armed Forces, especially the Army whose proximity to power is derived from its rigidly hierarchical organization. There is a form of "mystic power" or "invisible power" which runs parallel to the modern form of power represented by the state. We have, then, roughly two types of power which in theory complement each other but which can also compete with each other. Regarding the festivities and/or rituals, the formula of complementarity is standard, since in every ritual or order in Brazil - birthday parties, graduations, ceremonies of investiture of governors or presidents of the republic in their respective functions - there is a "table" and, before the ceremony begins, this "table" has to include representatives of the categories of power which are essential for the legitimization of the event. Thus in convocations and presidential swearing-in ceremonies a large "table" is formed including representatives of the clergy, the Armed Forces, and the people (deputies, senators, judges).

PATRONAGE AND MESSIANISM

If the study of national rituals indicates the above possibilities, what can be revealed by the study of the daily routine? The disjunction of categories and resources of power, whose values differ to the point of total incompatability, presents important problems. How is it possible for a society so divided to have a spirit of totality and a sense of identity? The question suggests its own answer. The system, as we will see in detail further on, is formed precisely by these complementary but dissociated lines or categories. What integrates these lines of power with different spheres of value into something possessing an overall meaning is the search for the perfect leader: the syndrome of messianism or the good master. In fact, in a system in which there is no single predominant ethic, the only way to obtain a sense of totality would be through interpersonal relations. In such systems the world is integrated by means of messianic leadership.

The opposite applies to modern and highly individualized systems. Exactly because personal relations are systematically restricted and delimited, it falls to institutions, not to persons or relations, to turn reality into a meaningful whole. The result is that in these systems the world seems to be divided in practice but united in ideal. Therefore, in highly individualistic societies, we know exactly whether or not one belongs to

a group, or has the right of access to certain prerogatives or privileges, because the social world is strati-
fied by means of gradations and relations between these
become the fundamental units of the system.

One of the results of the division of Brazil into
"double codes" is the phenomenon of messianism as a technique to integrate the world by means of personal links.
Thus the messiah is the one who knows everything and, because he makes all mediations and concentrates in himself
the forms of social relations, is able to do everything.
But, as a limit to this paradigm of integration through
personal relations and patronage, the messiah has to govern alone and in an absolute way - as an authoritarian.
Thus the movement in search of the totalization of the
system by means of one person becomes the search for the
messiah (who represents the essence of the system) but,
on the other hand, also gives rise to the chronic authoritarianism which is common to the Mediterranean countries. I am, in short, associating messianism and patronage as two moments of the same socio-political experience. My hypothesis is that these are not different
phenomena but rather are similar ways to deal with problems caused by a social system which is internally divided into multiple codes and social ethics. The Messiah
is only the ultimate case of patronage.

In highly divided societies in which power and authority are presented in so many different guises, the
obsession with totalization is a constant. I am suggesting that one of the ways to obtain this totalization
is through the search for an individual solution - the
only solution, in fact, which can overcome the multiple
ethics acutely disassociating the system. During periods
of crisis and competition between these ethics, when
their complementary aspects do not operate, the messiah
is called in. We have then two dynamics and two ways of
integration: (1) When the system is quiescent, the logic
of complementarity unites everything and allows for a
perception of totality. (2) When the system is in crisis
and the logic of complementarity collapses, the messiah,
or cosmic leader, is called in.

I will now expand this analytical framework to clarify the ethic of Umbanda, a messianic and hierarchical
ethic which allows for the division of everything in
"lines" of power and authority and for their rejoining
in terms of a powerful hierarchy and supernatural patronage. We should begin, however, from the beginning,
stressing the way in which, in Brazil, the social universe is delineated and acquires multiple planes and
ethics.

In Brazil we have the domain (or sphere) of the home
whose ethic is based on generosity, hospitality, tolerance, and love. It is at home that one recovers from
daily work and the demanding job. It is at home, also,

that we find and get in touch with persons who are like
us, who are from "our same quality and blood." At home
we have a sphere in which things are generously given
and received and to which we belong permanently, having
rights that are eternal. In Brazil, to break away from
this group and this type of relationship is impossible,
for in the home milieu we have an enduring connection
that does not depend on choices or on social laws. This
is the domain of the "natural" and of the "physical," as
these terms are understood in the Brazilian universe.

Alongside the home is a sphere that opposes but also
complements it, the world or the universe of the street.
In the street we are face to face with life in its most
surprising and broad meaning; that is to say, face to
face with a world that we cannot control or fully understand. In fact, it is in the street, in the real world,
that we meet the "raw and naked reality" of the world, a
reality that we are forced to discover without the protection of our parents or relatives. It is in the world
and in real life that we can be tricked, exploited, and
victimized. And, paradoxically, it is here also that we
find the instruments and sometimes the persons who help
us "win" and obtain a position which is independent and
even opposed to the one we had in the sphere of our home.
Brazilian expressions such as "to conquer life" or "women
of life" (prostitutes), and "the hard reality of life"
(an expression equivalent to "the hard reality of work"),
which recall the notion of work not as a vocation, in the
sense that Weber discusses the term, but as a punishment
should not surprise us. Therefore, logically, those who
have no choice but to work have, in the Brazilian social
universe, needs that must be complemented. The real
world is a sphere to be avoided as much as possible.

Besides the contrary but complementary axes of the
home and the street, we still have the sphere of the supernatural or the invisible. In this sphere we are
dealing with saints, gods, and spirit-beings who have
been through our world and who raise doubts about the
exact reality of the society in which we live. The supernatural world, thus, complements the real world but,
at the same time, makes it possible for us to see the
latter in relative terms. Thus, if a person is rich and/
or powerful, the supernatural can be immediately invoked
to delimit his wealth, indicating that in the area of the
invisible the logic is inverted: not all rich people can
be happy, nor can all powerful persons find true happiness.

If the first of these domains, the home, is governed
by a personal kind of morality, related to links of substance in which love and generosity are essential, the
second of these universes, the sphere of the street (or
of life) is perceived as being more individualized, impersonal, and competitive. In the third region of the

Brazilian social universe, the supernatural, we have the image of a world governed by an infallible justice and by just laws. If the logic of real life (here encompassing home and street) is the one of the old saying that "God helps those who help themselves" ("cada um por si e Deus por todos"), it denotes a kind of perverted individualism as it is not controlled by any rules or limits. The logic of the supernatural universe is based on an inverted supposition: what really counts is a disinterested relationship, the act of giving without expecting recompense, a pure type of reciprocity of long duration, or a universal love based on spiritual ties. The otherworldly universe, then, presents the concrete (even if invisible) possibility of relativizing the social world. This is why one of its clearest characteristics is that no one escapes its powers. And, because of this, it possesses laws externally valid and, even more important, valid for all. The irreducible point, always utilized in Brazil as the "final proof" of this ultimate reality of the "invisible world," is death and its caprices. What happens "after death" is the important point of this sphere in which one finds the roots of the two following points: (1) that all die and meet the end that relativizes everything and (2) that nobody can doubt or prove that "after death" the world disappears without any compensation for good and evil deeds. The final experience of death is thus used to establish a fantastic universe of moral compensation because in the sphere of the invisible we finally have the equality and justice that the social, political, and economic institutions denied to many in this world.

The transcendental universe leads us to an ideology of renunciation and relativization of the real world. This ideology is distinct from and complementary to the ethic of profit, of greed, and of tricks that operate in the realm of the street. In the realm of the spirits and gods that appear systematically in the Umbanda ceremony – the Exus, Pombas-giras, Pretos-Velhos, Indians, and Children, as well as a legion of African Orixás and Oriental and Occidental saints – we find a moral order in which good and generosity are the real winners. It is here that the so-called "law of Karma" (or "law of the eternal return") makes sure that each person receives exactly what he deserves according to his personal achievements. Here, we soon discover, it is not enough to be the son or godson of some rich or politically powerful individual. What matters is not the group, but the individual separated from his temporal attire. But perhaps the most basic feature of the Brazilian transcendental world is the realization that it is a world without transformations in which it is not possible to stage a "coup d'état" and in which the rich and privileged cannot change the rules of the game. In the supernatural world,

as codified in popular Catholicism and in Umbanda, nobody
rises or descends through the interference of godfathers,
friends, relatives, or a family name. In the Astral
there can be no cliques, nor "jeitinhos," or "patronage."
(13) There, the dominant feature is the ideology of merit and accomplishment. That is the reason why transcendental experiences can be associated with the gaiety and
immersion in the world which are characteristic of the
Brazilian case. I will elaborate this point as a conclusion to this essay, recalling some of the fundamental
issues.

MULTIPLE ETHICS, UMBANDA, AND PATRONAGE

My initial point was the thesis that in Brazil we are
dealing with a society with a "double ethic." In fact,
studying the Brazilian ritual system, such ethics emerge
clearly from the three basic ways used by Brazilians to
celebrate special events. But it was necessary to reveal
that this multiplicity of ethics could also be found in
Brazilian daily life, and this I showed by a study of the
various realms through which the social world in Brazil
is classified and divided. In fact, by studying the
realms of the home, the street and the transcendental
world, it is possible to show even more clearly how a
multiple system emerges. On the other hand, I have also
shown how the transcendental world ends up by becoming a
sphere whose basic function is to relativize differences
in order to complement and allow for a kind of moral compensation. The supernatural is an unchangeable sphere
in which the rules are fixed and the actions of an individual qua individual are basic. In this way, if in the
real world we are always classed according to families,
clans, cliques, and factions made up of ties of substance
and sympathy, in the "after-life" we will be on our own
and judged by individual performance in the real world.
This is a case similar to that in sport and in the arts
in the sense that in these realms nobody can be classed
according to family names or skin colour but simply according to performance following fixed rules that apply
to all. It is this fact which permits the transcendental
universe to fulfill its complementary role in Brazil.
On the other hand, study of the festivities in relation to Brazilian daily life permits the establishment
of an important postulate: it is by means of extraordinary occasions (such as rituals, commemorations, and festivities) that the fields and spheres of social reality
can be interrelated. It is clear that each one of these
spheres has its own celebrations. It was precisely this
that we saw in the first part of this essay. But it is
also necessary to say that by means of these festivities
a sphere can go beyond its particular domains and touch
all facets of the social universe. Thus it is the group,

256

the dances, the delicious food, the welcoming and seduc-
tive gestures, the physical and moral cleanliness of a
given space, the use of special attire, the drinks served
with utmost generosity, etc. which allow for the creation
of conditions such that the world can become a unified
whole once again. This creates the conditions for the
meeting and communication between persons whose status
had confined them to just one or two of the spheres into
which Brazilian social life is divided. Because of this,
it is a fundamental rule in Brazil to promote meetings
through parties, and to transform a party into a place
for rendezvous.

In this way there is a correlation between greater
festivities and greater social and moral distances. And
in the same way and by the same logic, the greater the
importance of the meeting and the greater the social differences between those who will meet, the greater will be
the encompassing character of the party. The consequences of this principle are that, in Brazil, the parties and rituals have an all-encompassing character,
contrary to those in individualistic or egalitarian societies. In Brazil, the festivity is an opportunity and an
excuse to meet, in the United States a party is an opportunity and an excuse to delineate the limits and distances between social groups that are undifferentiated in
the pursuit of the daily acitivities. In Brazil, therefore, the party's focus is on interrelationships (for the
individual as much as for the group that is celebrating),
while in the United States a party has as a focus not so
much the relationship as the individuals or groups with
whom they are concerned and who are their raison d'être.

If a festivity is a favored way to unite these
spheres and these ethics, then all contact between the
street and the home, the real and the supernatural, a man
and a woman, the old and the young, the poor and the
rich, the powerful and the oppressed, should be delineated and marked by means of parties and rituals. In this
way social life would take place in a cycle of parties
and meetings, each one, however, centered upon different
objects and objectives. The rituals that commemorate the
independence of Brazil, for example, create their own
zones of meetings in the same way that other meeting
zones are created by processes and "festas de santo."
In the same way, Carnival transforms the whole society
into a large arena characterized by the exchange of festive and irresponsible dialogues, hedonistic par excellence, between groups and social segments which are of
widely different lifestyles.

But, if each party has its own language and focuses
on its own domain, then the social world witnesses cycles
of tensions and relief, of anxiety and relaxation. For

each situation or sphere which creates an ethic generating uncertainties, acute distinctions, and individuali-
zations, there exists another situation or sphere able to
create the exact opposite. This formula is oversimpli-
fied and exaggerates the daily social reality, but it has
the merit of admitting the perception of social dynamism
in semitraditional societies involved in similar dilemmas between the impersonal formula which gives meaning
to the world once and for all and to the personal ties
that can reformulate it; between the real world that is
unjust and gives undue importance to family ties and the
supernatural world which is just but uncertain; between
Carnival parties that allow people to exorcise all their
fears and uncertainties and to turn the experience of
freedom and happiness into concrete and accessible realities, and the world of work and exploitation in which it
is known that by personal efforts alone one never reaches
the top; and between the personal and nontransferable
universe of faith and of mystical relations with spirits,
saints, and orixas in which we discover our personal
worth and acquire faith in the basic justice of the
world.

As an expression of all these divisions and of this
cycle which makes our anxieties vanish, the ethic of Umbanda (and of popular religiosity) appears as a paradigm.
It emphasizes tolerance, charity, acceptance of all with
equal generosity, and compensation for all social and political differences. This ethic also creates an environment conducive to a moral recovery that otherwise would
be difficult, especially during phases of acute social
change. The ethic of the Umbanda associates and incorporates itself with the spirit of patronage and messianism.
Thus it emphasizes social and moral relations, allowing
for the salvation of individuals from all social categories. If a person is poor and destitute of all secular
powers, being a true social nonentity with no acquaint-
ances to protect him from the most violent forms of exploitation, his mystical relationships with the orixa let
him be transformed into a "saint's or god's horse," - into "something."(14) He can be transformed into a man
who, because of a special spiritual relationship with a
transcendental entity, begins to control and manipulate
mystical powers which are very important in the Brazilian
social system. The same kind of mechanism comes into
play during Carnival, when involvement with the "school
of Samba" or with one of its groups of dancers ("blo-
cos"), or a special costume can become an escape from
anonymity by exposing an unknown individual to the eyes
of all - the media, the masses, the millionaires, and the
authorities in general.

The ethic of Umbanda seems to be similar to the one
that permeates popular Catholicism because this form of
spontaneous communication with the sacred is always in

the form of direct, intense, untransferable and, of course, personal association between someone from an inferior socio-economic position - be it an Indian, a slave, a child, or a woman - with a very powerful saint or supernatural being. The paradigm of the famous miracles of popular Catholicism seems to be the same as that which permeates the biographies of the new converts to spiritualism or to Umbanda. They also tell tales of how a person was disillusioned or desperate as a result of moral, social, or financial difficulties when suddenly he had a vision and a spirit or saint showed him the path to follow. Following the apparition, which signifies the exit from the daily world and the entrance into the transcendental world, the person began to feel better and obtained a permanent relationship with his supernatural contact. The sole difference is that in the Catholic creed apparitions of saints are zealously scrutinized by the Church's hierarchy and it is very difficult to obtain official recognition of an apparition. In the case of popular religions, and above all in the case of Umbanda, the ethic allows for a permanent routine of miraculous encounters. For Umbanda, nothing is impossible at the supernatural level. This is a kind of religiosity which appears particularly among the politically oppressed strata of society. It is as if unshakeable faith in frequent communication with the other world were a compensation for the skepticism that impregnates them from the social and political point of view. While the poor segments, or even the middle class(es), in the large urban centres have no hope for a sincere and efficient government or for a state that will be really determined to face the great social and economic challenges of our time, they are nevertheless unanimous in their trust in the mystical or even magic powers of a "father or mother of a saint" after they have incorporated their spirits. The ethic of Umbanda thus compensates for a daily life full of social and political frustrations by the blind faith in the powers of the mystical entities.

In the same way, the ethic of Umbanda allows us to relate individual creativity, visible at each and every center of Umbanda (and also of spiritism) in its most varied combinations, with the immutable laws of Karma that govern the world of the living and the world of the dead. In the universal law of eternal return, the law of the Karma, every individual is bound by a destiny which is adequate to his evolutionary level and from which there is no escape. However each biography or life leaves room for differential experience with the other world, permitting a varied spectrum of combinations and experiences. Therefore, alongside a group of fixed identities - the Orixás of African origin like Xangô, Ogum, Xemanjá, Omolú, etc. - there appear the "Caboclos" (Indians), the spirits of exslaves or Pretos-Velhos, and the

Pombas-Giras that represent unchecked feminine sexuality looking for self-satisfaction. In addition, in several Umbanda centers oriental entities are associated with the most popular version of Indianism and are important facets of the biography and mystical composition of many "mediums." As if this were not enough, there are also several entities from other planets. Thus, even though the cult is more influenced by traditional entities, the ideology of Umbanda is truly eclectic, integrating all important events of the social world into its cult. We have, thus, a nucleus of ideas and characters which is relatively simple but whose doctrine allows for a fantastic creativity which makes it adaptable to the most varied conditions of life, be it in small towns or large cities. From this adaptability arises the success of this form of religion.

In addition to this possibility of relationship, Umbanda allows for recuperation and contact with the world of the dead and the saints. This is also essential for a population which has no faith in the forms of social and political influence embodied in the right to vote and other forms of participation in the so-called "civil society." Skeptical of the process of change provided by political parties and professional associations, this same population believes, however, in the power of offerings and in the capacity of the saints to influence the social world. Thus, while the Church legitimizes funerals, weddings and christenings, Umbanda deals with conflicts provoked by contradictions in social life and between desires and laws, wishes and prohibitions, plans and accidents. Umbanda fills the space left vacant by a Church secularized by its competition with political parties interested in power.

Because it focuses on relations, on means, the ethic of Umbanda is characterized by a great degree of tolerance, by an embracing type of charity that integrates everybody into the same doctrinal nexus. There is room in Umbanda for all types of beliefs. Even those who do not believe are welcome because it is not Umbanda's objective to draw limits or to define areas. In the same manner, various forms of "possession" are acceptable, from the most theatrical in which the medium evidently controls his whole body and messages, to the most spontaneous and radical which cause much greater and intense dissociation phenomena. Thus, imitating its supernatural hierarchies (composed of powerful as well as of weak entities), everything in Umbanda is perceived in terms of gradations so that the relations expressed in and crystallized by the trances can be intense and intimate (when there is a total identification between the medium and his supernatural entity) or ceremonious and distant (when the "medium" and the Orixá are separated from each other, as a bad actor from a good text). As in the case of the trance, the distribution of the faithful in the Umbanda areas follows a similar gradation. There is, therefore, a focus – the altar and the area used by the "father and sons of saints" (the "mediums" and "ritual guides") – and a peripheral area occupied by visitors. (15)

As a result, Umbanda and many other Brazilian social institutions, such as Carnival and popular festivals, open up a new sphere in which the daily world can be radically changed. Here the poor and destitute in general can act powerfully and advise or cure the "rich," now in the subordinate position of "receivers." In this fashion, when a contact between mortals/mediums and gods is crystallized in the act of possession and trance, the weak become strong – the anonymous person gains a reputation. This is a strength that emanates from a concrete relation between the "other world" and "this world" in the service of an ethic of tolerance and universal generosity. Yvonne Maggie Velho, who wrote an important work about Umbanda in Rio de Janeiro, calls attention to this inversion when spiritual entities like Pombas-Giras (who represent the sexual freedom of women and behave like prostitutes), Exus (who appear as carefree individuals circulating between the spheres of right and wrong), the real "malandros" (bums), Pretos-Velhos (the exslaves) and Caboclos (Indians), give orders, demand favors and gifts, and perform cures. This is a phenomenon similar to Carnival in that those who are destitute and poor appear as gods and nobleman, incorporating and becoming possessed by their Samba and their costumes. In Umbanda we find the same type of inversion. Persons from the lower classes are transformed into powerful beings.(16) Thus, as all researchers have emphasized(17), the Umbandist group can reactivate intense personal links, allowing, as was said before, an escape from the excessive individualism and anonymity that permits the most violent and extreme forms of exploitation. As a result, one of the basic points of the Umbanda code is, it is worth repeating, the manipulation of personal relations and the "mystical sponsoring" or "mystical patronage" that allows the frail and unknown worker deprived of all secular power to have special ties with the almighty with whom he has a powerful and untransferable tie of protection.

CONCLUSION

Everything indicates that Brazilian society has a social system permeated by multiple ethics, and marked by a complementarity and hierarchical character. We saw that the task of unifying different spheres such as the "house," the "street," the "invisible world," the impersonal laws of the market, the economy, and the juridico-political spheres is accomplished through personal forms of relationship. The interrelations are constantly being

established between persons. Hence we suggested the
"messianic syndrome" of the Brazilian system, a syndrome
that expresses only those relations that are permanent
and instrumental and that many students of Latin America,
Brazil, Iberian, and Mediterranean social scenes have
classified as patronage. Taking as a basis some observations made by Weber, we suggested that there is a positive relation between the "ethic" of a religion such as
Umbanda, with its emphasis on personal relations and distinctive traits of "patronage" and "messianism," and the
structural phenomena of Brazilian society. We are,
therefore, confronted with a configuration of elements
and relations whose predominant characteristics arise
from the dilemma caused by a society always alternating
between its preference for personal forms of relationships (which are means and ends) and its support for a
body of impersonal and authoritarian legislation focusing
on the individual, the economy, and the market. There
is, thus, on one side the traditional code that embodies
as many ideals as a person possesses who is involved in
imperative and complementary social relations; on the
other side we have the liberalizing ethics, adopted from
the North American and French political experiences, emphasizing the individual as the normative center of the
world. Because Brazil falls between these two opposing
codes it combines contradictory and sometimes paradoxical
structures and forms of social relations and has thus
been able to avoid the violent institutional ruptures so
common in countries which faced the same dilemma but
chose to adopt abstract and impersonal laws and rules.
    The thesis which I presented was that the system in
Brazil has various codes and, precisely because of this,
means can be mistaken for ends in themselves. If the
means are personal interrelationships and rituals, then
we can understand the clanishness and hedonism of the
Latin countries in which, even during times of utterly
authoritarian dictatorships, personal relations are systematically activated and the aims promoted by the projects and plans of the iron-fisted governments can be
modified by the interplay of personal relationships. In
the same manner we can interpret, sociologically, phenomena like the Brazilian "jeitinho" and "malandragem"
which, in my opinion, are techniques to conciliate personal relations and universal laws.(18)
    All these phenomena belong to this special configura-
tion. The system, as we saw, operates through institutions which are able to simultaneously create and alle-
viate anxieties. The critical spheres in the formation
and accumulation of tensions are those found in the domain of the street; spheres that function according to
impersonal laws and which, in fact, upset the system's
basic and complementary characteristics. Given a modern
economic and political system based on individuality and

262

equality, it becomes difficult to avoid conflict with the
system's personal relationships which are based on hierarchy and privilege. The spheres of the home and of the
invisible systematically mitigate the tensions through
their encouragement of the role of personal motives and
influences. The tempo and rhythm of social life in countries like Brazil, as a result, is characterized by cli-
maxes and plateaus, and is very different from Weber's
presentation of the situation in societies in which the
Protestant ethic was adopted and consolidated. As Weber
said,

> The priest was a magician who performed the mir-
> acle of transubstantiation and who held the key
> to eternal life in his hand. One could turn to
> him in grief and penitence. He dispensed atone-
> ment, hope of grace, certainty of forgiveness,
> and thereby granted release from the tremendous
> tensions to which the Calvinist was doomed by an
> inexorable fate, admitting of no mitigation.
> For him, such friendly and human comforts did
> not exist.(19)

In Protestantism, anxiety is maintained because there
is a collapse of spheres and ideologies previously differentiated and complementary. Given this collapse and
rupture, society begins to function by means of a single
code and becomes eminently able to liberate the individuals from their family duties, which, in traditional systems, are the system's permanent ideals. It is through
this single ethic, impersonal and abstract, that one has
to relate to others and which then becomes dominant. It
permeates the home, the family, and the community, as
well as the organization of the states and of the business world. "The world," said Weber, "exists to serve
the glorification of God and for that purpose alone .....
/And this/ is expressed in the first place in the ful-
fillment of the daily tasks given by the 'lex natural'
...."(20)
This same point regarding the predominance of a single ethics in modern systems (or in the world that Protestantism has helped to shape) was also noted by Paul
Tillich when he said: "Just as there is no priest having
a special religious function, for everybody is a layman
and every layman is potentially a priest, so there is no
religion as a special spiritual sphere. Everything is
secular and every secular thing is potentially religious."(21) So for Weber, as for Tillich, there is no
distinction between the religious and the secular in
Protestantism. In modern systems these no longer exist
as separate entities, individual and parallel. The society is limited by the individual and we no longer detect
the segregation of personal relations and universal legal

systems. As Mauss observed in his unfortunately unfinished article, traditional societies are ruled by custom and not by "political laws" or by public rights "which are almost entirely religious." Mauss also observed that traditional legislation is always imposed from the point of view of the "powerful" or of the "king"; that is, from above. In these systems, society and individual are in opposition; they are complementary units but also in conflict and contradiction.(22) This also happens in Brazil where the "ethic of Umbanda" facilitates the complicated transition between these various domains which motivate and present multiple goals, or ends. Thus, where ends and means are confused and complement each other, mediations seem essential to abridge the various domains which together constitute a society.

Finally, it is curious to note that the recent interpreters of Weber's work, people like Bellah, Singer, Peacock, and Tambiah,(23) have not commented on the relation between "double (or multiple) ethics" and "single ethics" in terms of their sociological implications within the theoretical framework of Max Weber. I hope, therefore, to have called attention to this aspect because I am convinced that the "double ethic" is responsible for the tolerance which neutralizes the anxieties created by more dynamic and contradictory areas of the system such as the political and economic spheres. Conversely, the formation of a dominant "single ethic" is closely linked to the "spirit of capitalism" and to the market as the focus of all social relations,(24) and to the individual as the focus and normative centre of the whole system.(25)

NOTES

1. Roberto da Matta, "Sport in Society: An Essay on Brazilian Futebol." Manuscript, 1980.
2. Marcel Mauss, "Ensaio Sobre a Divida: Forma e Razão da Troca nas Sociedades Arcaicas," in Sociologia e Antropologia (São Paulo: 1974). Marshall Sahlins, "On the Sociology of Primitive Exchange," in Conference on New Approaches in Social Anthropology, The Relevance of Models for Social Anthropology (New York: F. Praeger, 1965). Claude Lévi-Strauss, Les Structures Elementaires de la Parenté (Paris: Presse Universitaires de France, 1949).
3. Max Weber, The Protestant Ethic and the Spirit of Capitalism (New York: Scribner's, 1958), p. 57.
4. Mary Douglas, The World of Goods (New York: Basic Books, 1980).
5. Weber, The Protestant Ethic, p. 57.
6. Ibid., pp. 56-57.
7. Karl Polanyi, The Great Transformation (Boston: Beacon Press, 1967).

264

8.   Roberto da Matta, "Constraint and License: A Preliminary Study of Two Brazilian National Rituals," in Sally Moore and Barbara Myerhoff, eds., Secular Ritual (Amsterdam: Van Gorcum, 1977).

9.   Roberto Da Matta, Carnavais, Malandros e Herois: Para Uma Sociologia do Dilema Brasileiro (Rio de Janeiro: Zahar Editores, 1979).

10.   Thomas Skidmore, Brasil: de Getúlio a Castelo (Rio de Janeiro: Paz e Terra, 1976).

11.   Da Matta, Carnavais.

12.   R. Rémond, O Antigo Regime e a Revolução: Introdução a História do Nosso Tempo (São Paulo: Cultrix, 1976).

13.   Anthony Leeds, "Brazilian Careers and Social Structure: A Case History and Model," in Dwight B. Heath and Richard N. Adams, eds., Contemporary Cultures and Societies of Latin America (New York: Random House, 1965).

14.   I.M. Lewis, "Dualism in Somali Notions of Power," The Journal of the Royal Anthropological Institute 93 (1963).

15.   Yvonne M. Velho, Guerra de Orixá: Um Estudo de Ritual e Conflito (Rio de Janeiro: Zahar Editores, 1975).

16.   da Matta, Carnavais; Velho, Guerra.

17.   Diana Brown, "Umbanda and Class Relations in Brazil," in Maxine L. Margolis and William E. Carter, eds., Brazil: Anthropological Perspectives: Essays in Honor of Charles Wagley (New York: Columbia University Press, 1979).

18.   da Matta, Carnavais.

19.   Weber, The Protestant Ethic, p. 177.

20.   Ibid., pp. 108-109.

21.   Paul Tillich as quoted in Herve Varenne, Americans Together (New York: Teacher's College, Columbia University, 1977).

22.   Marcel Mauss, "La Nacion," in Obras III (Barcelona: Barral Editores, 1972).

23.   Robert Bellah, Togugawa Religion: The Values of Pre-Industrial Japan (Boston: Beacon Press, 1957).

24.   Polanyi, The Great Transformation.

25.   Louis Dumont, Homo Hierarchicus: The Cast System and Its Implications (Chicago: The University of Chicago Press, 1970); "On the Comparative Understanding of Non-Modern Civilizations," Dedalus: Journal of the American Academy of Arts and Sciences 104 (1975); From Mandeville to Marx: The Genesis and Triumph of Economic Ideology (Chicago and London: The University of Chicago Press, 1977); da Matta, Carnavais.

Selected Bibliography

Books

Aguiar, Neuma. The Structure of Brazilian Development. New Brunswick, New Jersey: Transaction Books, 1979.

Bacha, Edmar. Os Mitos de uma Década. Ensaios de Economia Brasileira. Rio de Janeiro: Paz e Terra, 1976.

Baer, Werner. The Brazilian Economy: Its Growth and Development. Colombus, Ohio: Grid Publishing, Inc., 1979.

Baer, Werner et al. Dimensões do Desenvolvimento Brasileiro. Rio de Janeiro: Editora Campus, 1978.

Baer, Werner. Industrialization and Economic Development in Brazil. Homewood, Ill: Richard D. Unwin, 1965.

Bergsman, Joel. Brazil: Industrialization and Trade Policies. London: Oxford University Press, 1970.

Bittencourt, Getúlio. A Quinta Estrela. São Paulo: Ciencias Humanas, 1978.

Bruneau, Thomas C. The Political Transformation of the Brazilian Catholic Church. Cambridge: Cambridge University Press, 1974.

Cardoso, Fernando Henrique. Autoritarismo e Democratização. Rio de Janeiro: Paz e Terra, 1975.

Cardoso, Fernando Henrique and Faletto, Enzo. Dependency and Development in Latin America. Berkeley: University of California Press, 1979.

Chacor, Warwick. O Dilema Político Brasileiro. São Paulo: Convivio, 1978.

Cohn, Gabriel. Petroleo e Nacionalismo. São Paulo: Difusao Europeia do Livro, 1968.

Collier, David, ed. The New Authoritarianism in Latin America. Princeton: Princeton University Press, 1979.

Cotler, Julio and Fagen, Richard, eds. Latin America and the United States: The Changing Political Realities. Stanford: Stanford University Press, 1974.

Daland, Robert T. Brazilian Planning, Development, Politics and Administration. Chapel Hill: The University of North Carolina Press, 1971.

266

Diniz, Eli and Boschi, Renato Raul. Empresariado Nacional e Estado no Brasil. Rio de Janeiro: Forense Universitaria, 1978.

Dos Santos, Wanderley Guilherme. Poder e Política: Crónica do Autoritarismo Brasileiro. Rio de Janeiro: Forense Universitaria, 1978.

Erickson, Kenneth. The Brazilian Corporative State and Working-Class Politics. Berkeley: University of California Press, 1977.

Evans, Peter. Dependent Development: The Alliance of Multinational, State and Local Capital in Brazil. Princeton: Princeton University Press, 1979.

Fagen, Richard, ed. Capitalism and the State in U.S. - Latin American Relations. Stanford: Stanford University Press, 1979.

Fajnzylber, Fernando. Sistema Industrial e Exportação de Manufacturados: Analise da Experiencia Brasileira. Rio de Janeiro: IPEA, 1971.

Faucher, Philippe. Le Brésil des militaires; l'État et la structure du pouvoir dans un régime autoritaire. Montréal: les Presses de l'Université de Montréal, 1981.

Fernandes, Florestan. A Revolução Burguesa no Brasil. Rio de Janeiro: Zahar Editores, 1975.

Fiechter, Georges André. Brazil since 1964: Modernization under a Military Regime. London: Macmillan, 1975.

Fitzgerald, E.V.K. The State and Economic Development: Peru since 1968. Cambridge: Cambridge University Press, 1976.

Flynn, Peter. Brazil: A Political Analysis. Boulder: Westview Press, 1978.

Góes, Walder de. O Brasil do Presidente Geisel. Rio de Janeiro: Nova Fronteira, 1978.

Hewlett, Sylvia Ann. The Cruel Dilemmas of Development: Twentieth-Century Brazil. New York: Basic Books Inc., 1980.

Knight, Peter et al. Brazil: Human Resources Special Report. Washington: The World Bank, 1979.

267

Humphrey, John. Labour in the Brazilian Motor Vehicle Industry. Liverpool: University of Liverpool, 1979.

Lafer, Celso. O Sistema Político Brasileiro. São Paulo: Perspectiva, 1975.

Lamounier, Bolivar and Cardoso, Fernando Henrique. Os Partidos e as Eleições no Brasil. Rio de Janeiro: Paz e Terra, 1975.

Leff, Nathaniel H. The Brazilian Capital Goods Industry: 1929-1964. Cambridge: Harvard University Press, 1968.

Linz, Juan J. and Stepan, Alfred, eds. The Breadkdown of Democratic Regimes: Latin America. Baltimore: The Johns Hopkins University Press, 1978.

Lowenthal, Abraham F., ed. The Peruvian Experiment: Continuity and Change under Military Rule. Princeton: Princeton University Press, 1975.

Martins, Carlos Estevam. Capitalismo de Estado e Modêlo Político no Brasil. Rio de Janeiro: Graal, 1977.

Martins, Carlos Estevam, ed. Estado e Capitalismo no Brasil. São Paulo: Hucitec - Cebrap, 1977.

Martins, Luciano. Nação e Corporação Multinational. Rio de Janeiro: Paz e Terra, 1975.

Martins, Luciano. Pouvoir et développement économique: formation et évolution des structures politiques au Brésil. Paris: Anthropos, 1976.

Matta, Roberto da. Carnavais, Malandros e Herois: Para uma Sociologia do Dilema Brasileiro. Rio de Janeiro: Zahar Editores, 1979.

Motta, Fernando. Empresarios e Hegemonia Política. São Paulo: Brasiliense, 1979.

O'Donnell, Guillermo. Modernization and Bureaucratic-Authoritarianism: Studies in South American Politics. Berkeley: Institute of International Studies, 1973.

Overholt, William H. The Future of Brazil. Boulder: Westview Press, 1978.

Pereira, Luiz Carlos Bresser. O Colapso de uma Aliança de Classes. São Paulo: Brasiliense, 1978.

Pereira, Luiz Carlos Bresser. Estado e Subdesenvolvimento Industrializado. São Paulo: Brasiliense, 1977.

Pinto, Anibal et al. <u>Inflação Recente no Brasil e na América Latina</u>. Rio de Janeiro: Graal, 1978.

Rezende, Fernando, ed. <u>Aspectos da Participação do Governo na Economia</u>. Rio de Janeiro: IPEA/INPES, 1976.

Robcock, Stephan H. <u>Brazil: A Study in Development Progress</u>. Lexington: Lexington Books, 1977.

Roett, Riordan, ed. <u>Brazil in the Seventies</u>. Washington, D.C.: American Enterprise Institute, 1976.

Schmitter, Philippe C. <u>Interest Conflict and Political Change in Brazil</u>. Stanford: Stanford University Press, 1971.

Schneider, Ronald M. <u>Brazil: Foreign Policy of a Future World Power</u>. Boulder: Westview Press, 1976.

Schylowsky, Daniel M. and Wicht, Juan J. <u>Anatomia de un fracaso economico: Peru 1968-1978</u>. Lima: Universidad del Pacifico, Centro de Investigacion, 1979.

Selcher, Wayne A. <u>Brazil's Multilateral Relations: Between First and Third Worlds</u>. Boulder: Westview Press, 1978.

Skidmore, Thomas. <u>Politics in Brazil, 1930-1964: An Experiment in Democracy</u>. New York: Oxford University Press, 1967.

Smith, Peter Seaborne. <u>Oil and Politics in Brazil</u>. Toronto: Macmillan, 1976.

Stepan, Alfred, ed. <u>Authoritarian Brazil</u>. New Haven: Yale University Press, 1973.

Stepan, Alfred. <u>The Military in Politics: Changing Patterns in Brazil</u>. Princeton: Princeton University Press, 1971.

Stepan, Alfred. <u>The State and Society: Peru in Comparative Perspective</u>. Princeton: Princeton University Press, 1978.

Suzigan, Wilson. <u>Crescimento Industrial no Brasil</u>. Rio de Janeiro: IPEA/INPES, 1974.

Suzigan, Wilson, ed. <u>Indústria: Política, Instituicões e Desenvolvimento</u>. Rio de Janeiro: IPEA/INPES, 1978.

Tavares, Maria da Conceição. Da Substituição de Importações ao Capitalismo Financeiro. Rio de Janeiro: Zahar Editores, 1972.

Tello, Carlos. La Politica economica en Mexico, 1970-1976. Mexico: Siglo Veintiuno, 1979.

Tolipan, Ricardo and Tinelli, Arthur Carlos, eds. A Controversia Sobre Distribuição de Renda e Desenvolvimento. Rio de Janeiro: Zahar Editores, 1975.

Touraine, Alain. Les sociétés dépendantes. Brussels: Duculot, 1976.

Villela, Annibal and Suzigan, Wilson. Política do Governo e Crescimento da Economia Brasileira: 1889-1945. Rio de Janeiro: IPEA/INPES, 1973.

Articles

Araújo, José Tavares de and Dick, Vera. "Governo, Empresas Multinacionais e Empresas Nacionais: O Caso da Indústria Petroquimica." Pesquisa e Planejamento Econômico 4, no. 3 (1974).

Bacha, Edmar. "Issues and Evidence on Recent Brazilian Economic Growth." World Development 5, nos. 1-2 (1977).

Baer, Werner, Kerstenetsky, Isaac, and Villela, Annibal V. "The Changing Role of the State in the Brazilian Economy." World Development 1, no. 11 (1973).

Baer, Werner and Beckerman, Paul. "The Trouble with Index-linking: Reflexions on the Recent Brazilian Experience." World Development 8 (1980).

Bennett, Douglas and Sharpe, Kenneth. "The State as Banker and as Entrepreneur: The Last Instance of the Mexican State's Economic Intervention, 1917-1970." Comparative Politics 12 (1980).

Bonelli, Ricardo and Malan, Pedro S. "Os Limites do Possivel: Notas sobre o Balanço de Pagamentos e Indústria nos Anos 70." Pesquisa e Planejamento Econômico 6, no. 2 (1976).

Bruneau, Thomas C. "The Catholic Church and Development in Latin America: The Role of the Basic Christian Communities." World Development 8 (1980).

Dos Santos, Theotônio. "The Crisis of the Brazilian Miracle." Working Paper 20, Brazilian Studies/LARU (April 1977).

270

Dos Santos, Theotônio.   "Economic Crisis and Democratic Transition in Brazil." Contemporary Marxism 1, no. 1 (Spring 1980).

Faucher, Philippe.   "Industrial Policy in a Dependent State: The Case of Brazil." Latin American Perspectives 7, no. 1 (Winter 1980).

Fernandez, Paul and Ocampo, José F.   "The Latin American Revolution: A Theory of Imperialism, Not Dependence." Latin American Perspectives 1, no. 1 (1974).

Fishlow, Albert.   "Flying Down to Rio: Perspectives on U.S. - Brazil Relations." Foreign Affairs 57, no. 2 (Winter 1978-1979).

Fox, Jonathan.   "Has Brazil Moved Toward State Capitalism." Latin American Perspectives 7, no. 1 (Winter 1980).

Humphrey, John.   "Operarios da Indústria Automobilística no Brasil: Novas Tendéncias no Movimento Trabalhista." Estudos Cebrap 23 (1979).

Mantega, Guido.   "Expansão e Crise na Economia Brasileira: O Papel do Capital Estrangeiro." Cadernos Cebrap 28 (1977).

Martins, Luciano.   "La joint-venture état-firme transnationale - entrepreneurs locaux au Brésil." Sociologie et Sociétés II, no. 2 (1979).

Matta, Roberto da.   "Constraint and License: A Preliminary Study of Two Brazilian National Rituals," in Moore, Sally and Myerhoff, Barbara, eds. Secular Ritual. Amsterdam: Van Gorcum, 1977.

Meireles, José.   "Notes sur le rôle de l'état dans le développement du capitalisme industriel au Brésil." Critique de l'économie politique 16/17 (avril-septembre 1974).

Mericle, Kenneth.   "Corporatist Control of the Working Class: Authoritarian Brazil since 1964," in Malloy, James, ed. Authoritarianism and Corporatism in Latin America. Pittsburgh: University of Pittsburgh Press, 1977.

Moises, José Alvaro.   "Current Issues in the Labor Movement in Brazil." Latin American Perspectives 6, no 4. (Fall 1979).

Moises, José Alvaro. "La huelga de los 300 mil y las comisiones de empresa." Revista Mexicana. de Sociologia 40, no. 2 (1979).

Munck, Ronaldo. "State, Capital and Crisis in Brazil, 1929-1979." The Insurgent Sociologist 9 (1980).

Munck, Ronaldo. "State Intervention in Brazil: Issues and Debates." Latin American Perspectives 6, no. 4 (Fall 1979).

Oliveira, Francisco de. "A Economia Brasileira: Crítica a Razão Dualista." Seleções CEBRAP 1 (1977).

Rezende, Fernando. "A Produção Pública na Economia Brasileira." Dados 18 (1978).

Serra, José and Cardoso, Fernando Henrique. "As Desventuras da Dialéctica da Dependéncia." Estudos CEBRAP 23 (1979).

Souza, Herbet and Afonso, Carlos A. "The Role of the State in the Capitalist Development in Brazil (the Fiscal Crisis of the Brazilian State)." Working Paper 7, Brazilian Studies/LARU (1975).

Suzigan, Wilson. "Industrialização e Política Econômica: Uma Interpretação em Perspectiva Histórica." Pesquisa e Planejamento Economico 5, no. 2 (December 1975).

Tyler, William G. "Brazilian Industrialization and Industrial Policies: A Survey." World Development 4, nos. 10/11 (1976).

Villareal, Rene and Villareal, Rocio R. de. "Las empresas publicas como instrumento de politica economica en Mexico." Trimestre Economico 45, no. 2 (1978).

Warren, Bill. "Imperialism and Capitalist Industrialization." New Left Review 81 (September/October 1973).

Theses, Reports, and Unpublished Material

Abranches, Sergio Henrique. "The Divided Leviathan: State and Economic Policy Formation in Authoritarian Brazil." Doctoral dissertation, Cornell University, 1978.

Grabendorff, Wolf. "West Germany and Brazil: A Show Case for First World - Third World Relationship." Washington: Johns Hopkins University, Center of Brazilian Studies, January 1980.

Guimarães, Cesar, ed. "Expansão do Estado e Intermediação de Interesses no Brasil." Rio de Janeiro: IUPERJ
mimeograph, 1979.

Lessa, Carlos. "A Estrategia do Desenvolvimento 1974-
1976: Sonho e Fracasso." Thesis, Federal University of
Rio de Janeiro, 1978.

Malan, Pedro Sampaio. "The Brazilian Economy: Its Directions in the '80s." Washington: Johns Hopkins University, Center of Brazilian Studies, January 1980.

Mello, João Manoel Cardoso de. "O Capitalismo Tardio."
Doctoral thesis, Universidad Estadual de Campinas, 1975.

Newfarmer, Richard S. and Mueller, Willard. "Multina-
tional Corporations in Brazil and Mexico: Structural
Sources of Economic and Non-Economic Power." Washington:
Government Printing Office, Report to the Sub-Committee
on Multinationals, Committee on Foreign Relations, U.S.
Senate, 1975.

O'Donnell, Guillermo. "Reflexiones sobre las tendencias
generales de cambio en el estado burocratico-autorita-
rio." Buenos Aires: Centro de Estudios de estado y so-
ciedad, August 1975.

Pfefferman, Guy and Webb, Richard. "The Distribution of
Income in Brazil." World Bank Staff Working Paper 356
Washington: The World Bank, 1979.

Sercovich, Francisco Colman. "State-Owned Enterprises
and Dynamic Comparative Advantages in the World Petrochemical Industry." Cambridge: Harvard Institute for International Development 98, 1980.

Tavares, Maria da Conceição. "Ciclo e Crise: O Movimento Recente da Industrialização Brasileira." Thesis,
Federal University of Rio de Janeiro, 1978.

Trebat, Thomas J. "An Evaluation of the Economic Performance of Public Enterprises in Brazil." Doctoral dissertation, Vanderbilt University, 1978.